LET'S-READ-AND-FIND-OUT SCIENCE®

STAGE 2

Elephant Families

ARTHUR DORROS

HarperCollins*Publishers*

For more information about elephants and to find out how to help protect them, contact:

IUCN, World Conservation Union
Avenue Mont Blanc
1196 Gland
Switzerland

Conservation International
Suite 1000
1015 18th Street NW
Washington, DC 20036

Wildlife Conservation International
195th Street and Southern Boulevard
Bronx, NY 10460

National Geographic Society
17th and M Streets NW
Washington, DC 20036

African Wildlife Foundation
1717 Massachusetts Avenue NW
Washington, DC 20036

World Wildlife Fund
1250 24th Street NW
Washington, DC 20037

There are also organizations in almost all African countries.

The *Let's-Read-and-Find-Out Science* series was originated by Dr. Franklyn M. Branley, Astronomer Emeritus and former Chairman of the American Museum—Hayden Planetarium, and was formerly co-edited by him and Dr. Roma Gans, Professor Emeritus of Childhood Education, Teachers College, Columbia University. Text and illustrations for each of the books in the series are checked for accuracy by an expert in the relevant field. For a complete catalog of Let's-Read-and-Find-Out Science books, write to HarperCollins Children's Books, 10 East 53rd Street, New York, NY 10022.

Let's Read-and-Find-Out Science is a registered trademark of HarperCollins Publishers.

Elephant Families
Copyright © 1994 by Arthur Dorros
Typography by Christine Kettner
1 2 3 4 5 6 7 8 9 10 ❖
First Edition

Library of Congress Cataloging-in-Publication Data
Dorros, Arthur.
    Elephant families / Arthur Dorros.
        p.   cm. — (Let's-read-and-find-out science. Stage 2)
    Summary: Describes the unique qualities, status as an endangered species, and familial behavior of elephants.
    ISBN 0-06-022948-9. — ISBN 0-06-022949-7 (lib. bdg.)
    ISBN 0-06-445122-4 (pbk.)
    1. Elephants—Juvenile literature.   2. Elephants—Behavior—Juvenile literature.   3. Familial behavior in animals—Juvenile literature.
[1. Elephants.]   I. Title.   II. Series.
QL737.P98D66   1994   92-38972
599.6'1—dc20   CIP
                                                         AC

For Alex

With special thanks to Sandy Andelman

Out on the grasslands of Africa, a baby elephant is born. Mother helps the baby stand up. Sisters, brothers, cousins, aunts, and grandmother watch. They are all part of a family. Elephants live in families.

The baby takes its first wobbly steps. Big sister helps the baby along with her trunk. She helps take care of the baby. She is a baby-sitter.

Sometimes the baby-sitter is a cousin or an aunt. Almost all baby elephants have baby-sitters.

You can tell elephants apart by differences in the shapes and sizes of ears and tusks. Tusks grow larger as elephants grow older.

The baby drinks milk from its mother. The older elephants eat grass, seeds, fruit, leaves, even branches and tree bark.

Elephants eat almost all day. An elephant can eat more than three hundred pounds of food each day. You would need to eat a lot, too, if you weighed three or four tons like a grown elephant. That's as much as a large truck!

Elephants often wander far to find enough to eat. An elephant family may walk forty miles a day, looking for food.

Grandmother elephant leads the way. She knows where to find the best food. The other elephants follow her. Each elephant family is led by the oldest female elephant.

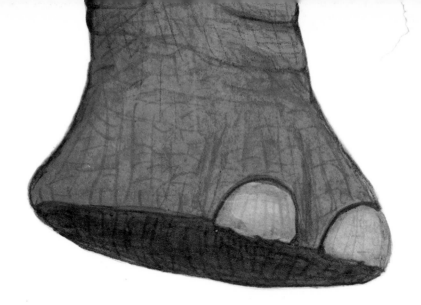

Elephants can walk very quietly.
The bottoms of their feet are soft,
and elephants walk carefully on their
toes! A family of elephants could walk
right by you and you wouldn't hear
them.

Elephants are surefooted. They can
walk on logs or narrow trails.

Mother and big sister help the
baby up a steep bank. They show the
baby where the trail is.

Grandmother leads the family to trees full of fruit. She remembers how to get here for ripe fruit every year.

The elephants shake the trees with their trunks and tusks. A trunk is like a nose and hand combined. Elephants can pick leaves or peel fruit with their trunks faster than we could with our hands. Tusks are useful too. Elephants use them to dig, to push over branches or trees, and to strip off bark to eat.

The small elephants wait for fruit to drop from the trees. Babies run and play. A baby-sitter pushes apart two babies who are banging heads too hard, playing.

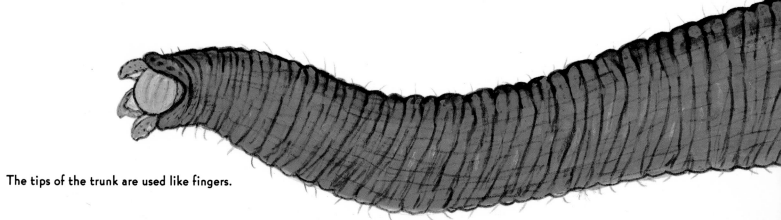

The tips of the trunk are used like fingers.

Suddenly the elephants spread their ears and hold their trunks in the air, sniffing. They stand perfectly still.

They hear and smell lions. Lions could attack a baby elephant. The babies stand in the middle of the circle of big sisters, brothers, mothers, aunts, and cousins.

Grandmother elephant raises her trunk and trumpets loudly. The lions disappear into the shadows. Not many animals will bother the big elephants.

Some elephants live in wet forests. But this family lives in dry country. They travel far to find water.

The bigger elephants dig holes in a riverbed. A little bit of water seeps into the holes from the wet sand below.

Most of the elephants are still thirsty. Some rest in the shade. The elephants will need to travel to find more water.

Elephant skin may look tough, but it is sensitive enough to feel an insect on it. Elephants take dust baths to protect their skin from the sun and insects.

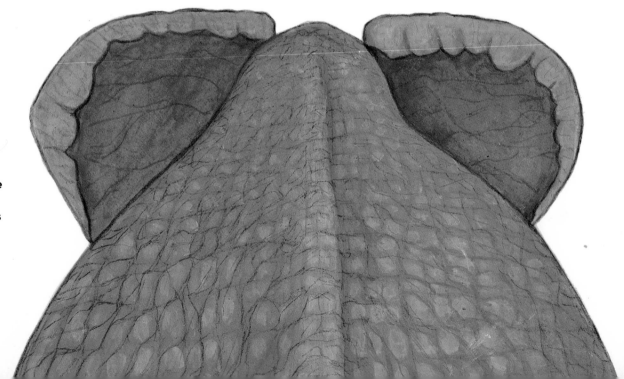

Grandmother elephant is listening again. She is listening to faraway elephants. Elephants make some sounds that people cannot hear. Other elephants can hear the sounds from miles and miles away.

Some of the elephant noises people can hear sound like rumblings from a huge stomach, or faraway thunder. Elephants cannot see as well as people, but they hear and smell very well. Smells and sounds help elephants keep in touch with each other.

Another elephant family is calling from miles away. They have found a pool of water.

The family walks toward the rumbles they heard. Near the pool, they start to run. Tons of elephant go thundering across the grassland. Elephants can run more than twenty miles an hour. That's faster than people can run.

The two families trumpet to each other as they meet. Babies chase and screech. The elephants touch trunks with their old friends. They will share the same watering hole.

The elephants drink and play for hours. They suck water into their trunks and squirt it into mouths and over dusty backs, and take baths. The elephants splash and swim. They even swim underwater, using their trunks like snorkels to breathe through.

Then they bathe in the mud. The color of an elephant family changes depending on the color of the mud or dust they bathe in. Elephants can look orange or brown when they are covered with orange or brown mud. But underneath, their skin is gray.

One baby elephant gets stuck in the mud. Two older sisters pull and push their baby brother to lift him out.

The baby brother will leave the family when he is grown. Adult male elephants wander alone, or join herds of male elephants for a while. They rejoin families only for short times.

A herd of male elephants comes to the pool to drink. Many small groups of elephants may gather together for a while in a large herd. But female elephants spend most of their time with just their own group or family. The older female elephants take care of the younger elephants. The oldest and wisest female leads the family.

Elephants can wander into places where people live, looking for food. The elephants may get into crops, gardens, even houses. Some elephants have been killed because they destroyed people's food. But many more elephants have been killed for their ivory tusks. From 1980 to 1990 over half the elephants in Africa were killed.

The people who kill elephants look for the biggest tusks. Families are left without the bigger, older elephants who lead them.

Now many people are trying to protect elephants. And people try not to buy things that are made from the ivory elephant tusks.

One elephant tusk could be sold for thousands of dollars.

There are two kinds of elephants on earth—African elephants and Asian elephants. They live in different parts of the world. Asian elephants have smaller ears than African elephants, and only males have tusks you can easily see.

Some Asian elephants live with people and haul logs and other heavy loads. But wild Asian elephants live in families, too.

African elephant

Asian elephant

Mammoths were ancient elephants
that lived in North America, Africa, Europe,
and Asia five million years ago.

Elephants have lived in their families for millions of years. With people's help, elephant families will live on earth for many, many years to come.

Acknowledgments

This book would not have been possible without the help of those committed individuals who volunteered to put time aside to tell their stories. The energy and enthusiasm that they bring to the Mexican American communities they represent are truly an inspiration.

I also want to acknowledge the significant amount of time that Sarah Goenne and Mark Burnette dedicated to this work. Sarah transcribed the interviews, while Mark ensured that they were all catalogued and saved electronically. In addition, Esmeralda Dominquez translated and transcribed the one interview that was conducted in Spanish.

Alvaro Obregon was there from the start and introduced me to those in the community who would generously share their stories. He also conducted and recorded the Spanish interview. Without his assistance, I would not have had a place to start. Laura Bauer was also there at the start to help formulate the questions and conduct an interview.

1

Fabian

I met Fabian when he attended National Louis University as part of the Bridge Program. This program allowed public school students to take college courses while still attending high school. Everyone at the university knew Fabian because he was persistent and hungry for a supplement to his high school work. He constantly wanted to stretch the expectations and enroll in more courses than allowed in the program. His determination to move ahead often created obstacles for him, as he tried to take on too many courses. Fabian is dreaming forward for his community.

Background

I went to high school at a career academy. Yes, that's where I graduated from, and I still have an interest in the school. I plan on running for local school council as a community representative this coming April. A lot of things are going on in the school. I constantly hear negative things, and it's like, *That's the school where I graduated from.* It doesn't feel good when you hear negative things about stuff like that. We need to change that status, and I believe we can. If we have like-minded people who want to change things, we can do it. But as far as it is right now, I don't think that there's any likelihood that people are interested in trying to change things. We just plant the seed so that further more down the line, someone else can come down the line and say, "Hey, let's continue the legacy."

I have an older brother, two younger sisters, and a younger brother. My parents are separated, so they kind of have different children with different people. I share a full brother who's older than me and two half sisters and a half brother who are younger than me. My older brother's twenty-five years old. He went to school, and he got a bachelor's in telecommunications management. He's right now in their CTI [College of Computing and Digital Media School]. He's in the graduate program for network security. He's the first in the family to go to school, and I'm following behind. He's been very helpful to me with some of my questions I've had about school and picking the right program. With computers, especially, he's been very helpful. He's an IT specialist. He works for IBM now. He's a very good person if you have any questions about computers and stuff like that.

My sisters are entering their teens, so they're at that stage where their hormones are going crazy; their feelings are just everywhere. My brother–he's in a private school; my younger brother, Matthew–he does academically well. He's performing above average. My younger sister–she's in the public school, and she's not performing as good as she should be doing. We're encouraging her to do well–to go to school, do homework, get involved. It's hard to make a child realize that you have to do something unless they see a concrete reason why I should do this. If they don't see anything, like there's no interest. You have to sort of instill it in them that, hey, if you don't do this, what are you going to do with your life? You got to do something. You just can't do nothing. Everybody does something.

My father went as far as high school–never finished high school. My mother went to high school, dropped out, went back to get her GED, and took some course work at the university. She never completed her undergraduate degree, but I encouraged her to go back, and I'm telling her, "Hey, go back; it's only going to be best for you. It will only do you good. It can't do you any harm."

I'm in my third year of college, and it's way more challenging than high school. It kind of makes you want to come to school, whereas in high school, it was like you didn't want to be there, because it was wasting your time. In college, the material is more interesting. You read lots of different points of views. You get different arguments, different sides of the debate. Not everybody thinks the same way you do, and I think that's good because you're open to discussion where not everyone's going to agree on the same topic. You'll have debate; you'll have argument, and people can express their opinions in a good way, not disrespecting anybody, not offending anybody. This is what you believe, and you hold a strong, firm belief in that matter.

I think being exposed to college while in high school [in a dual-enrollment program] was something that took me away like I was taking a class or two, and I enjoyed it. I need to be here. This is where I belong. I don't belong in high school. I had to come to college, and I think what motivated me is having the opportunity to participate. And taking classes while in high school kind of gave me that extra push to finish and come out to college.

Educational Experiences

The parents, I feel, are sort of discouraged from getting involved with the schools. A lot of times, they feel that they don't have the resources, the power, to make change, and there's not much information out there available to them. A lot of times, they're not English speakers. They don't have access to information, so it keeps them from knowing things—what they can do and what they can change. Students—I feel like they can change things. They're young, they have the potential, and if you encourage them and coach them appropriately, I think they can revolutionize a lot of things—the situations in the schools right now.

I think the teachers are overwhelmed with the work that they do. A lot of times, their course load, their workload, is so heavy they just want to get the day over with and go home; they're not really concerned with what the issues are affecting the school community, especially the environment that their students are exposed to. Some do care. I know I met a few that were willing to stay after school and work with students and give their time to form a group or committee to sort of encourage students to participate and get involved in community affairs. Administrators and principals—their work consists of more management-level stuff; they're not really concerned. I want to say a true, a good educator would be interested in every student's life—what they're exposed to at home, what they're exposed to in the community. But a lot of times, I feel like some of those administrators lack ability to truly understand or to connect things—truly connect. That kind of keeps them separated from the environment that they're supposed to affect.

For the most part, there were counselors at the high school who were supposed to be encouraging you to stay in school and, if not, to give you alternatives to what you can do. A lot of time, I felt like the counselors there were not very supportive. They sort of said, "Hey, if you feel you can't do it, then don't bother wasting your time, and don't bother wasting the teacher's time. Let them focus on the kids who do want to truly learn." And I understand that's how they felt. I don't think that's what they should have said to somebody, because their role as a counselor is to keep you and retain you in the school and help you advance, not discourage you and forsake you and just kind of like forget about you. There were some people who were encouraging. Some teachers were like, "Hey, you gotta do it; you gotta keep up with it." There was a social worker there that I really liked. She was very instrumental to my staying in school, because she told me, "This is what you need to do." She kind of guided me. And I highly respect her because she was a major figure that kind of made me realize that you have to do this. You need to do this. There's no *and*, *if*, or *but*s. You got to do it.

My experiences in school were good and bad, more bad than good. I felt that teachers that I went to school with really didn't pay much attention to the students. They didn't really care. They kind of said, "Hey, they are not going to make it." When I would be in a classroom and I had a teacher like that, it kind of upset me. I wanted to say, "Hey, you're getting paid taxpayer dollars, and you are supposed to be teaching us, and you're telling us that we're not going to make it." I don't know if it was a tactic that they were trying to use to make you want to come to school and show them you could do it or if they were being truthful about that. They were really exposing themselves to us; I didn't think that was appropriate. I didn't think that was the right thing to do, and my impressions were not very good. I felt I could have done a better job if I were in a teaching position. I could have motivated students more. They're going to want to come to my classroom because I'm going to make it fun, interesting. They're not going to want to skip my class. And if they do, they're going to want to come back and do the extra work because it's going to be that enjoyable in my classroom. If I were the teacher, like, I feel I could have done a better job than they could. That's how I felt.

The teaching was very traditional lecture, open-book test. They weren't very visual; they weren't. We did have a lot of technology resources, but we lacked an adequate library. We lacked a lot of other facilities that other schools were plentiful in. We were an underperforming high school, and we were always underperforming according to state exams. Our dropout rate was about 50 percent. If you have a class of, let's say, a thousand freshmen entering, maybe four or five hundred will graduate out of that class. That was pretty depressing, and the truth of the matter is that's how it is now. We're trying to change things.

Dropping Out

I sort of went through some situation where I wasn't interested in education; I wasn't interested in school. I wasn't interested in having any business doing this until I realized how important it was to have an education. I dropped out of high school when I was a sophomore, and I wasn't able to get a job, and that was what kind of opened my eyes. I need some education. I need to go back to school and finish high school and go on to college just to be a competitive individual in the marketplace—just to be able to say, "Hey, I have some type of skill. I can do something." I didn't want to be another statistic. I didn't want to be a low-wage earner. I wanted to have a good quality of life and that made me realize that education was the key for me—a key to anything for anybody, so that's what made me go back to school and motivated me to get involved.

When I dropped out of school, my parents were very, very upset. They didn't know what to say. They were disappointed. They wanted me to go back. I really didn't want to go back. Then I had a good job. That's when I realized I could get a job. You could get a job, but it wasn't going to be a job that required you to use your mental abilities. It would be a labor job, getting paid very minimal, and I just couldn't see myself doing that. That's a motive to go back to school. I have to do something with myself. I wasn't thinking at the time. I was thinking, *I don't have to get up every day, go to school, seven o'clock in the morning, and go through what I go through every day.* For me, it was so bad I would say, "I'm getting up to go through another day of hell," and I just couldn't do it anymore.

Going to school was like walking into prison, where the environment is so negative people don't respect you; people look down on you. There's no encouragement. It's like, why are you here? It's like, why are you wasting time? Do yourself the favor and go—just go. Nobody wanted to deal with you, and that was not a very good experience for students. It made you think about things like is there a purpose to this? Why am I really here? So you start thinking about stuff like that, and one wonders, *Should I really be here?* Then you start thinking other things that make you take actions like drop out of school. Then you realize that was not a smart move. Then you have to go back. The hard part is really taking the action going back to school.

> Going to school was like walking into prison, where the environment is so negative people don't respect you; people look down on you. There's no encouragement. It's like, why are you here? It's like, why are you wasting time? Do yourself the favor and go—just go.

For a lot of students who don't return, a lot of times, they are more interested in getting a job that pays—that just pays, and they're not really thinking about the future. They're not thinking about how they want to live. They're just worried about how they don't want to open up a textbook and read boring material and do boring assignments. That's not what they wanted to do with their time. Too many times, I see in the community where minority girls sometimes get pregnant. It happens a lot, I think, in the Latino community, and that becomes the top priority–their children–and they lose focus on education. It's like, how do they expect their lives to get better? You want to give yourself an opportunity. You want to give your child a better future than what you had. The school's not going to help. And it's sad when I see stuff like that.

Too many of my friends went through that situation. I can recall the number of people who I went through grammar school with who later on went to high school, got pregnant, and just never went back. And it's so sad to hear about that, because I thought they could have done something if they had had it in them. It's just unfortunate that they had to leave.

Some mothers do still go to school and still care for their child. I look up to those women, but then the ones that don't, you're not giving yourself the opportunity. In the long run, you're going to wish that you stayed in school, and you're going to wish that you did something with yourself. My mother was an example of that. She dropped out of school because she got pregnant with my brother, and she went to go back and get her GED when she was pregnant with me. When she had me, she was taking courses at the university. She never finished. I think one of the reasons was she had to work. She had to take care of her kids. She was a single mom. So it was kind of harder for her. I think that kind of impacts people's lives as well.

I was out of school for three months. I think the hardest part of going back was actually having the courage to want to go back and say, "Hey, I want to come back." When I did, they were very supportive of me. They didn't reject me. They didn't send me away and say, "You have to go to an alternative high school," or "No, you can't come back." They made it really easy for me. I walked into the principal's office; I stated my reason for being there. And they pretty much knew what I wanted to do. It was a no-hassle kind of situation. Like "You want to come back? Okay, fine, come back." It was that simple. I've heard of other situations where other students were not given an opportunity to come back–where they were rejected and sent off to a special school, an alternative school based on their performance or their disciplinary record, that they just said, "No, you can't come back in." I was fortunate to be given an opportunity to come back.

Sometimes I think it's hard for minority students to stay in

> Sometimes I think it's hard for minority students to stay in school, especially when you have other factors like having to provide for the family and having to work to help pay bills to put food on the table. Especially when there's little ones involved where you have to sit there and care for them. Sometimes there's not adequate child care available for them. So often, that can hinder them or take them away from schooling. That's not the priority at the moment.

school, especially when you have other factors like having to provide for the family and having to work to help pay bills to put food on the table. Especially when there's little ones involved where you have to sit there and care for them. Sometimes there's not adequate child care available for them. So often, that can hinder them or take them away from schooling. That's not the priority at the moment.

Elementary school was more enjoyable. It was more fun. I think the learning environment in elementary school is higher; it's better because teachers sort of feel like they still have an influence over the child. We're still developing our skills, our social skills, our mental abilities, and at that point, I want to say, students still respect the teacher. They still look and say, "Hey, that's the teacher." It's like a second parent almost. You have your mom, dad at home. But when you're not at home, you have your teacher to listen to, and that's who you pay attention to. You don't question them. It was a better experience for me in elementary school. I felt like I learned a lot, a lot with reading books, engaging in discussion. They should have applied some of those models in high school as well.

Moving from elementary school to high school was definitely not a smooth process. When you start switching classes in high school, like you have different classes for a period—science is a class; English is a different class—that has an impact on the student, the stress, the anxiety that they experience, having to deal with different courses of homework. You've got eight different classes, and you've got eight different assignments in one day. It's a lot for kids to do. I know in other countries, education is better. In Japan, I think, they're more serious about their education. They're very, very competitive about doing their work, and they don't waste time. They don't waste any time with their students. They expect them to learn. I don't know what went wrong here; we have the right ideas. I don't know where we're failing. I don't know how we're not closing the achievement gap, how we're not creating a sense of staying in excellence.

Making It Better

What would have made it better for me? I would say more encouragement from educators, from the teachers, more support from counselors—true support, like giving you a scenario, options. I think we lack the supports, and that's why a lot of the children often quit school. It's because they feel like there's no purpose to it, and I feel like the educator's role is to put a purpose to it. "The reason why you're here is because you want to go on to something else, whatever it is that you want to do. You can do anything." They never said that to us. They never encouraged us to want to go on, above and beyond. They would say, "Oh, you're just, you're just nothing." They would belittle people, and that was not very nice. It makes people feel very small and very insignificant.

I don't think closing down underperforming schools is a good way to handle the situation. That's going on right now with underperforming schools or underutilized schools. It's going to impact the student's performance when you disrupt the child's education. Anything can happen. They'll lose interest; they're going to lose their information that they were supposed to be taught. I don't think that phasing out or transforming schools is going to help out. It's just another strategy that they want to use. I think the

> In the high school that I went to, we didn't have a big library. We didn't have books, but that's something that we should have. Why don't we have this stuff? You go to other high schools, and their libraries are beautiful. There's some schools that don't have that.

results are going to be the same; nothing is going to change. They're just trying to put a new face to it, a new label to it, and that's about it. But the down side is the same thing, same schools, same students. You might have a different staff; you might have a different administration, but you're probably going to have the same results in the long run.

I would advise the head of the schools to create smaller learning communities, to have smaller classroom sizes, to offer different kinds of programs. I believe in community schools. I believe in alternative education, whatever will get the child's attention, whatever will encourage the child to want to learn–that's what I would set up. You have to survey and find out … the child's interest, what the parents are thinking about for their child's education, and kind of set up different kinds of programs.

I think we're too cold-minded, and we're just trying to fix things for the moment, trying to patch things up. We're not trying to look at the big picture. We need to say, "Hey, we have to have a long-term solution for this," and not just fix it for the moment and let whoever is going to take this position later on deal with that. So I would suggest to him not to close down schools but to create smaller classrooms. You can't go wrong with smaller classrooms. The teacher has more time to focus on children individually; interaction is more central. You interact; everybody shares your thoughts and ideas. I think that would be a better way of addressing those thoughts and situations than closing down schools and phasing them out and then merging schools. Yes, it's true they're nonperforming, they're underutilized, but you're not doing any favor to the students.

In the classroom, I would like to see more group type of instruction where you assigned a number of students to a group. They can work together sort of as a team, and they could share their ideas together and work out their solutions to the assignment. I would do group activities if I were a teacher. I would use technology in the classroom. I would encourage them to use the outside resources of library use and provide them with the tools that they would be able to access the resources. I think that in this time of society, we have to be computer literate; we have to know how to use technology, and if we don't know how to use technology, we're falling behind–way behind. Something that I would implement in the classroom is technology skills and learning how to navigate through the web pages. There's an immense amount of information out there–Library of Congress, public libraries, even your own school library. In the high school that I went to, we didn't have a big library. We didn't have books, but that's something that we should have. Why don't we have this stuff? You go to other high schools, and their libraries are beautiful. There's some schools that don't have that.

To have a full-functioning library is really important. I mean, I don't think that having a plasma TV screen in the library is appropriate. Why don't we invest those dollars in books or computers? Their way of thinking is "Let's make it look nice; let's make it look catchy." Then buy a few plasma screen TVs and put them in the library and have C-Span or CNN showing throughout the whole period. Why would people want to do that? Our shelves are empty, and our students are not reading at grade level. Let's put up programs–after-school programs for reading, for education. You know, we could do this. That's possible. Nobody ever thinks about that. Not there.

There needs to be change, and I just don't want to run away from the problem. It's easier to run away, to just leave: "Forget about that; I'm moving on." It's easy to do it, and it's harder, it's tougher to say, "Hey, you know they need to be changed." Someone's gotta do it, and if no one's taking the initiative–like I said, someone's got to plant the seeds. If it has to be me or somebody like-minded, a seed or two won't hurt. It will do people good. So I'm trying to change things in there. It's hard; it's not easy. It's very hard. It's especially hard when you have parents who don't see eye to eye how you see things. Trying to convince them of certain policy decisions the school makes, what's best for the students–not what's best for the administration, the teachers–is hard. We're worried about decisions. That's our prime concern. It's student development. That's why I want to get involved. I am involved.

Reflections

Fabian's contribution to the overall mosaic was significant. His insights into the overall culture of the public schools was framed around the elements of encouragement and respect. He was committed to making the schools more responsive, supportive places for students. He reflected deeply on his own experiences of not being challenged or encouraged and wanted to make a difference by serving on the local school council. He was fortunate to have his older brother as a mentor, and this seemed to make a difference in his level of motivation and future goals. He found little stimulation in the public schools but continued to look for challenges by enrolling in a College Bridge Program, which allowed him to attend a local university while still in high school. Fabian spoke to the necessity of looking at the big picture when it comes to transforming the schools, and he felt that too many of today's problems are being addressed with short-term solutions. [Tragically, Fabian was killed in a car accident in 2013.]

2

Christine

C hristine and I met at her school, which is on a small side street off a busy avenue that bisects two Latino communities. When I arrived, I walked through several areas bustling with students of all ages, including adults learning English and computer skills along with adolescents. We found a quiet room to settle into for our time together, but Christine was always alert to the swirl of activity close by and ready to intervene if needed. Christine believes in her students and their abilities. She knows that personal encouragement and respect are significant factors in their success. She is dreaming forward for her students.

Background

My name is Christine. I'm thirty-three years old, and I'm a principal at the Academy, an alternative school. Basically, our mission is to serve students that were not successful at a traditional school system for various reasons. We're giving them another opportunity to get their high-school diploma and pursue their dreams.

Actually, by trade, my background's engineering, and I used to work at Lucent Technology. I did some counseling work; I tried to recruit more Latinos into the science fields and just fell in love working with youth. I decided I was no longer happy working in the corporate world and really wanted to work with youth, so that's what brought me to Rudy Lozano. I didn't start off as a principal; I was program director of the College Bridge Program here. Six months later, the principal left, and they asked me to take over the high school. So almost seven years later, I'm still here.

My father is a career military man, in the army twenty-one years. My mom—both of them just completed high school, and that was it. My mom was a military wife and just followed my father. She moved up in her career as time passed, but education in high school was the furthest she was able to accomplish. I think I'm the second person in my family to go to college at that time. Now there's probably two more persons. When I entered college, I was only the second one in my family. I have three sisters. Me and my sisters were all born in Texas, and then we just went back and forth from Texas to Germany, back to Texas, back to Germany, and then New Jersey, where I graduated high school; I went to college in Florida and landed here. Lucent Technologies recruited me when I was out in Florida, looking for a job.

I knew I was going to go to college. Actually, my dream when I entered college was to work for NASA as an astronomer. Where that came from, I have no idea. I was just always interested in what was out there. The one part about that is at the end of my four years, I got a job offer from NASA, and I turned it down. Things change over time, and at that time, the government wasn't really a stable work environment, and I didn't want to take that chance. I had a lot of offers on the table, so I went with the most exciting one. I found the corporate world just wasn't fulfilling. I'm working on telecom switches, and I'm working with other telecom providers and making sure they can provide services to their customers, but so what? What's the big deal?

I just didn't feel any impact from what we were doing, so when I was working on a subcommittee—RESPECT team was what we called it—I was working with the high schools, the local high schools. That was pretty impactful because high school was as far as the students were going, if they even got that far. And I just found that amazing, because how could that be? Living in a military household, you're very cocooned, and I didn't realize that until I went to college. There's no question in my mind, or in my family's mind, that we were going to go to college, so I didn't understand how other families could not support that. That really opened my eyes, and so it was a challenge. I started to take on challenges, and I said, "How do we—or how do I—offer support for those really interested in college and let them know that it is possible?" That really caught my attention. I felt that I could probably do something there that might be helpful.

Joy of Teaching

I wanted to leave the corporate world as quick as possible. I just wasn't happy there at all. There was a posting of a math position here. So I applied, and I was a part-time math teacher and part-time program director for the College Bridge Program. I was hooked right away. I had never taught before. I worked one on one with a lot of different Latinas because of the work I did at Lucent Technologies. I just enjoy teaching, especially with math; so many students are afraid of math; they think that it's just a scary area. I tell them no, that's possible, because I was bad in math up until college. I was really bad at math, and it wasn't until my second or third year in college that I learned how to be good at it. And I was like "Oh, it's not so bad." I just didn't know how to attack it.

> What I find amazing is that they're labeled as troublemakers leaving the public school, and they're leaders here. And what's curious to me is what makes that difference. Our students are wonderful here.

In college, I was in the tutoring center every day all day long, studying my butt off. Finally, the aha moment, the lightbulb went off, and it's just like, as long as you know the process, it doesn't matter the problem. Just follow the same process. What you've got to solve—one-step, two-step, multistep equations—just follow the same process, and you're good. I didn't realize that until finally one day, and I just wanted to give back.

Giving Back to Community

I didn't know anything about the Pilsen community. So I've learned a lot coming here, and you fall in love with the community. I think what attracted me the most is the population that we serve. It really upset me how unsuccessful the students were or how they felt or how they were being treated in the regular system for whatever reason, whether the students said teachers weren't great or they just didn't get along. What amazes me is that unfortunately, with the Academy being considered an alternative school, some people don't even like to give us a second chance or even a second look. There's a lot of negative connotations. What I find amazing is that they're labeled as troublemakers leaving the public school, and they're leaders here. And what's curious to me is what makes that difference. Our students are wonderful here.

I did some research a couple of years ago when I was finishing my training program, and I probably interviewed about eight to ten kids about why they left the public school. The biggest reason was lack of academic support. Whenever they needed some additional help, if they weren't understanding anything, the teacher was like, "As soon you lose attitude," or "You were here—too bad; I don't have time for you. Either you catch it the first time, or that's it." Or if they say they will be available—"Can you be here at lunch?"—the teachers were never there. So that trust factor was just broken from the beginning, and once you lose that trust with the student, it's really hard to get it back. The student just gives up. That was the biggest reason.

The other reasons that I would hear were just very condescending, very disrespectful language toward the students. From teachers, counselors, administrators, just a mix, but comments such as, "You might as well go back to Mexico because you're not going to do anything here. You're good for nothing here. All you Mexicans are always late." It was very disrespectful. I was floored with some of the comments I would hear. I'm like, "Wow, did they really say that?" Again, not just from particular people—it's across the board. And that just hurt! How can you say that to somebody?

I'll look at the school that I lead, and I know that I'll treat these kids as if they were my child. I hope that's how it really should be. Unfortunately, that's not the case. So that really hurt me, and I get excited by just taking, giving additional time, the space, additional support that the students need and just help them grow because unfortunately, this is the only home for some. They come from situations we will probably never understand or we will never go through. They go through more crisis and more real-world and adult experiences than we will ever face. It impresses me how well they have been able to survive. They have a lot to offer. Our students have a lot to offer, and we need to mention that just a little bit more: "Just keep going. You're doing great—you're awesome; you've been so great this whole time." Just push them on to go the extra step. It's just really rewarding.

Here they have the trust and the respect. Some love me; some hate me—and that's okay. I'm not here to be your friend. I had a confrontation with a student the other day, and she thinks I'm out to get her, that I absolutely hate her, I'm trying to pick on her. It's not that. I will hold you to high expectations. This is what you're going to need to be successful. They don't see that yet. They think I'm out to get them all the time. I'm going to be hard on you because I know you can do better. I know you're better than how you're behaving out here. And to see them grow is just awesome.

I keep in touch with them when they leave. I see alumni. We don't have a formal alumni coordinator. We tried a couple of years ago, but it's not really a funded position, so it's really difficult to do so. But they come back. They'll give me postcards and tell me, "Oh, I have a baby now." The student that just came—she graduated three years ago already. I had another one a few weeks ago; she's going to college now. She asked for a letter of recommendation. So that's really nice. We have to socialize more, an alumni-association type of event or program, but we haven't been able to do so yet.

I hope there are more schools like us. I just think there needs to be choice. Some students thrive in a large city; some students thrive in a small city. I'm a small-city type of person. I think that's why I'm out here so much. The university I went to is a small school. It was four thousand students. I just prefer a smaller city, and I like to know people that I'm working with. That's helping me because I want my teachers to know me. I hope there are more schools like us. It saddens me how overcrowded the schools are. The local schools around here are. I wish we could do something more, and unfortunately, it's difficult to make some real change. I hope there are more small schools that are being developed, not just another two-thousand-student school. That would be a dream.

The Next Challenge

I think the next challenge for us, especially because of the age of the students that we serve, is that unfortunately, the parents may just not be available—not that they don't exist, but they're living a lifestyle that is not positive. In some cases, they're living with Grandma and an aunt, which is good if they're involved. We're trying to redefine how instead of parent involvement, that it's more family involvement, because even if you don't have a specific mom or dad, you have an uncle or cousin that wants to see you succeed and to find that motivation and that guidance for it.

> We're trying to redefine how instead of parent involvement, that it's more family involvement, because even if you don't have a specific mom or dad, you have an uncle or cousin that wants to see you succeed and to find that motivation and that guidance for it.

So we're trying to attack it in that sense more.

We haven't put a big push on it yet, but it's something that next year, it's one of our major goals to really increase involvement because we just so desperately need the families to be involved, either by helping the students get here on time, knowing how to go to college or how to apply, or to support them by saying, "Yes, you can do it." We're building more parent workshops or family workshops or just awareness training on how you can support. Even if you didn't go to college, but this is what your child or nephew or niece is doing. They need to finish their résumé: can you help make sure they submit it on time, make sure they get a good night's sleep the day before the test, get a good breakfast, and things of that nature? Because I think … the biggest challenge that our students face is they just don't have the push to say, "You can do it." They don't have anybody to believe in them.

I think the majority of the reason is just because they didn't experience it themselves. Most of our parents only went through sixth grade. They don't even know what a big deal it is to graduate high school, much less go into college or finish college. They just see money and say, "Go and get a job because we can't pay our light bill or gas bill." I think there's a lot of discouragement because of what they have to deal with just to survive. It's like, "You know what? Going to school is not even for you. You got to go to work."

It's tough. I think that's beautiful about us: you can serve the entire family. If an adult is lacking English language skills or math and reading skills, you can enroll the student in high school but also give Mom and Dad some additional training. They can go to the Job Center for Working Families. You enroll the student, and you can serve the entire family—now you can really start transforming the community.

By working here in the community, working in the school, and realizing the challenges and obstacles that are facing our students and our families, we got to do something. I would really like to open up another school, serving the general population from eighth grade. There are eleven elementary—public elementary—schools here and only one public high school. I guess I didn't realize how one high school is fed with all these elementary kids; that's impossible. I've always known we need more high schools in the area. That's a no-brainer. I just didn't know how significant it was. We need another high school to help with the overcrowding situation, but my dream would have it to be small. If it must be a large school of two thousand kids or what have you, you've still got to go where it's smaller communities, because their relationships, the personal relationships one develops with the student, makes all the difference in the world. If you don't have those relationships, sound and stable and trustworthy, you're not going to make a difference at all. So I could see that happening.

> If you don't have those relationships, sound and stable and trustworthy, you're not going to make a difference at all.

Safety

But I would love to be able to open up straight out of eighth grade going into high school, because there's a lot of need there—a lot of need. And I have parents coming to me all the time: "My daughter's fifteen. I don't want send her to X school, because it's unsafe, and she's already been bullied and beaten up." I'm like, "I can't take you until you're sixteen," and they're just heartbroken. The charter won't allow me to take her at fifteen years old; you have to wait until you're sixteen. The student is out of school for a year-plus.

The parents would rather risk getting in trouble with the law—and I would too—than send them to the designated district high school. It's just incredibly violent. They have to cross between Eighteenth and Twenty-Sixth Street; there's eight different gangs. In a six-mile radius, there are approximately eight different gangs. If you're going to a certain high school, you may cross four different gang zones, and so they're like, "I'm not going there." We've still got a lot of growth to do here at the alternative level as far as making sure we're getting our students the high-school diploma, but we still have to bridge that post-K–8 piece; we still have a long way to go in transforming just that.

I definitely think there's a fear that I probably would never understand of leaving the neighborhood. Growing up in the military, I've traveled, seen different cultures. I love doing that. I'm the type of person who can get up and go in a heartbeat, and it doesn't impact me whatsoever. My husband, who is Mexican, had a different experience. He grew up in this community. Right now, his family's close by, but when we started dating, his whole entire family's on the same block—one in the basement, one upstairs, one next door. That is weird to me because in the military, I saw family once every four, six, eight years, because we were living in Germany. We can't afford to go from Germany to Puerto Rico. It's just me and my sisters. Right now, we're all scattered. But here, it's where you're rooted. You can't just get up and go; there's a huge fear. So I could partially understand but not fully understand, because if you're not safe, move. That would be a no-brainer for me. But if your whole family's here, you just don't want to go anywhere else—the fear of change.

The students—they're afraid to change as well. I even see it moving to the university. They want to stick with the Latino crowd. They're afraid to move out, and I see here they've never been to the lake. They've never been at the airport, because everything's at Twenty-Sixth Street, and this is their home. It's the closest they're ever going to get to Mexico without living there. So this is their home, and I can understand you don't want to move to a community you're not familiar with. Unfortunately, this city is very segregated.

I don't think I'll ever fully understand that part, so I'm always a big advocate: move out of state; live on campus. I will push, and I will get a lot of resistance back because they don't want to leave their parents, or they can't imagine themselves not living with close family. But I tell them it's a different world, a different experience totally. I'll always push for that because especially among females, I'm going to push for your independence. So that's where my background does come in. My mother's a very strong, independent woman;

that's how she raised me. Don't ever depend on any man. Whatever you can do yourself, you do. So I sort of push on the girls here. So when I see them, they often say, "No, my boyfriend said I can't do this." I tell them, "If that's what you want to do, you go do it." So that's an interesting battle.

Knowing the Culture

In the Mexican culture–if you're in the old-school Mexican culture, I should say–at eighteen, you start getting married and start having babies. I remember one student particularly telling me, "Mom wants me to have another baby." She's eighteen years old; she already had two kids, and her mom was pressuring her to have a third. She hadn't even graduated high school yet. So she eventually had the third; she eventually graduated, but it was tough. It was very tough, so we

I remember one student particularly telling me, "Mom wants me to have another baby." She's eighteen years old; she already had two kids, and her mom was pressuring her to have a third. She hadn't even graduated high school yet.

have to adapt. We have to adjust; it doesn't matter what I think is right or wrong. We have to take what the community issues are and their culture and just equip them to meet their needs. Because I can't say, "Mom, that's not right." We're just supposed to be educators. I can't say, "Mom, you're wrong." That's disrespectful. So I try to work with this family to have it a win-win situation where Mom and Dad are happy, the home is stable, and they got their income, but their child can start pursuing their own path. Maybe not the first year, but maybe at least you give the strategy so when she is ready, she knows where to go to and the resources. So maybe two years down the road, she is ready to go to college.

It's interesting about this community, because my husband, for example–he grew up here, and so he hated the idea of me working here. He hated the idea because of the safety issue. My husband's very old-school Mexican. We're completely opposites. I'm the type of person where I'll trust you until you're proven to be untrustworthy. My husband's the exact opposite. He's "I don't trust until you prove to be trusting." So he didn't want me to work here and highly discouraged it because he was very concerned. Of course, as the husband, he's the protector of the family, and he was doing his husbandly duties, I guess. But I find this community so amazing because of how culturally rich it is. And given how I grew up, that was significantly lacking in my childhood because we had to move around so much.

I've lived in my suburb going on six years, and I don't know anything about my community over there. I'm more invested over here. Moving here would be a fight with my husband. My husband wouldn't want to. We have interesting conversations because he is one of those persons that would not agree to give our students a second chance. It angers him how innocent people are always being killed or hurt by the community violence. And because of that, he feels that if you're in that lifestyle and you're affiliated or in the gangs, "I don't want to talk to you; I don't want to see you. Just get out of my face—move out."

I'm Puerto Rican, and I know very little about Puerto Rico, about Puerto Rican history, what it is to live on the island. My Spanish is not even that good, so I just find that so beautiful. I live in a suburb, and my son goes here to a Catholic school because I want my children to learn the Spanish language, and it's just so culturally rich; it's just beautiful. I feel that's getting lost. Our schools have to capture what this community is known for. People come here because it's *X, Y,* and *Z.*

Now we're making some changes for next year. To give you an example, we don't have Mexican studies or Latin American studies courses in school. We're going to change that next year—also the arts program. We've always known we have to do it just for our students. They're wonderful artists. And we got to take what they're known for and make it to be turned into a positive, like the mural design—like that. I need to figure out how to make the arts a priority in the school. In any school district, the arts—the fine arts program—is the least prioritized of English, math, and social studies. It's the first to go. Art is a form of therapy for the students, and I have seen such a tremendous change in the students when they're able to do artwork and express themselves. Their demeanor, their attitude just changes. You see the lights in their eyes, and when you can find the passions in that student, you can change. So I'm going to try very, very hard to bring the art, not only for my students but also to help contribute better to the preservation of the Pilsen community. I think it's what keeps me here. I've had offers to go to the public schools and things like that, but I won't. They would have to be a pretty awesome school.

Power of Relationships

It bothers me right now that I don't know my kids' names. I've always been very good about knowing all the kids' names, and it's because we've grown from 60 to 130 now. I'm not as involved anymore. Whenever we brought new kids in, I interviewed every single one of them. I did all the orientations; I met all the parents. Now that we've grown, I can't do all that by myself anymore. I have a team of people. So I don't meet everybody all the time. So I have to say, "Who are you?" That bothers me, because again, we're about relationships. And if I don't know your name, we're not holding up to our own mission. And that drives me insane. I got to figure out how to not lose that.

It's unfortunate because people here are really underserved. They're in the gangs for a reason; they're not getting the support at home. They're using that for extra income. They're looking for a home. They're looking for someone to love, and unfortunately, they're finding it in this negative lifestyle; we just need to gear them away, show them there's a better way to do it. It's extremely hard. We have had some success, but it's a long process. It's a very, very long process. They're recruited by the gangs at nine or ten years old–very, very young. By the time they come to us, they're already five, six, or seven years in the gang. They've already seen a lot. They've done a lot, so they realize they're already on their own. A lot of times when they come to us, they're already on that crossroads: Do I want to continue, or do I want to move to something better? So we just give them the extra push: use this pathway instead. For those who haven't reached those crossroads yet, it's very, very tough. And we have to really give them tough love. And so what I mean by that is we lose some kids. They're just not ready to be in school, because they're only here to socialize or check out who's here or recruit, and that doesn't belong here. You want to do that? Unfortunately, you're going to have to move out.

But overall, considering the amount of gangs that are in this community and where our school resides (we serve three different gangs), we have maybe one fight a year–maybe. But our rules are tough. As soon as we know, we cut you off. I don't care if you started it; I don't care whatever. You swung; you're out. And I swear it hurts me a little bit. I never worked with the public schools, so I just wonder if the policy could just change–what a difference that can make for the students, because if they know they could get suspended for fighting, that they can do without the vacation. It's curious to think: my students know–you fight; you're out. So they don't fight. Versus over there in the public schools, they just get suspended, and they're back the next day, and they fight on the next day. It's curious.

We try very hard, and it's my mission that whenever we have to remove a student from the school, we will not leave each other on bad terms. I think in six years, I've only had one student leave that way. Everybody else has taken ownership of what they've done. They understand where we're coming from and why we've got to do what we've got to do. We hardly ever, ever, ever leave on bad terms. And so I don't close my doors. Once I dismiss you from the school, we don't close your doors. We say it's more of a long-term suspension. You have to be out for the semester. If you want to come back, these are the stipulations.

Basically, we want to be more restorative in that sense to where the student is taking responsibility for their actions. Are they reflecting on how that hurt somebody or themselves and possibly … put the school in jeopardy of serious safety issues? Providing that they show sincere remorse and/or responsibility for their actions and also depending on what the situation is, we'll say, "Okay, we realize this is what you're struggling with. I'm going to send you to this counseling area. They're really good. What do you think?" If they want to come back, they will agree to it. If it's not a counseling need—if it was a fight situation, for example—we'll bring both parties back together, and they have to talk it out. Until they talk it out and resolve it, they're not allowed back into the school. And they're actually surprising me. They always do it. Very rarely do we have "I'm out of here."

They trust us. We have a good team here. We have an awesome team here. I was telling the teachers just today at the teacher-appreciation assembly that they're extremely dedicated and committed. It takes a special person to work in this school. It's a 24-7 job. I think because our teachers—my counselors too—have a whatever-it-takes attitude, that makes the biggest difference. And I'll tell anybody—you come to this school; you pick out any student you want. Ask them if they're happy. I guarantee they say yes. I'd be curious to see if other administrators could say that about their schools.

I feel really good. There are parts that I wish we could do better, because we lose students for different reasons. But they know what is expected of them, and they know what we're going to tolerate and not tolerate. They know even the smallest things. What was I dealing with the other day that I was upset about because I had to waste my time on a stupid thing? A student was at lunch, and she put her books down. When she came back, her books were gone. She became upset obviously, because all her homework and everything was taken. And I pretty much dropped everything I was doing, and we went searching for her books. And the students were coming and saying, "Christine, why are you making it such a big deal?" I said, "Books. If it was your property and your homework, wouldn't you want your stuff back? We're going to make every effort."

We eventually found it. It was in the trash. Somebody took them, and playing a joke on her—a nasty joke—threw them in the trash, but we found them. A student gets their cell phone taken away, believe me—we're doing a hunt. I will slap down all the classrooms. I will search you. We do everything. It's a small thing that probably any other administrator would say is a waste of time: "I got more important things to do," "I got a business meeting," or whatever. But that's how you build the trust with the student.

They're not afraid to come to me and let me know the smallest thing that's bothering them, a safety concern or whatever it may be. And you know we're going to do something about it. That's the biggest difference.

The students are awesome, and I wish I could do more—I really do. But I take just one day at a time and one student at a time. I just have to keep that perspective there.

Reflections

Christine emphasizes the importance of building personal relationships with students and their families. She believes that this inspires trust and allows the students to see that they are, indeed, valued by the school. This contributes to their level of self-confidence and also to their sense of belonging, which can be a significant factor in leaving the gang life behind them. Personal relationships go beyond the individual students and include the entire family. Christine articulates that families need to provide support and encouragement to their children. She also believes that the school shares in the responsibility of ensuring that it happens.

Christine begins with a student's strengths and works from there. Her strategies include continuous reinforcement for both the students and her staff. She truly believes that her school can make a difference, even while recognizing that it takes a long time. One significant component of her approach is recognizing the importance of culture. Christine realizes that the curriculum should build up the students' pride in their cultural and ethnic backgrounds. This belief pervades her personal life also, as she ensures that her children attend school in a Latino community even when they don't live there. She respects the family expectations in the community and also understands the reasons behind gang membership. Understanding that these factors all enter into a student's commitment to school ensures a holistic approach to education.

3

Rafael

I met Rafael at a community program for male adolescents that focused on guns and violence. The organizers were art therapists and were trying to get the boys to express their feelings related to violence through art. Rafael began to speak as a police officer and quickly moved over to a drawing board, where he drew a picture of a flower to emphasize the boys' potential; I was hooked on his ability to connect immediately with a hard-to-reach group. Later, I asked Rafael if I could interview him, and he invited me to his home. I arrived, and his son greeted me at the front door and then proudly showed me the bookshelf that was the most prominent object in the living room. Rafael constantly buys him books to read, and he was pulling them off the shelf for me to see up close. As we sat down at the dining room table to start talking, Rafael's wife began serving us a multicourse hot meal. She would quietly enter the room while the children watched from behind the door and then leave. They were clearly proud that their father and husband was talking to me about his background. Rafael is dreaming forward for his children and community.

Background

My name is Rafael. I was born February 23, 1979, so I'm thirty-one years old. I am a police officer and was born here in the city. At the age of two, my family decided to go to Mexico, so we moved to Mexico and a state called Michoacán. I lived there from two years old to ten. When I was there, it gave me the opportunity to learn the culture and the language and just really a different lifestyle, of course–different of what I'm having now. At the time, my grandfather had passed away, and I feel–it hasn't been confirmed 100 percent, but just reading between the lines, I think that my father felt that he had to move back to Mexico. Why? Because of his dad passing away and because he wanted to raise us in Mexico, just for us to have the language and the culture, which I really thank him for.

I don't think my parents are fluent in English. I think my mom is now more than my father. They do understand; they do understand the language, but they're not fluent. So I mean, my dad's highest education is probably second-grade level. And my mom probably sixth grade; both went to school in Mexico. They stopped going to school more out of necessity, more on my dad's side. They were really poor. I hear stories from my uncle. He says that my father–they put him in a bag, a bag that they used to put food in–you know, like animal food. Basically, that was his bed, so the point is that they were really poor. You know, the house was made of a type of brick made of mud, the most inexpensive material. So they were building their home little by little. My grandfather at the time–he worked in the forest, getting glue from the trees. You know, the rubber trees.

They were moving a lot because they were looking for him. It was a group of criminals, outlaws, looking for him, so my grandfather had to move them a lot. And basically, that was dad's story. My mom–she was upper-middle class. My grandfather inherited land from his father, so basically, my mom had the opportunity to go up to sixth grade. My father–he had to work at a young age to help his family bring food to the table. He said he worked carrying water to different homes, and they paid him five cents. And he would just help out by doing that. He left school at a young age. When he was fourteen or fifteen, he started preparing; he said he started swimming a lot, learning how to swim, getting good at swimming because he knew he was going to cross the border. His oldest brother was in California already, working in the fields, so he knew he was going to come here. And the funny story is that, you know, when he got to the border, there was no big river or ocean.

He met my mom when they were young, actually; my mom–she was seventeen, and she got married.

They got married at a young age. They met in Mexico, but they started like kind of seeing each other here. Then my grandfather moved and went back to Mexico because he didn't want his daughter to marry my father, because he was poor. So my father started following them, and basically, they got married. So they got married in Mexico, and then they came here, and my dad–I remember from the conversations I hear that they bought a house on the north side. He was able to sell that house and just gain equity; he made $50,000 in less than two years. So he used those $50,000 to bring that money to Mexico. He bought a house. He started a business, a store.

I went to school in Mexico from kindergarten to fourth grade. I think it was a great experience. When I was eight years old, I was already taking transportation–public transportation–because we lived far from my school, so I needed to wake up early to take transportation. The life in Mexico was very, very peaceful. I don't remember ever seeing a squad car patrolling the neighborhood. And I don't remember seeing graffiti or gangs, and it was very safe.

I think I felt community involvement. It was a great respect for the elders, teachers, and grandparents; there was a lot of respect. You respected them no matter what. It's something like, let's say there was an accident at school; the teachers were allowed to discipline us. They didn't take advantage, because they knew they were there to teach us, to discipline us to a certain extent, and we knew that. Basically, I think that that really helped me a lot

> The life in Mexico was very, very peaceful. I don't remember ever seeing a squad car patrolling the neighborhood. And I don't remember seeing graffiti or gangs, and it was very safe.

personally because I knew the teachers had that permission from home. It's part of the culture, I think, that teachers are allowed. As a matter of fact, I remember one incident where my teacher–my fourth-grade teacher–said, "I don't want you guys to be running around during recess, because last time, you guys, you know, pushed around the girls." And we didn't listen; we ran around. So he was pointing at every single one of us, and we knew that something was going to happen; we're going to have a consequence. And we knew the consequence was a stick, but he was really different. He actually had a vote, you know. As we come in, he said, "Now, guys, you heard when I said not to do this, and we're going to have a vote. Everyone's going to vote. Let's have a vote to see if you're going to get a couple of swings with the stick or not." So that was the first time I learned democracy–the democratic approach! Of course all the girls voted yes. I mean, again, that was part of just respecting our elders and respecting the authority of a teacher.

I liked going to school. Academically there were ... I saw the difference when I came in the middle of fifth grade here. Academically, as far as math, I mean, I was more advanced, and it was fun. It was really fun. I think I remember my fifth-grade teacher in Mexico telling us to go in the front and having competitions in multiplications. So someone would ask me seven times seven, and I had to respond, and back and forth in front of the class; you don't want to get embarrassed in front of the class, so you better know your multiplication.

So basically, it was a good approach, and it was fun; it was fun. I mean, discipline was really all over the table there. Every morning, we had inspections. They inspected our hair, our nails, our uniform. And we sang the national anthem, so it was a public school. It was a public school where education was treated as high importance.

Move to the United States

One of the reasons that we came back was because my brother finished high school, and he took a small technical career; he was driving a cab. So my brother—he told my dad that he didn't want to do that, that he wanted to have a better opportunity, and he wanted to come study here. Since we were born here, he wanted to come here to study in the United States. My brother, at the time, he was fourteen. So basically, my dad had kind of like a switch, you know—a lightbulb came up. And so he came here, came here by himself, you know; he saved some money, and then he came here, the community where my family has been for years. My uncle, the oldest brother, was heavily involved in the community. My other uncle—they all got together and really started just working to get a community center, and then, obviously, they started working on the high school. Why here? Because there was roots here. My uncle, he had like set the roots, so anyone that was coming here, they would come because that's where he was, and he was kind of like our grandfather in a way.

He was here for a year, and then he sent for us. So I was in the middle of fifth grade. That was a big change for me. I was excited to come here. I had an image in my mind: Hollywood. I think I expected—I don't know; it's hard to explain. I mean, sometimes when I see the buildings here, like made of brick, those big three floor, three flats—that's kind of like the image I had.

So basically, when I came here, I was crying. It was a new world; I missed Mexico. My youngest brother at the time—he was five. He was born in Mexico. So I mean, he actually had to come in legally, you know? And so we needed to wait for her, and my mom wasn't there. It was the first time my family being separated. So it was painful. It was really painful, a new world. My cousins were all born and raised here, so they didn't, they really didn't embrace me, because I wasn't part of the "club"—you know, I wasn't … I was new. I didn't speak English; I mean, they spoke Spanish, but I think they were more comfortable speaking English. So we just didn't bond. And I felt pushed out and, again, a new country. I saw a lot of graffiti, and we were living in the third floor in a really, a tiny apartment. And my dad had a lot of dirty clothes because he was living by himself. So we needed to, the next day, do laundry. A big change—a truly big change for me.

Entering School

I was in fifth grade. So I started school, and my class was in one of those trailers outside. The class was mixed, you know? It was bilingual and regular. So I remember that day 'cause the day before, we had went to the thrift store to buy just clothes. And I had bought like one of those sixties' jackets—you know, those leather jackets with square pants? I mean, it was totally off from the fashion at that time. So everyone is turning and looking at me, so again, it was different. It took me a lot to adapt. I have to say. It took me a while. And I constantly just was thinking about Mexico and just the thought of maybe going back, you know—the hopes of my whole family going back to Mexico.

Through time, I was able to just make friends and started to adapt to this new lifestyle. It was really tough because in Mexico, we were so used to, since my parents had a business there, and for the most part, a lot of businesses they close for—they call it recess—for like a couple hours. So that time is like family time. You know, people, like, eat; they have their meals in the middle of the day, you know?

I think it's so needed. You know, because family is like the heart. And if you have family and you don't have that communication and bondage, it disrupts a lot of things, and it disrupted my life

I never, I never took part of a gang 100 percent, but I mean, they were the neighbors around. You knew them; you knew their parents. And when I will go to, to my school, you know, the kids in the other blocks knew that I lived away from that school, so they would chase me. And it was just a struggle. It was like, like survival. Just struggling to get to school—I walked to school.

because it was so fast. My parents—they were working. They had to wake up early in the morning, just an hour or two to get home, another hour or two to get back once they were here. I mean just enough time to make a meal and go to bed for the next day. The environment was very negative—I mean, gangs outside. At that time, I was ten years old, and you're in the preteenage years and looking to belong to something. I mean, you need attention in, I think, every year. But a lot of thoughts are going through my mind—I mean, a lot of changes. You feel alone, and then there is the environment outside. You know, I think you're looking for love. I was looking for acceptance and love and just to be part of this new lifestyle. The neighbors, I mean, were not the best company, and those are the people that kind of like embraced me in a way and gave me the opportunity to belong, to feel welcome. I remember my parents actually had to send me back to Mexico because I was getting in trouble. I had bad company, bad friends.

Well, I mean, not necessarily in a gang, but these kids–they were born and raised here. They were in a gang. I never, I never took part of a gang 100 percent, but I mean, they were the neighbors around. You knew them; you knew their parents. And when I will go to, to my school, you know, the kids in the other blocks knew that I lived away from that school, so they would chase me. And it was just a struggle. It was like, like survival. Just struggling to get to school–I walked to school.

I think sometimes adults are so focused in the daily routine that they forget to step back and just look at the whole picture. As adults, we're responsible, and we forget to think and just analyze, stepping back and saying, "There's more than what we see." And again, I think that, personally, for me, I didn't feel that people understand my situation, that teachers didn't understand my situation. They didn't understand that I was in the middle of the ocean, trying to understand all these changes. And because teachers at the time–and I'm sure now–have so much expectations, that I feel that part of the curriculum does not give them the opportunity to step back and analyze and, and see– look at emotions. Consider emotions. You know, have more time with students, and just, again, look beyond what they see.

Teacher Impact

So again, I finished fifth grade, and then I went to sixth grade. Because of my age, one of the instructors said that I needed to repeat fifth grade. So I had already finished fifth grade, and they put me back in fifth grade. I've always been a big boy–you know, taller than most of my classmates. And again, I don't think that they consider that. They don't consider that I was bigger, that I was going to get bullied, you know, by bigger kids. Because they're obviously going to see it as

> Our primary goal is to raise children to have good character, and the only way to do that is to have relationships. And you cannot have relationships if we're living fast, and we're not looking at them or listening to them and just paying attention, you know?

this kid that is way bigger than the other kids and all the other students. I'm going stand out. So sure enough, I started getting bullied. I've always been a person that is easy to get along with. It didn't take much before people stopped, because I have never been like a fighter–you know, someone that gets into fights. But I struggled again with that year. Consciously, I didn't feel that I belonged in that grade.

Well, there was a teacher, and I don't forget her name; it was Garcia. She, when she heard the news, she actually pulled me aside and said, "If you get straight As, when you finish fifth grade and go to sixth grade, I will pick you up and take you to seventh grade." So I think she gave me a purpose–hope. She gave me hope. So that's what I did. I worked very hard, and I got straight As. I think she was sent from heaven, like an angel, so again, that was in the back of my mind. I finished fifth grade. I worked really hard, and sure enough, the year came–I went to sixth grade. My second week, she came and picked me up for seventh grade, and she was a teacher there; she became my teacher.

So I think I'm never going to forget her name, because it's those teachers that really, I think, that go the extra mile. And I think anyone has the ability to, to make an impact on someone's life–anyone. But it's just a matter of stepping forward and doing it. And not only that, but I think we have to have integrity. Because if we say something, we must, we must respect that and do it. Because I think right now, we're moving so fast. We need to go back to basics and look at the foundation. Look at the foundation. We're talking about education. Our primary goal is to raise children to have good character, and the only way to do that is to have relationships. And you cannot have relationships if we're living fast, and we're not looking at them or listening to them and just paying attention, you know?

Everyone is accountable for that. The school has, to an extent, a responsibility because the students spend a lot of time in the schools. So basically, I think the administrators of the schools–they need to realize what's good for them, what's good for the students, and not just go by policies and things that they want to enforce in their schools; speak up on behalf of their schools. They have a responsibility to their communities and to make, you know, a difference. Basically, if the administration doesn't speak up and say, "Listen, we have a problem here; we have so much percent of behavior problems in my school. I need to change this curriculum. I need to spend more time on conflict resolution." A cookie cutter with everything the same all around the city doesn't always work. The schools are also accountable in that sense that administration has to speak up, and don't be afraid to do that. And also to have your teachers, you know, understand that that they can make that impact. So again, I think the school has–they have a big role in making this change.

Sent Back to Mexico

My family sent me to Mexico because I was getting in trouble, and I came back with a different mind-set because it was painful. It was truly painful. I was helping my grandfather tending the cows and stuff, so I was working. I came back, and when I was in high school, I started a youth group in high school. At the time, people–they had dancing clubs, you know? So I started one to make fun of that new thing; it grew so much–it grew. We had over 250 members–all over the city! So I took advantage of that. And what we actually started doing is we started doing dances in the community at a church. At the time, it was Father Chuck. I said, "Listen, I have this group. We want to help," so he lent us the basement. We started having dances. We raised like $8,000.

I was the president of that youth group, and it was mandatory to go to Mass on Sundays. I had rules, of course, of when we would go out: no drinking, no smoking. I mean, at the time, I was already maybe like seventeen. Yeah, I made up the rules, and we had the meetings in the basement in my house. And we will talk about community service and helping the community and stuff, you know? So again, a lot of those kids–a big number of those kids–were kids that were in gangs. They were leaving the gangs to come to this group.

I think it goes back to wanting to belong to something, wanting to be recognized, wanting to be part of something, you know: freedom and independence. I think everything was there because, I mean, the dance was like flippy, and I mean, it was different. It was like freeing. You know? And like independent, because there were–it wasn't adults. It was young people, you know?

Yes. I mean, at the time, I remember someone from a local community-based organization–he came to one of our meetings, and he saw this basement full of kids. The next time he came, he brought a guy from the local newspaper, so they did a story on us, you know, and then FOX came and did another story. And then ABC, on national television–they did a story. So the kids–they felt recognized. They did a paper, and then I put my number there; I started getting calls from everywhere. And they wanted to be part of this group, and that's why the group grew so much.

The High-School Difference

Things changed in high school. I went to the community high school. It wasn't too far from where I was, and so I think it was a great experience. I think my troublemaking years were when I was younger. At the time, what helped me a lot was that I, that I enrolled in the wrestling team, and I was practicing. You know, I was going to practice, and I actually got a job too after school. So it kept me busy. I don't think that the school, academically, was, you know, the best school. I don't think they really pushed the students to the highest potential at the time. I also think that there were so many great teachers, but there were so much limited resources that they could only do so much.

An example is the music teacher. All the instruments, you know–I'm sure the music teacher would appreciate a new piano and nice violins and nice instruments, but he only had those, and he needed to work with what he had. Another example was the biology teacher; I mean, we were working with equipment that was old. I would probably take a guess, but it was probably even, you know, fifteen, more than fifteen years old. I mean, as we think about technology now, it's so fast that we need to constantly be, you know, just bringing in materials and bringing resources to the schools.

My school adviser was so detached. She didn't even know my name. I mean, she was my counselor for four years. I think counselors–they have a pool of names. They have to reach out to the students. If they don't come to her, she should come to them. You know, by sending them a letter. I mean, maybe they're doing that now, but I mean, she didn't know my name. She didn't know who I was. The police officer in the high school–she come to me one day because there was gang fights, and she thought that I was a leader of a gang. She would say, "Hey, you need to talk to these people." And I say, "I'll talk to them, but I just want to let you know, I'm not part of that gang." Actually, I met that officer. I met her six months ago at headquarters at the police department. She always spoke to me with respect, you know? She thought that I was in a gang, but she always talked to me with respect, and I respected that. And I felt that she was a good officer, just the way she would speak to me. She would get more things by speaking to me like that than just, you know, disrespecting people. And I told her that. I told her that I would look up to her because of the way she approached me. And I would talk to those gangs without being in them, but I would talk to them because this group was so recognized that even the gangs respected this group.

I would start relationships with people. I would talk to people. Like, a good example is in my drafting class–there was a student there, and he would just come once. We would be working every week all week, building this drafting plan, drawing and making measurements, and basically, he will come once a week, and he will finish a drawing before time. He would give it to the teacher, and the teacher would say, "This is amazing; this is great." One day, I just approached him, and I said, "Listen, I've been here all week, and not only me. Other students here–we've been here all week, trying to make this drawing. You come here one day, and you finish it. And with all the glory the teacher's giving you, why are you in a gang? Why? You're very smart." He didn't know what to say. You know, he pretty much just said that it was part of the community; it was part of his environment.

A lot of people–they see a group of young men, and they cross the street. They avoid them. They actually oughta go in there and make some contact some way or another. If it's "Good morning," that's a contact. That's it because those kids–you never know who's watching you, who's looking up to you, you know? So I think that was, again, a great opportunity to do that with students in high school. The drafting teacher wasn't noticing. I mean, obviously, he was noticing that he was absent, but I think that was a great opportunity for the instructor to engage with him, you know? And maybe he did. I don't know. But I mean, it wasn't obvious.

I don't think I noticed that at the time. I think when I got older, I started just maybe realizing my life. But I think I should have been past that. One of my counselors when I was a senior in high school ... I wanted to go to college, so I went to get advice. I went in with my counselor, and she was instructing me to, to apply at Coca-Cola. Basically, she could have gave me an option to go to a community college, improve my grades, and then try college, university. But she basically flat-out said that I didn't have my grades and maybe the capability to go to school. I don't think teachers or counselors or anyone in general should be in a position where they have the opportunity to help someone and they're doing the total opposite. Because I think that it wasn't her fault; it was the principal's fault because ultimately, at the end of the day, it was the job of the principal to make sure that everyone's in the same boat. So when they lose focus–when they lose track–other things happen. You're going to have, again, people that are like that–you know, discouraging people instead of helping them. At the time, I felt embarrassed. I felt that it was really my fault, that she was right.

Planting the Seed

Actually, when I graduated, I started working in a factory, making soap, because at

> One day, he pulled me to the side, and he said, "What are you doing?" What do you mean what am I doing? I'm working. I'm a father now. My brother said, "You need to go back to school." I said, "Listen, school's not going to buy me Pampers." And my brother says, "Yes, it is. It's going to buy you more than Pampers in many ways." I didn't even hear it; I walked away, but I think he planted that seed.

the time, in my senior year of high school, my son was born already. So it was a combination of things–that conversation with my counselor, my son was born, and I say, "You know what? She's right. You know, buy Pampers, and start working." At the time, my brother—he was at the state university. He was getting an accounting degree. One day, he pulled me to the side, and he said, "What are you doing?" What do you mean what am I doing? I'm working. I'm a father now. My brother said, "You need to go back to school." I said, "Listen, school's not going to buy me Pampers." And my brother says, "Yes, it is. It's going to buy you more than Pampers in many ways." I didn't even hear it; I walked away, but I think he planted that seed. And I thought about it, and I enrolled. I enrolled in community college that same summer. I took a placement test, and it was so low that I was in ESL classes, you know, with folks that were just coming from China. I scored that low, so I had to spend a year or so just to get on that one-on-one level. But I realized that I needed to do it; I needed to work hard and just stick at it and continue.

I was working, and I was working there and going to school, and then I think I was just very, very fortunate, very blessed. Because you know, I started getting, you know, a job—better jobs. I started working at the planetarium; it was a job, but it was flexible to go to school, and so I continued school. I transferred to another college because mine had become more like high school, and I didn't want it to be like high school anymore. I was serious. I wanted to learn. So I figured that if I went to downtown, it was going to be a different crowd. And sure enough, it was. And it was actually in the evening, so older people. And I just stayed there. I got my courage, and I wanted to study psychology.

I wanted to help people. I think my heart has always been service and helping—always. But as I start checking different classes one day, I saw that they had a criminal-justice class. So I take that class, and I thought it was really interesting. And you know, just growing up, you know, what I saw in my community. At the same time, there was also an opportunity to take the test for the police department, so I took it. Before that, of course, I had different jobs. Since I was fourteen years old, I've been working with young people that have behavior problems. Learning from my own experience, you know, going to Mexico.

There was also an incident from my past: I was with my cousin, and an officer came. And there was an officer that didn't like the response that was given to him. He actually, he put me in the squad car, and he took me to the projects. He left me there, and he told the guys there where I lived. And those guys—they pretty much told me to go ahead and walk. They let me walk. I really didn't understand why that officer did that, but I think there was a reason. I think he felt that he was offended, you know? He felt offended by the response. And it wasn't really my response. It was my cousin's response, but obviously, he thought it was me. I think he wanted those young men to beat me up, you know? Maybe to give me a lesson, give me some discipline.

So basically, I walked home. I walked home; I think a guy was with me. I could have been really angry at the police, but I think that was another reason why I decided to, when I realized that I wanted to be a police officer, that I wanted to, to help and make a difference. And I notice many officers have the same mentality and have the same passion. I see more in the officers than people might think. You might not see it. There's a saying that in every tree, there's bad apples. But again, that experience also helped me push this dream a little bit further and understand that I really wanted to be a police officer.

I was studying at the state university, and I was working security. One time, when I was doing my homework, one of the officers saw my books and State folder, and she said, "Ah, you're in State." And she referred me to another program. It was a law enforcement management program. It's a bachelor's program, like an accelerated program. And she said, "Why don't you check this program out and get all your credits?" So I did. I started. It was mainly for police officers, but since I was working in security, they accepted me. So I enrolled in that program. I was in that program for a year, and I had already submitted my application to the police department, so they called me.

Before being a police officer, I was a volunteer in the Alternative Policing Strategy Program, a facilitator. And we were doing block clubs, street cleanups, and there was an incident where they killed a kid–a thirteen-year-old by the name of Yen. On Sunday morning, he was helping us clean, and they killed him. And I felt responsible for him, too–for his death. Because I was the one kinda like passing the flyers and telling the principals, "Hey, you know we need eighth graders. They need hours." And he was one of them eighth graders.

I was so ready to make a difference with this kind of activity; I was so ready to be in the police department. I started there in September 29, 2003, and I've been there ever since. I'm still active in the community. I think it was a great experience being in the academy–a tremendous experience. And I started working in the seventh district. I started working there on midnights. Then I went to evening shift, then mornings. Then I went to another unit, another specialized unit, working all over the city, responding to high crime calls, responding to big incidents. Then after working there for two years, I went back to the seventh district. And I started working there in the Community Policing Office, working with youth programs, building new programs. I built a program called the Senior Ambassador Program. And all the programs that were reached–they were basically geared toward different age groups. We were doing workshops every couple of weeks–bringing professors, attorneys–and then I left the youth programs and just started working directly with all the schools, just building communication with all the principals and the commander. You know, setting up meetings with them; doing strategies to implement different preventive programs like the Officer Friendly Program, the Gray Program; doing workshops for the high-school students; and working in mentoring programs for high-school students, too.

Community Engagement

So I'm working on my doctor's program. It's an EdD. It's a doctor's in education. The focus is organizational leadership. I want to continue to learn. I'm doing it for the community, for the service. I'm not doing it for money. I'll be honest to you, in my first class, my assignment was to do a project, and that project was to develop an organization. I implemented that project, and I built an organization; I followed through.

> A student from a local high school was killed. So this student lived across the street from an elementary school, a school where the principal is refusing to open the doors to the community–the only school that can give an opportunity. This really can be a lighthouse to the community, and the administration is refusing to do that. So basically, this student could have just walked across the street to have a program. But he needed to go to another territory, and he got killed.

I made a flyer. We made a community center. I started reaching out to community leaders here in the church. And I said, "Listen, we have to do this. We have so much work to do–can you help?" People started getting on board and said, "Yes, I will help you." I asked my priest in the area, "Can we use your space, your gym?" "Use it." So we started a soccer program, a martial-arts program with volunteers, and today that soccer program has more than two hundred kids. It's a league; it's a soccer league, more than twenty teams.

This all started from another death. A student from a local high school was killed. So this student lived across the street from an elementary school, a school where the principal is refusing to open the doors to the community–the only school that can give an opportunity. This really can be a lighthouse to the community, and the administration is refusing to do that. So basically, this student could have just walked across the street to have a program. But he needed to go to another territory, and he got killed.

So I mean, we needed a task force from this incident. From the class I was taking at the time, I learned to do that. And then we started reaching out to partners and key people that help out. So we named it Inner City Task

Force. At the time, when I was working at the seventh district, the chief from organized crime, I was also working on the Extended Antiviolence Initiative. He was told what we were doing: we had a meeting, and we united. So we're united in this task force now. We have the police department and, you know, different agencies. A lot of the projects that we do, it's in partnership with the police department and, you know, their agencies.

I mean, I feel that this is very rewarding. I think they're just going to have to take me out in a casket from here. This is very fulfilling, you know? I think when we started this task force, one of the things we highlighted was that we're all responsible. There was a group of young people, and we kinda like told them the same thing–the Englewood group: "This is not your fault. You know this community, you know, the way it is is not your fault. And from this point on, it will be your fault, because now you're responsible. Now you're accountable, you know?" So until the time that they're unaware that they can make a difference, it's okay. But once they know that they can make a difference, it's different now. Now people are responsible. So again, accountability is all over the place. We should hold people accountable for their responsibilities. If it's just cleaning up the alley, if it's just cleaning the neighbor's–whatever it is, we need to work on those different things that we have to do in the community.

Thinking Ahead

I think about my own kids every day, and I bring them with me. Because I think one of the things I think about is I'm responsible for what they're going to inherit. My inheritance is going to be this community, whatever I did here. Now they're going to be responsible, taking it to another level. So I want them to come and see these events. For example, the soccer ceremony–I asked them, "Do you guys wanna go?" They said no, but it wasn't an option. And then on the way over there, my daughter asked me–she said, "Can I be the vice president of the organization?" And I said, "Why do you want to be the vice president?" It just sounds cool, you know? And she wanted to be the vice president. And I said, "In order for you to be the vice president, you need be a volunteer first." She said, "Does that mean that I have to go to, every month, to the meetings–the organization meetings?" And I told her yes. She says, "I'm going to miss my"–whatever show she watches. I said, "Then you can't be the vice president or a volunteer. So at this point, you're not even a volunteer because of being with me."

I think you have to understand my daughter's nine years old, but I think that was an opportunity to have a conversation. Together, we watched the program director for the soccer program in the rain; he was wet, with his son, you know, taking apart the goals, the goalies. And families with their kids that volunteer–they are getting wet and picking up garbage, and I told my kids, I said, "Look at those families, okay? Because they could be home watching movies or doing other things, and they're here. Everyone else left, and they're here, and they don't get paid, you know? And that's what matters. That's what matters the most–is people that do it for love, you know?" So I think, again, it was a good opportunity for them to hopefully, when they get older and they become professionals, that they could come back and continue to make a difference.

I think we need to get back to basics. We need to reconnect with the community. I think every organization is built from the ground up, and in this great city, it is made by the great people that live here, you know? Not by the great corporations but by the great people. The mayor's father started a grass-root community effort. He was connected. He was engaged in the community. It doesn't mean just coming to a march. It means engaging, you know? Coming here to the community and really hearing, listening to the people in the community–not only listening but going back to basics, and we are able to implement community centers. They bring resources to encourage, you know, the kids to continue education.

And not everyone is going to a university, but maybe they could be carpenters or electricians. We need technical schools. We need opportunities, and the CEO of the public schools–I think he needs to understand that we cannot, we cannot put it in one big cookie cutter, and everything's going to be data driven. I don't think it works like that. I think we're dealing with, with emotions. I think we're dealing with broken families. I think we're dealing with broken communities–communities that have no options. If I go right now, in this moment, if I go to this corner on Forty-Eighth and Loomis, and I tell the group of kids there, "Why are you there? Do something," that kid is going to tell me, "Okay, show me what." And I don't have anything–anything. Why? Because the school across the street is refusing to open doors and because there is no church, and there's no community center–because there is nothing. There's no option for that kid. I'm not saying that should be an excuse, but again, most likely, his father and mother are not at home, because they're working.

Reflections

From a young age, Rafael experienced the importance of relationships. He understood the lure of gangs from his early days in the city, when he was lonely and simply wanted to be part of a group; in his neighborhood, the group was structured around gang membership. In school, he felt the lack of attention from counselors who didn't know his name or anything about him or his family. They made assumptions about him and held low expectations as they advised him to get a job following high school rather than to think about college. The fact that his proficiency in English was not high enough to allow him to register for regular classes at a community college following high school is a significant example of the system holding low expectations for many of its students and making assumptions about their future potential.

Rafael tells about the significance of the one person who stepped forward to help him when he was told to repeat a grade due to his age. He says he will never forget her. Her confidence in his abilities helped him raise his own expectations and achieve his potential. He emphasizes that there cannot be a cookie-cutter approach to helping kids. In order to make a difference, adults need to feel accountable and get to know the youth they encounter in a more comprehensive way. They must find ways to make connections so that children don't turn to gangs for support.

4

Jose

To get inside the elementary school where Jose works, I pushed a buzzer on the outside wall. The security guard in the hallway let me in just as he does all visitors, including parents, who come to visit during the day. He directed me to the reception area, where there was a frenzy of activity along with school announcements continuously punctuating the air. This is where Jose spends his days, and despite other employment opportunities, he wouldn't trade this job for anything else. He believes in the power of the schools and is committed to raising his family in the community.

Background

My name is Jose, but they call me Chuy. I was born on December 25, 1962, and that is where my middle name, Jesus, comes from—the Jesus. I was born in San Juan, Texas. My parents would migrate here to Chicago for work, and my dad found a construction job here. We've been here since I was about twelve years old.

But we did live half the year in Texas and half here. It was hard. It was hard because I always felt more comfortable living here in the city. Going back to Texas was always a little bit harder. The community in Texas was a lot more rural. You know, the houses are a little bit further apart, whereas here in Chicago, you're really close to your neighbors. I feel like your neighbors are your friends, and even your aunts and uncles sometimes because they are the ones who are seeing you at every move. Whether you're outside doing something that you're not supposed to be doing—your parents will hear about it. It was more of a more close-knit connection with neighbors, whereas in Texas, there were just certain things I didn't feel comfortable about. The school itself—I never felt like I got a good start in the school year, because we'd go there in the middle of the school year. In other words, we'd be here in September, start the school year off here, so even if I was new, everyone else was too. In Texas, it would be in the middle of the school year, like November. Everybody there had started in September, when the school year began. I would come in the middle, so it was kind of hard for me to make that adjustment. It was okay once I was there, but then I was leaving again in April. So I was there for four months and come back to the same classroom I was in here in September, so it was easier coming back. It was always hard going to Texas.

In Texas, the language was mainly Spanish, but there was also English. The kids in the neighborhood knew the English, whereas the Spanish part, I think the parents spoke mostly Spanish. At home, we spoke English because my mom understood it. My dad, however—he understood it, but we always felt more comfortable speaking to him in Spanish. So English was probably mostly our first language, I would say. We would use it a lot; however, my grandparents didn't speak any English. My grandparents only spoke Spanish, so we always had communication with our grandparents. I think it was just that when we thought we knew someone who was speaking in English, that understood English, that was what we would use, like with my cousins, like with my mom. Like, I had aunts who didn't speak English, so I would speak to them in Spanish. Like with anything else, I was more comfortable with English because I was surrounded by it all the time with my friends.

Spanish was never discouraged here in the city when I was in school. I never had any problem when we'd speak Spanish or we'd speak English. In Texas, we could not speak Spanish at school. It was to the point where if I was to say something out on the playground, I would have to be very careful if I spoke Spanish to one of my friends, because if there was an adult or another student who didn't speak Spanish who overheard that, we would get in trouble.

It happened to us quite a few times. Maybe at that moment, I wanted to express myself, and I couldn't to my friend. I could remember the word in Spanish, and I would say it in Spanish. I would want to say, "Hand me that pencil," but I couldn't remember the word for *pencil* in English, so I would say, "Hand me the *lapiz*." If you didn't understand it, you would take offense, or at least it was an opportunity to get somebody in trouble who did speak Spanish.

There wasn't any detention or anything like that, but there was some scolding involved by the teacher, or even the student himself would make you feel uncomfortable. Because it would be as bad as saying you swore. If you said something in Spanish, fingers would point at you: "You spoke Spanish! You spoke Spanish!" That made you feel, *Oh my God, I did say something in Spanish. I wasn't supposed to.* Then you felt like you did do something wrong, so you were afraid that he was going to go back and tell the teacher, and the teacher was going to come down on you. I don't think there was any harsh punishment, but just the fact that they made you feel like you were doing something wrong was enough. It made you not want to say it again.

Here, we did use Spanish. We're speaking English, and all of a sudden, one of us would start speaking Spanish. And the conversation would change to Spanish. There were both languages being used here with no problem.

Well, here's the thing—when we went back to Texas, you would always feel like you're doing fine. Here in Chicago, as a student, I thought to myself, *This is easy.* So I would do my homework, start the school year here with no problem. Go down there, and if I was in third grade here, I would be placed one year back in Texas and go into second grade. So that, in itself, made it difficult starting second grade—starting in the middle of the school year but starting at an age where everybody's one year younger than you are.

Choosing a Community

I live in the Pilsen community and have never left, not since we came here to live. I guess the question is really why haven't I left? A lot of people would say, "Why are you still here? Why did you buy there?" Because I'm now a homeowner. People were wondering fifteen years—no, twelve years—ago, when I purchased the home, why I was purchasing in this community. Maybe it's because I've liked being close to my neighbors. You know, I still will have neighbors who have lived here since I was young, and they're still here. I know these are my friends' parents, and I see them all the time. I was comfortable here. I think first of all, my parents and my in-laws were here. I was the first one to get married on my side of the family, from my mom's side. Maggie [Jose's wife] was the first one that got married from hers. She's the oldest, so she's the first one that got married. We knew our brothers and sisters were still here, so obviously that was going to make it comfortable for us to stay here. But there was that question where friends and even neighbors said, "Why are you buying here?" We wanted to stay close to the family. All my in-laws have moved out now. So it's just us and my father-in-law and mother-in-law.

When my sisters-in-law decided that they were going to move out to the suburbs, they got good schools. Your children will probably have a good opportunity out there. Not that they couldn't find it here, because I think it still has a lot to do with how they're reared, and it has a lot to do with home.

Education and Expectations

If you move into an area where there's a good school and your home-attendance school is going to be a good school, I think it makes it a little easier for you. You don't have to be as involved, be as persistent. Definitely your surroundings have a lot to do with it. The students that you hang out with or your friends that you're with—if that circle tends to be toward education or being interested in some type of sport, that's the way you tend to lean. And I think we still—and when I say "we," I mean the parents—have to push the children into that education. I don't think it comes natural. I don't think it does. I guess we're kind of lucky to some point, because we were able to do that with Jessica, and we were able to do that with Alex. Alex is my son, who is twelve years old now. So we expect a little bit more from them than, I guess, our parents would have expected from us. Or at least maybe not expected, but they were able to provide for us.

Definitely my mom thought I would be college material. I just wanted to graduate high school—that's it. And if you were to ask me now do I regret any of that? No, I do not. Will I change any of that? I don't see that in my picture tomorrow. Am I considering going back to school now? No. Do I want the same for my children? Of course not—right now, I want them to go to college. I just think they're going to have a better opportunity.

When it was my turn to go and look and take the ACT test, I never even did that. I just had it set in my mind that I was going to graduate from high school and not go on to college. I don't think that it had anything do to with my parents, if they could provide that for me or not. I was just one of those students that thought I wasn't going to go. I wanted to work construction with my dad. That was what I thought I was going to end up doing.

Of course your parents don't think that's the best for you. Just like I don't think—I think there's always more out there. But once I started working and started, I guess, providing for myself—I should say not having to depend on my parents so much anymore—I lived there until I got married, and I was twenty-four years of age. I wasn't independent up until that point. I was working; I had my car and bicycle and everything I thought I needed at that time. And it wasn't till I got married and moved out. Neither one of us had an education outside of high school. My wife, I think, went to college for a few semesters, but that was about it. And no, we don't want the same for our children. We want our children to—I don't know why; that's just our goal. Now it's get our kids to go a little bit further than we did.

And my daughter is surrounded by it. I don't know if I mentioned to you earlier—she's at a magnet school. So her surroundings, 90 percent of the kids are saying, "We're going to go to college." So it rubs off on them. They start hearing, and they start thinking, and they start pulling out applications, and they start helping each other out. So I think it has a lot to do with that too.

Experience with Gangs

When I was in high school, this community had a very bad reputation for gangs back then. They probably still do, but when you're a teenager growing up around them, you're just happy not to be involved in that. You come across incidences like that. I did. I've had guns pulled on me where I've actually been threatened or hurt or something like that, but just the fact that you're able to make it past that, you feel like you're successful already.

When I attended high school, I wasn't completely past it, because I ran into incidences at the high school. I'm not blaming the school; I think it's just, how would you say, the student population. That's what the problem was there. You probably had at the beginning, when the school first opened, a large majority of students that were related to gangs or were in gangs. That large population of students made it difficult for other students in school who didn't want to have anything to do with gangs.

> You probably had at the beginning, when the school first opened, a large majority of students that were related to gangs or were in gangs. That large population of students made it difficult for other students in school who didn't want to have anything to do with gangs.

It was difficult to stay out of gangs, because my freshman year, when I was walking home one day, I heard somebody call my name out as they drove by in the car. I saw the car, and I didn't think anything of it. When they pulled around a second time, some guy got out that I knew from grammar school. And he says, "Hey, Chuy, how have you been?" And I thought, *Oh, good*. I was happy that it was him when he got out of the car, because I knew they were gangbangers; I just didn't know who they were. When I saw it was someone I knew, I thought, *Oh, good, it's someone that I know*. He asked me for my book. These are his words exactly: "I hear a lot of guys are turning RBs on me." RBs are a gang that was being formed at that time called the Racine

Boys. And I was like, "Oh, really?" I was just happy to see someone I know. "Can I see your book?" I give him my book, and he's looking through my math book. Again, at this point, I'm just relieved. I don't care what he's doing with my math book, but he's standing with another taller gentleman, and he says, "You're cool," and he gives me my book back. And he says, "Okay, you're on your own." And I said, "Baretto, what are you talking about?" That was his nickname–Baretto. The other gentleman that was with him grabbed me by the collar of my coat, just like this.

Baretto was, "Okay now. You're not an RB; you're a King." That wasn't enough for the other guy, who grabbed me by my coat and says, "Remove your coat." Now, at that time, I wanted to be in style, and if you wore a long coat, that was the style, but it also made you look like a gang member. So that was probably the first reason they stopped me. The color of the coat had no significant color. It was just beige–a long beige wool coat, warm, nice. It was late in the fall, probably early November, so it was time to wear that coat. It was cold. And he grabbed me, and he says, "Remove the coat." And I says, "Baretto, you know me–tell these guys." He said, "No, you're on your own now. I just wanted to make sure you were not an RB." So he gets back in the car, and another young man gets out. I didn't see the other young man, but when the other guy told me to remove my coat, I said, "I'm not taking off my coat." It was brand new. My older brother had just bought it for me. My older brother was hardworking. He was working. He had just gotten out of high school, and he was working midnights at Ryerson. And his theme was "If you ever need anything, I'm going to provide you with it. Ma and Pa can do that, but I want to help." So he did. That was what he got me for that year. So they made me remove it; he closed-fisted punched me in the face. I said, "My coat's not worth that much." So I did remove it, and I gave it to him. And then he got in the car and took off.

They all left together. There was a carload, so there must have been at least five in there. But I do know the driver was there; Baretto; the guy who made the contact; the guy who hit me; and a fourth person who was looking out of the car corner window. So I go into Dvorak Park, and I go in there, and the rec leader tells me, "What are you doing without a coat?" And I says, "Well, they just took it away from me." And he said, "Who took it away from you?" And I said, "Well, this carload of guys–they got out, and I know who they were." "Why don't you call the police?" "You think I should?" So I thought about it a little bit. *Wow, okay, I'm going to call the police.* So I called the police.

Well, here I go the next day back to school, and my mom says, "You might be running some dangerous spots." She introduced me to this gas station, and the gas station attendant said, "If you run into a situation, just come into the gas station, and we'll take care of it." But I was a freshman, and there was some sophomores and juniors near us that came to me and said, "We live on your side of the neighborhood, and we understand that you ran into a problem. Why don't you walk home with us tonight just to make sure that everything's okay?" I started thinking to myself, *Well, okay,* because I knew these sophomores and juniors and knew they weren't in trouble, and I knew they weren't troublemakers. I said sure, I'd like that.

But then I also had the RBs come to me and say, "I heard you ran into some trouble yesterday." I said, "Yeah." He said, "Chuy, do you want to join us?" "I don't think it's the best thing I could do right now." They actually asked me or invited me. "Now is the time when you can join us. You can be protected by us. Hang out with us, and you won't have to worry about those types of problems." I said, "No, I think I'm okay." And I was, because the following day, I got home, and we got a call from the police station, saying, "Come identify your coat. Make sure it's your coat." So I went into the police station, with my parents this time. And this is Barreto: "This is your coat." They took it out of a plastic bag. And they said, "Is there anything else?" This is the police talking. "Is there anything else you'd like for us to handle here?" I says, "What am I going to do now? They know who I am." And they told Barreto, "If anything happens to this young man, whether you are in the area or not, it's going to come back to you." That's the words they told to my friend–because I thought he was my friend. He said, "Okay," and they kept away from me. Well, first of all, they weren't in that high school. So they weren't going to be coming back to the school anyway. But I think they stayed away when they heard that the RBs kinda said, "Okay, keep away from him; let him do his own thing." And I did.

So I walked home with these sophomores and juniors and then started getting involved with baseball and softball. It was a totally different atmosphere. And of course, being a freshman, knowing all the freshman that are from your class and knowing the sophomores and knowing the juniors became a popularity contest for me. So I was like everybody's little brother, and everybody's brother that was at my age level. And it was nice at that time, and I thought it was great. But it didn't help with my focusing on high school. That might have had some backfire on it.

The school was so new; there was gang fights in the lunchroom–big ones: garbage cans being thrown. You've got a new school. By the way, maybe I didn't mention, but when I went to the high school, my freshman year was the first year they opened. So you can imagine how many new students came there from every side of the neighborhood and how many of them were involved in gangs that were trying to take over the school, 'cause that's what they were trying to do. At first, I was glad not to be involved in any of that, even though it came this close. Could the school have done anything different? I think so.

This is something I will always blame the school for, but maybe they were just too new to know what to do.

High-School Experience

I spoke mostly English. I could speak Spanish, and I could read it, and I could write it. But when it comes to understanding it, I had the problem of I couldn't sit down and have a teacher teach me in Spanish. It was easier for me to learn in English. So I was in an honors class for algebra my freshman year, and they took me out of the honors class because my first-quarter grade was a C; my second-quarter grade was a C, so it averaged out to a C. The reason for them pulling me out of my honors class was they thought I'd do better in a regular classroom and maybe score a little higher and get a better grade. Initially, the teacher's request was a good request or an okay request. The problem is when they put me in another algebra class, there was no more room in a regular classroom. So they took me out of the classroom that I could understand and put me in a bilingual classroom where even though we were working with numbers, the teacher was always speaking Spanish. And I just focused out, focused out.

> The problem is when they put me in another algebra class, there was no more room in a regular classroom. So they took me out of the classroom that I could understand and put me in a bilingual classroom where even though we were working with numbers, the teacher was always speaking Spanish. And I just focused out, focused out.

So that is where I got an F the third quarter. Again, that wasn't my biggest worry at that time. I just wasn't worried about it. What they told me and all the other students was, "If you fail, you're missing half a credit of algebra, and you can't take geometry next year." "What do you mean I can't take geometry?" "If you don't pass your algebra class, you can't go on for your geometry. You're not supposed to." I don't say nothing, because I've got a geometry class; I'm signed up for it. Maybe they don't know. The teachers don't know; they got eight hundred students to worry about. I go to geometry class. Geometry class is okay. I get passing grades in geometry class in junior year.

My senior year, they tell me, "You're missing half a credit in algebra." Then I start blaming the school. That's when I said, "You guys moved me out to geometry; you were supposed to let me know. You moved me out of an honors class to put me in a regular classroom. You didn't find any room, so you put me in a bilingual classroom, and that backfired on me." Whatever I said was not going to make a difference. Eventually, I was going to have to make up that half credit. "Good, I'll make up the half credit. What do I have to do?" "You have to go to night school." "Okay, what do I have to do?" "Go to night school at a college located in a completely different section of the city." I went there and took an English class to make up that algebra credit. So I took an English class for like six months, and I made up an algebra credit.

So guess what? My goal was to graduate, and my dad was going to help me graduate. At some point, even when I was a junior, they were talking high-school rings, about ordering your high-school ring. I'm not going to order it. I knew I was missing a half credit, and I was afraid; I was almost embarrassed that if I do order a high-school ring, I wasn't going to graduate. There I am with my 1981 high-school ring, and I'm graduating in 1982. I just said, "Forget that. I don't think I'm going to graduate; forget my high-school ring." And then, of course, college is way out of my question. I'm not thinking I'm going to go to college anyway. But I graduated, and I was happy with that.

Following Graduation

After graduating, then it was like "What are you going to do now? You graduated." But can I work with dad? "No, you can't work with dad." My mom said, "You're going to Spanish Coalition." I don't know if you've ever heard of this community-based organization that taught basic job skills directly related to employment. "Why don't you sign up for Spanish Coalition?" Why would I want to go to a class for typing and this and that? Basically, that's all it was. I shouldn't say that, but most of it, that's what it was: learning typing skills. I don't want to go to Spanish Coalition, but they gave us incentive: "Go there, and we will pay you minimum wage for going, for taking this class." So I did. And I picked up some typing skills, and I picked up some general office skills. And then they help place me in a job. They help place you in a good job, in an office-environment job. I did that, and I liked it. Then, of course, I'm nineteen or twenty years old. Now, I'm actually–how can I say that?–making money in a decent way. I'm not making a lot of money, but I'm making money in a decent way. And I bought a car. That's what you think of first. Actually, I didn't buy a car; my brother bought me the car, which was nice of him. He tells me, "Pay me back when you get a chance." I think his goal was he knew I could easily fall into trouble out there, and he wanted to keep me focused away from that. He thought buying me a car would probably keep me focused in keeping my job, because now I got to pay him back. So I did pay him back.

What happened is that my car was eventually going to be customized and become a lowrider. That was my goal, and I knew that in high school, and that's what I did. I saved my money, and I don't regret doing it, because I got it out of my system. But when you're forty-three years old and looking back at what you did when you were nineteen, you don't know if it was always the smartest or the best thing you could have done. Right? But I look back at when I was nineteen and twenty years old, and I bought my car, and what I did with my paycheck after I gave it to my mother for whatever they needed, because I did live at home. And I started investing in my car, getting a paint job and buying wheels for it and thinking to myself, *This is cool*. And it was; it was for me back then. A lot of the guys that I hung out with thought it was cool. Not everyone was able to buy a car and do this with it, because some of them may have been in college and had other things on their mind.

So that's what I did—customized my car—and I met other friends, new friends who liked to get into customizing cars. Not bad people—good people like me, who are married, who are having children but didn't have that focus on college. My brother-in-law was one of them. I started hanging out with him and then met his sister—my wife, Maggie; I met her by stopping over at his house, picking him up. I was twenty years old. What was I going to do? I already had a car. No, I shouldn't say that. It's just to be a little funny. I liked her; she was interesting, and we had a lot in common.

She doesn't like my car. I still own it. I mean, that was something to me. My wife tells me, "You love your car." That's not true, because I haven't done anything to it in years. I mean, there's this thing about that car; I don't sell it, because I don't have to at this point. It's not the most important thing to me. It carries a lot of history with me, and people tell me if you ever sell your car; one day, if I have to, I will sell it. It's a classic '63 Buick Riviera; it is a big car, heavy car.

I went through a lot of problems when I was nineteen to twenty years old, driving a car like that. I got stopped a lot. I was harassed. I actually felt I was harassed a lot because, again, I was working. This is all legal. I wasn't doing something illegal to purchase my car, to drive around in it. I had a driver's license, but I got stopped a lot by the police. First of all, back then, when I was nineteen, twenty years old, I would hear a lot about "You look fifteen, sixteen years old." So that probably was one of the reasons they stopped me. But my car was always turned inside out by the police officers. They honestly thought they were going to find something. But when they'd ask me for my ID and ask me if I was old enough to drive, they would see they got nothing else to do. "Well, we stopped you; we might as well search your car." So they would search my car.

But there were times where I was actually harassed by them. What I mean is I would get stopped, and if I would have either my wife or my girlfriend or a date or just a friend in the car that was female, I was called everything in the book. They would actually talk to the girls and say, "What are you doing with this bum? He's this; he's that." They don't know me personally, but they were judging me by what I was driving because it was a customized car, and it was a lowrider. If you had a lowrider, you were either a gangbanger or you were dealing drugs, or you were just a no-good nobody. So that's what they would tell these girls. I'm not the type of person that swears, my friends know, but the language that they would use about me made me feel so bad, but I told myself I got to respect. They were in uniform, and if I say something wrong, I'm going to catch the bad end of it. "Okay, Officer, whatever you say." They would literally try to get you to say something wrong to have that reason. That's all they wanted was the reason. And I would never give it to them. I'd never give it to them.

Inside, it was eating me up. Inside, I wish that he was just an average person. First of all, they're older than me. But if they had been an average person, I would have handled it different. But I had to respect that it was a police officer and the consequences I would suffer if I had done something or said something. But they did make me feel this small in front of my friends.

My Children

I've told my children my stories, but I've seen that my daughter tends to be more curious about what my mom says than what I say. Maybe because she feels I will be able to repeat it ten years from now. Where my mom— hopefully she will be able to remember half the things she does now. But yeah, Alex—I don't think there's the necessity of telling him about that yet. He's still too young. I don't want him to go out and think to himself, *Policemen are bad*. I don't want him to think, *I'm not going to drive my dad's car, because police are going to stop me*.

My daughter, Jessica, is at a selective-enrollment school. Her grades, I guess, got her a scholarship to a private school. She went there for seventh and eighth grade. Why wouldn't she go to the community high school? Because we feel—at least I feel—that she has a better opportunity being surrounded by something that has that positive feeling toward education. I'm not saying that students at the community high school do not. I just definitely know that the students at her school, 90 percent do have that interest, and I think being surrounded by that influence is important.

Our parents were fighting for the community high school the same year her magnet school opened up, so I had classmates who chose to go to there because they got accepted in the selective enrollment. I'm sure had

I applied there and if I had the option, I'd have gone there because it was supposed to be a better school.

Many of us stayed at the community high school, made the best of what we could there. I'm sure they didn't have the problems at the magnet school that we were having when they opened. They didn't have the gangs. You're talking about a magnet school, talking about a school that's drawing from every area of the city. Did that make a difference? Yeah, that made a difference. Because here the guys that were coming because they had to come to school, because they had to be enrolled in a school. Some of them, whether they were interested in being in school or not, were going to be there, and you're going to come across them. But if you're involved in a gang, if you're a gang member, and you live in the attendance area, you get to go to the community high school, whereas a selective-enrollment school, if you're in a gang, you're going to keep to yourself because you're traveling to get to that school. And if you are involved in a gang, you are not going to make it open there.

But if you're involved in a gang, if you're a gang member, and you live in the attendance area, you get to go to the community high school, whereas a selective-enrollment school, if you're in a gang, you're going to keep to yourself because you're traveling to get to that school. And if you are involved in a gang, you are not going to make it open there. Because you don't know who half these people are. It makes it a little bit harder.

I don't think it'd be tougher for Jessica to go to the community high school, but it's not as safe as where she is. I can tell her to go ahead and catch the bus, because I know she's going down Halsted. But if I tell her to walk to the community high school, I myself know what that walk is like 'cause of what happened to me–the experience I told you about earlier. So what I would do is say, "Let me drop you off." Where it's a shorter walk, it's a shorter distance from the community high school from my house than it is from the magnet school to my house on public transportation, but I know what it could be like out there.

And if you're going to tell me that it's different fifteen or twenty years ago, when I went to high school, than what it is now, not really–not really. Not what's out on the streets, no. Maybe the school itself has changed. Maybe you don't have those big brawls we used to have. But what's the commuting part? That scared me. It does–not because I think she's going to look for anything but just getting caught in the crossfire. You heard what happened just recently. I think about it all the time.

Safety in the Community

When I first bought here, it wasn't because I thought my property was going to skyrocket. I bought here because outside of the gang activity, I liked the neighborhoods. I liked the people. But there has been times–I'll tell you an incident that, that I literally wanted to fall to my knees and cry. [At this point, Jose asked that I turn off the tape recorder so that he could calm himself.] My daughter was about twelve years old–you know, seeing Jessica in the middle of the night having to jump to the, you know, off the bed and to the floor because she heard gun shots, something awoke me emotionally; it did. I just felt bad. It was funny at first, but then I thought to myself, *God, it's very likely that something could come in through the window and hit her.* You know? You don't hear this every night; it's not like you hear them every night, but if you hear this two times a year, that's a lot. That's more than enough. So you really don't want your children to grow up around that–you don't.

There was already one incident when I was coming home. These are now children or grandchildren of the same people I love seeing and who say hi to me, and they talk to me–the grandchildren of them who may be hanging out on corners, you know, and they're thirteen, fourteen years old. I tell you when we first moved into our house, I came home with Alex, who was probably about a year old. I still had to carry him to get in and out of the car parked right in front of my house. As I'm coming out, these guys that were out there, about fourteen to fifteen years old, who were gangbangin'. It wasn't the first time they were there; it wasn't the last time they're going to be there. It's right in front of my house, and here in front of my house, it's fifteen yards–no, fifteen feet–not very far from the corner where they're standing to the actual first wall of your house; it's not very big. As I'm walking in and I'm getting ready to open door, the car rides by, and they start flashing gang signs and representing to the car that's driving by.

> I'm telling them, "What are you doing out here? Don't you know that I'm getting out of the car, and if these guys decide to shoot back at you, they're going to hit one us?" Of course, they understood, but they weren't thinking what they did when they did it.

Of course, I take the kids inside the house and come back out, full of rage, and I start getting on these kids' backs. These are fourteen- and fifteen-year-old kids. I'm telling them, "What are you doing out here? Don't you know that I'm getting out of the car, and if these guys decide to shoot back at you, they're going to hit one us?" Of course, they understood, but they weren't thinking what they did when they did it. They weren't thinking; I know they weren't thinking. But when I went out there and told them what could have happened, what could have resulted out of their stupidity, they understood. They said they're sorry: "We did not realize it." They're sorry; they don't realize it because they live it every minute of that day until they grow out of it. They're focused in on what they're going to do, and they're focused in on who's coming up behind them and what cars are passing by. So as soon as they say something, they're going to duck down as soon as they see any reason to, and those innocent bystanders like myself are going to go out there, and we're not going to realize it.

I think the schools try to get at this problem. I mean, I think every school wants to be free of that. I don't think there's a school that doesn't give it the attention that it has to, but it's hard for the school to do that and everything else that's expected of a school. You know, this thing about, I guess, the police officers are the ones who have to be out there during dismissal time. 'Cause they're the ones who can make it a little bit safer. You know, our security officer here does a real good job. He's out there, and he walks and makes sure the students go home and that no incident takes place. He can't do it by himself. I think if the police officers are out there, it makes it a little bit easier because he knows everybody. It makes it easier for him to show his authority. The school can only do so much in that sense.

A lot of the things I'm telling you about had nothing to do during the school hours. If Jessica had to commute by walking, I would still be careful about that. "Come on—I'll drop you off, and make sure you call me when you get home. Get to school, and give me a call," because you want to get to that comfort zone once you get in to work. You want to focus on your comfort zone once you get in to work, but if you don't know if your child's okay or not, you can't focus.

Family Engagement

You know, my mom was involved in a lot of community organizations. I wish I could do what she did. I still have a lot of my own self-interests—not my car anymore, but my kids and the fact that they played soccer; they played baseball. I coached the soccer; I coached a baseball team—fills up my day and then things I like to do, you know, things I like to do that also has a lot to do with why I don't focus into community organizations. I have in the past, and then I haven't, but I, I try to tell Jessica, "Do what you want to do." Jessica does a better job of it than I do or than me and my wife do. I think she plays a very big part in—she teaches catechism classes, which is at the church, which is the same place I grew up in.

We're Catholic; we go to Catholic church, and she's now teaching catechism classes because we tell her, "It's good for you to do this," you know. My mom was just glad I went, I think. I don't think she expected us to teach. I think she was like, "Okay, great. They're going; that's good." We're not just saying you gotta go. You gotta help–you gotta reach out and teach what we think is right. So we always tell Jessica, "Do community service. Go help the neighbors set up for this; go help them with that." Even though we don't do it ourselves, we think it's the right thing to do. We don't get involved much in community organizations.

You know what? I think my main goal is getting my children in higher education, and if I lose focus in that or both me and Maggie lose focus in that–I always think that once they're set, it might drive me to do the same. I don't want to lose focus in that right now.

Reflections

Jose begins his story by talking about how difficult it was for him to switch schools midyear due to his parents' work. As he moved between states on a regular basis, he was often put back a grade with no consideration given to his skills or achievement. At the same time, he was also receiving mixed messages about his native language, Spanish. In Texas, speaking Spanish was punished, while in his current urban community, it was allowed. Later on, he attended the community high school, which was a school that his mother and other community organizers had spent years fighting to establish. Jose was a member of its first class, yet when it came time for his daughter to attend high school, he did not consider it good enough for her. This was a consequence of his personal experiences, which included witnessing gang fights inside the school, receiving little personal attention, and being sent across the city to receive enough credits to graduate as a result of poor advising. He was not convinced there was enough emphasis on education and encouraging students to go on to college.

Despite Jose's personal experiences with gangs and fearing for the safety of his family, he is committed to living in the Pilsen community. It is here where he feels at home. He knows everyone and feels as if neighbors watch out for neighbors. He is close to family and works in the office of one of the neighborhood elementary schools. Jose works hard so that his children can have the education he believes they deserve.

5

Zulema

Z ulema was a college student at the time of her interview. Her family brought their children to the United States in order for them to have more opportunities and an education. The public schools discouraged Zulema until she followed the advice of her older sister and discovered teachers who cared about her. She talks about the challenges she faced due to her undocumented status and how she wants to be a mentor to other young women who face similar struggles.

> The biggest difference between the schools, I think, was the fact that the teachers seemed interested in us. Like in high school, I was known as a number in a lot of the classrooms. When they would pass attendance, I was number twenty-seven or number sixteen, and the teachers—I guess because they had a lot of students—they didn't really try to interact with us as much.

Educational Background

I'm twenty years old. Right now, I'm working with a nonprofit organization that focuses on immigrant rights, and I am also working with another program in the community. What we do is teach kids from elementary schools, and right now, I'm teaching them theater; I'm also a student at a local college.

I have two brothers. One is twenty-six, and the other one is ten, and then I have a sister which is twenty-five. From all of those, only my sister went to college. I wasn't really planning on going to college, because when I was in high school, I was not really interested in education for me. I thought it was boring. My freshman year, I went to high school, and I would always ditch school. I would never be in class. Maybe it might have been the people I was hanging around with, but for me, school was boring; I didn't find the point of it. So my sister would always tell me, "You have to go to college because that's the only way you're going to succeed in life." She motivated me a lot, and then I actually went back to school. I transferred schools. I went to a smaller school with smaller students in the classroom. And my report card just changed so much. I went from having straight Fs to As and Bs. And I just took advantage of every opportunity I had.

The biggest difference between the schools, I think, was the fact that the teachers seemed interested in us. Like in high school, I was known as a number in a lot of the classrooms. When they would pass attendance, I was number twenty-seven or number sixteen, and the teachers–I guess because they had a lot of students–they didn't really try to interact with us as much. But at the community-based high school I transferred to, there was about thirteen to fifteen students in each class, and the teachers knew my parents. The principal knew my parents. I felt more comfortable there.

My parents would go to school to see how I was doing a lot. And sometimes my adviser, which was my teacher–he would sometimes call my house and find out how I was doing or talk to my parents and let them know how I was doing as well. I saw the connection between my family and my teachers, so that made me focus more on school as well.

My mom did go to the high school a lot, but it was an issue because a lot of the time, she would go to see how I was doing, and I wasn't there. I would come in through the front door and leave through the back. I guess I took advantage of the liberty I had, because at home, my parents were very strict. They didn't want me going out; they didn't want me being outside after eight o'clock. I had to let them know who I was going to be with–everything, right? That's good, now that I think of it; it's good. But back then, I was really mad. All my friends had more liberty than I did. I would think, *How come I can't be like her? She's out until ten.* So I guess I took advantage

I was the only one who didn't get pregnant, and I was the only one who continued my education without getting in trouble anymore. And I'm thankful for that. It was because of my sister's and parents' support, because they never gave up on me. So I thank them a lot, too.

of the fact that once I was in school, it was easier for me to leave and go places with my friends, like to the park.

There was security there, but I don't know; students do that [leave school] all the time. It would be hard sometimes when security would be walking down the hallways, but we would find our ways and would leave. And a lot of teachers would never call my house or anything like that. You know how a lot of public schools have that machine that calls home to let you know your student wasn't there? I used to disconnect the phone because I already knew around what time they would call. And I would just connect it back, and my parents would never find out. I mean, I know that students find ways. They're always going to find ways to get away with things. That's wrong, but I really feel like we need more schools like the community-based high school, because that really changed me a lot. I know there's a lot of students out there who were just like me and never had the opportunity to go to a school like I did and just ended up dropping out and maybe getting pregnant.

Honestly, all my friends at the high school—all the girls were always together. All of them are pregnant or have kids already; only two of them are going to college right now. It is really hard for them because they already have a baby. I was the only one who didn't get pregnant, and I was the only one who continued my education without getting in trouble anymore. And I'm thankful for that. It was because of my sister's and parents' support, because they never gave up on me. So I thank them a lot, too.

Actually, they kicked me out of my first high school. I got kicked out because of all my cuts and absences, but they actually gave me a chance to come back. And I told my mom I didn't want to go back, because I already knew how it was going to be. So my mother talked to the priest in my neighborhood from the church we go to, and he was the one who mentioned the community-based high school. Because they were actually planning on sending me to Boys Town, which is this school in Nebraska for troubled kids, and they're very strict. You cannot come home for like years and stuff like that. But my priest was like, "No, she's not a bad girl; she's a good girl. We just have to find the right school for her." They took me, and since I got there, I changed everything around.

I got involved with community work just because I wanted to be involved; I wanted to do something after school. I didn't want to hang around with the same crowd of people. So I started teaching catechism in my church. I started joining after-school programs in my school, like theater, because I'm very into theater. And then through the teachers that I met through my theater classes, they are the ones who told me about how there's more theater programs in the community. So that's when I went, and then I met more people there, and then I started doing more community service there.

Since I was young, I remember I would always, like in elementary school, be the main character in plays because my voice is really loud. I also love dancing. I've always liked it. Since I was a little girl, I love being on stage. So when they mentioned that we're having a theater program in my school, I decided to join, and the theater teachers were like, "Wow"–they were amazed. They're like, "You have something. I can see your passion; you should keep pursuing it." So I did. So right now, I've already done a lot of plays here, and we perform at different universities, and I love it. I want to continue.

> I know a lot of the kids that I graduated from elementary with–a lot of them are not in college right now. And that's sad because in my neighborhood, it's awkward when you find somebody talking about college.

A lot of teachers did stand out. I graduated from kindergarten and eighth grade from that same school, so I had actually had the same teacher in kindergarten and in third grade. I guess she changed from kindergarten, and she went to third. And she was the one who also motivated me a lot to love theater and to perform. She would always put me as the main girl to sing or the girl to dance. And in third grade, the play we had–I also had the main part of it. So I visit her often, and I tell her I'm doing theater, and she's gone to my plays.

When I was at the high school, actually, I was very ashamed of what I was doing, and I stopped visiting her for a while. Because I knew she was going to ask me, "How's school?" and I didn't want to lie. But I think the best thing I could have done was I should have gone to somebody to talk. A lot of the times, I guess I regretted what I was doing, and I did not want to talk to anybody; I just, like, wanted to stay on my own. Because I didn't want anybody to know I was doing wrong, just leave me alone. I was ashamed of it, but the best thing to do is always have somebody there. And I'm glad that I had someone like my sister to motivate me and to tell me, "You're doing things wrong."

I know a lot of the kids that I graduated from elementary with–a lot of them are not in college right now. And that's sad because in my neighborhood, it's awkward when you find somebody talking about college. Like I found myself, when I talk to my old friends that maybe pass by my house, because I don't go out a lot or hang around in the park or anything, and we started talking about school, I noticed a lot of them just like walking away: *Oh, I have nothing to do with that conversation; I'm just going to walk away.* But it's, like, I think it's sad. Why do things have to be that way? Why?

Documentation Status

My dad came to the United States because he wanted to give us a better life, and then later on, my mother, me, my sister, and my older brother came. I lived my whole life here undocumented. I just recently became a resident. It's made such a difference, because first of all, I had a lot of people from my family tell me, "Oh, what's the point of you going to college?" I have a lot of cousins who dropped out of high school because of the fact that they were undocumented. The way they see things is like, what's the point

> I just recently became a resident. It's made such a difference because first of all, I had a lot of people from my family tell me, "Oh, what's the point of you going to college?" I have a lot of cousins who dropped out of high school because of the fact that they were undocumented.

of going to college? You're going to get a degree, but what's going to happen when you do? They are not going to take you at a job unless you have a social [social security number], right? They get to me a lot, but I would be like, "No, I know that there's going to be something; there's just a plan that's going to happen, and I am going to be able to do something with my life." So I didn't give up.

I realized I was undocumented when I was in elementary school, because there was a lot of programs we could join, and I wasn't able to. I was like, "Why can't I join?" "It's because you don't have a social." "What's a social?" I didn't know anything about this. I realized I was undocumented, and when I went to Big Picture, I realized, *I have to go to college. I have to do all this.* I would think about my friends that had a social and that were able to go to college and receive scholarships or receive financial aid, and I would get mad, like why couldn't they take advantage of that? I would tell a lot of my friends, "You have the opportunity to do so much. Go for it." I never paid for college from my pocket. Everything I paid for college–this is my second year in college–and I've been paying through nothing but scholarships. That's because I work hard. They don't have to work as hard as I have. They could just apply for financial aid; it's so much easier for them.

I started taking College Bridge classes. I kept doing good in school. I kept going to different programs, and I did not let my social stop me for anything. And right now that I received the social, I'm able to apply at jobs– good jobs. I was working at a supermall, and the guy I was working with was so rude. I felt like I don't have to be dealing with things like this. I have so many skills; I have so many internships. I deserve a better job than this. But I was aware of the fact that I couldn't get a better job because I didn't have a social.

So that gets to me a lot, and I know that gets to a lot of people as well. But I stayed there. And I knew that sooner or later, I was going to get my social, and everything was going to be okay. I remember the day that my social arrived at my house. I was so happy. I remember I used it right away. I told my mother, "Nothing's going to stop me." I texted the world, and I was just so happy.

My mom speaks a little English because of her job. She's a housekeeper, so she speaks English; she knows a few words but not a lot. We don't really speak it in the house, though. In elementary school, I took bilingual from kindergarten all the way to fifth. I didn't really know that much English until fifth grade. That's when I really started writing it. I guess it was good, and I'm glad I could take it, because now, right now, I can speak Spanish with a lot of confidence. That has helped me a lot. Because of the people that I've met and because the place where I'm working right now, it requires us talking to a lot of people who only speak Spanish, because I'm working with the immigrant community. I need to know a lot of Spanish; I speak in front of a lot of people, like a lot of parents. I feel comfortable doing it. So that's helped me a lot. I think if I would have just taken English since kindergarten, I wouldn't have been able to do the things I've done now.

Mentoring

I talk to a lot of my friends. They're like, "Oh, I don't know; maybe I'll go next semester." I don't know what it is. Like, right now, you cannot get a good job unless you have education. And I guess they're just used to the life in the neighborhood.

Just recently, I was talking to one of my cousins. She is fourteen years old, and she doesn't want to go to high school. And I saw myself in her. It's like, you know what? I see myself in you. That's how I was. I thought it was boring. She said, "Yes, I went for the whole first week, but it got boring." I'm like, "Of course it's boring. It might not be what you want, but try to sit in the front of the class, and try to listen to the teacher. And sooner or later, you are going to find something you like, because that's what happened to me at Big Picture." She goes, "Yeah, I guess." And I was asking her, "Why don't you want to go to college?" "I don't know. I just feel like just working." "Okay, where do you

> Oh, just because they have a nice car, and they want to be just like them. Sometimes it's the gangbangers who are the role models for these kids. I wish I could talk to all of them in a room and show them my straight-F report card and let them know everything I've done.

want to work?" "I'll probably work right there at that *supermercado*," which is like a grocery store. I'm like, "Oh, that's good. I guess you see yourself working there for the rest of your life, huh?" She's like, "Yeah, maybe." I was like, "How much are you getting paid?" She's like, "I don't know. It doesn't matter." I'm like, "It does matter. If you're going to work there for the rest of your life, just think about it. You're going to end up having your kids. You're going to end up having bills to pay. You need more money than that." And I was like, "Don't you want to explore? Don't you want to travel? Don't you want to meet new people, meet new friends?" But she's like, "No, I don't know. I like it here."

And then she has a boyfriend, and he drives a car, so obviously, he dropped out of high school. He's older than her. I got her really mad, but I still wanted to talk to her, so I still kept going with it. And she was like, "Yeah, my boyfriend–he doesn't go to school; he has a nice car, and he has nice rims and a nice system in the car. All the guys in the neighborhood want it, and they all look up to him." And I'm like, "Yeah, I'm pretty sure that's right, but I bet he's not happy with his life. He probably works at a place where he doesn't like to work, and he probably wishes he could have done something else." And she's like, "Well, I don't know." Just talking to her made me realize–why do kids look up to these kinds of people? Oh, just because they have a nice car, and they want to be just like them. Sometimes it's the gangbangers who are the role models for these kids. I wish I could talk to all of them in a room and show them my straight-F report card and let them know everything I've done.

Gang Impact

These are kids that come out of the school and a lot of times walk home. And as they're walking home, they see these cool guys riding in their cars–their cars, the way they have their rims, and the way they have the sound system, the way they're playing music really loud to attract all the girls' attention. And they see that they probably have money, and it's not through hard work. It's probably by selling drugs or easy things like that, which I know is going to get them in jail or something like that. The kids don't see that. All they see is "Wow, look at how cool he is," and it's bad. I just wish they could look up to people like teachers: "Oh my God, that's so cool. Look at her–she's so happy; she traveled. She showed pictures of her family in Hawaii," or something like that. We need more role models in our neighborhood.

Just the simple fact of the teachers motivating the kids: "Join this program after school; it's great." Even three hours after school makes a lot of difference because those three hours keep these kids from walking around and seeing all the gang activity in the neighborhood. These could help a lot.

So that, and then also, we need more programs anywhere. Right now, I was talking to one of my friends, and I told her, "Why don't we get a group of girls together and maybe meet like twice a week and just talk to them? It doesn't have to be like a lecture, but maybe we could take them to like downtown, take them to ride the train." Things like that help because you get to see new things. I know it could make a difference.

I think my family had raised us pretty well, because my older brother's not into any gang activity. He always stayed away from that crowd, even though he does talk to them, of course, because we've lived there all our lives. But my mom was after my brother: "Hey, come inside already; it's late." If she would see him wearing shirts too long, she would cut his shirt to make sure he would not buy long shirts. She would make sure he would not dress baggy either; that's how gangbangers dress. Another thing also: you don't want to get confused. I've friends who have been shot and killed because of the way they look, and they're not gangbangers. So it's very dangerous. My mom always made sure my brother never dressed like that, or he never shaved his head bald.

She saw it, and I have cousins that have been gangbangers. So she saw how they were, and she did not want my brother to be like that. My brother's one of the ones that said," No. School's not for me; I don't have a social. I'm just going to stick at working whatever I can work at." So he's not going to school right now, and he's still working. And I'm guessing he's doing a pretty good job, because the money he gets is decent money. He's worked hard for it. I think my parents did a good job, and I think other parents can do that too. Parents can do that. My mom did it. I think anybody can do it. It's hard because kids fall into the influence, but I think if you have your parents' support, you can go over anything.

Expanded Boundaries

When it was time for college, I was going to go to one of two city colleges, but then a lot of the kids that I knew were going there. And when I got to the community-based high school, I learned to let go of the fear of going places or meeting new people. Like, for example, I took advantage of all those programs where I had to travel on my own. And I received scholarships for them. My whole view of life changed. Nothing could stop me.

And then I went to Wyoming through the World Less Traveled Program, which is a program which takes students or kids for summer programs, and you learn leadership skills. You don't stay in a hotel or anything. You stay in the wilderness for like the whole three weeks or whole two days. It was so cool; you shower for once a week. I liked it a lot. It was a challenge, but

I loved it. And then my last trip was to Hawaii. It was through this program, the World Less Traveled, but since I didn't have the money, I had to apply for scholarships and grants. And I went around my neighborhood, going to banks, going to all these different businesses, just letting them know who I was and how I could serve the community.

So when I went to these programs, it was me and another Latina. And everybody there, of course, had money, because these are expensive programs. And I did feel kind of weird at first, because I was like, "Oh my God, I don't have new shoes," or "My tent is used," or "My sleeping bag is dirty." But I really cared. I let them know: "I'm here, and I'm honored to be here. I'm here because I got scholarships. I'm not here because my parents would never afford a trip like this for me." No, I made sure they knew who I was and why I was there. And at the end of the program, everybody fell in love with me. The leaders were like, "Oh my God, you're the one who always took advantage of everything." When we went out snorkeling, I was the last one in the water to come out; I learned how to swim over there.

When I first started to travel, my parents were scared because of immigration. "What if they say something to you at O'Hare?" "Mom, I'm going to be okay. I'm going to be okay. I'm going through a school program." And she was scared, especially when I was going to Washington.

For one of the workshops we had in Washington, DC, we had to pick from the issues. One of them was immigration, another one was abortion, and another one, I think, it was like health insurance or something like that. I chose immigration, and I was aware I was going to be in a room with a lot of people who didn't know I was an immigrant, but I just wanted to hear what they had to say. And my plan was to just sit there and listen, right? But I ended up being the main one who argued against the ones who were against immigration. I was going back and forth with people, and my teacher was there because we had a teacher from school to go with us. And when we came back to the community, she was sitting here: "Oh my God, you should have seen Zulema in Washington. She was talking, and it was great." I lost my fear. I lost that fear of going places where I didn't know anybody and just meeting new people. I feel like that makes anybody stronger.

So back to why did I choose my college? I just wanted to go somewhere new. It felt good. I had already the college experience thanks to my College Bridge classes. So I was not scared anymore. I liked it a lot. I liked that there was not a lot of students in the class. I felt real comfortable there. I noticed that there was a lot of Latinos there, and that made me feel so happy and so proud. It was like, "Wow, there's so many Latinos here. I love it." It made me feel so happy, and so far, so good. I guess once you're in college, you don't see it as boring anymore. You just see it like, "I have to learn to–I have to."

In four years, I will graduate; this is my second year already. But I'm still undecided about a major because I have so many passions. I don't know what to do. I think it makes it so difficult because of the fact that I'm still undecided on what I want to major in, but I definitely want to stay working in the Latino community. I wish I had somebody like me when I was young to talk to, and I feel like I can give so much to those girls who have no one to talk to. And especially, I want to focus on the eighth graders who are not going to high school yet, because I want to show them my report card and be like, "You don't want this." My GPA affected me throughout my whole four years of high school because of my freshman year, and you don't need that. I could have probably been at a good university right now, but it was so hard for me to bring my GPA back up after having my two semesters at the high school with nothing but straight Fs. I could have done something better about it, so I don't want anybody making the kind of mistakes I made. I'm not ashamed of saying this, but I want to share the things I've gone through, because I know a lot of people can learn from that. So I'm willing to do things like that.

I would love to do everything I love, but it's so hard. So far, I am doing it. So far, I'm teaching theater, and I'm in this organization that I'm helping my Latino community. And I'm in school, and I'm also planning on starting the little thing that I told you where I just want to get a whole bunch of girls and just talk to them. Hopefully, I can continue to do this, but I don't know.

Advice to Others

If I could see my old friends, I'd tell them to go back to school. To go back to school, it's never too late. I know it's going to be harder, but I admire them a lot—don't take me wrong—even though they, some of them, are not in school anymore. I admire them because of how strong they still are right now. Because a lot of these girls are not with a husband—I mean with the baby's father—but they're still working, and they're still bringing up their kid. They're making sure he eats and everything. But I know it's going to be easier if they go back to school, so that would be my advice. I know it would be really hard for you to maybe not be there with your kid twenty-four hours. But if you really want something better for this baby, go back to school. I just feel like everybody has to stay in school and keep going to school, because that's the only way of success.

I'd also like to talk to the teachers, to one day be able to go back to the high school and talk to whoever's in charge of all this and just talk to them. We need more–either if we're going to have a big class with kids, we need to make sure we do not call the kids by a number. That is the first thing that I would change. Not call a kid a number, because how is this "number" going to feel comfortable to ask a question to the teacher? If we are going to have a class with big [numbers of] students, we should have one-on-one with them at least once a week. I understand that these teachers have a lot of classrooms. At least once a week, just ask, "How's it going? How's your project?" Ten minutes a week–it's not hard, because students need this. Maybe they don't get any attention at home. Maybe ten minutes once a week can help a lot. I only spoke to my counselor once throughout the whole time. And that one time was because he was letting me know that I was no longer going to be able to be there because of my cuts. That's when it hit me. That's when I was like, "Wow." I had the opportunity to do something good, and now I have to find a job. I honestly thought I was going to start working somewhere, and I was not going to go back to school. But I honestly felt like, "Hey, man, maybe this is the right thing to do. Maybe this is my life; this is what I was meant to be." I was hurt because I knew my sister was in college, and I was like, "Man, that could have been me." Once I heard I had the opportunity to continue high school at Big Picture, I was like, "Nope, I want to change my life around right now."

Safety Issues

I am watching out for my brother because he's ten years old, and he already sees these gangbangers, and he always asks me a lot of questions. Like I remember when I was fifteen, I ran away from my house with my friends, the ones from the high school. So he remembers those things. He was, what, maybe five, I think. And he remembers all these things, and he's like, "I remember that day when all the police was here, and they were looking for you. I remember the days when our mother used to get mad because you used to talk to the gangbangers. Did you ever wear those colors?" He tells me things like this, and it hurts me, but I talk to him. When a cool car passes, he's like, "Oh, I want a car like that." I'm like, "Ooh, that's an ugly car. Why do you want that? It might look nice from the outside, but it is probably not going to work in two more weeks. It's going to break down. You want a good car, like a Lexus or something like that, but those are expensive, and you don't have to put rims on those or anything. They already look nice. From the inside, my God, you feel like you are in paradise. You have to stay in school so you can get a cool car, not those ugly ones that pass by here that only look cool because of the rims."

And next to my house, I have gangbanger neighbors. So my little brother's always playing on the sidewalk. A lot of times, their kids ask him to play with them, and a lot of the times, he's in the crowd with all of them, and I get mad at him. I tell him, "Don't do that, because you never know when another gang is going to come by and start shooting, and what if you're there? It's not good for you to hang around with those people." So I make sure he's in programs; he's in boxing right now. So after school, he comes home. I help him with his homework when I'm there. If not, I'm in class or doing something else. And then he goes to boxing, and he comes home, and he plays downstairs with my cousins. If he's on the sidewalk, my mom always tells us, "Your brother's on the sidewalk; someone has to be there to be making sure he doesn't go too much to that side." But I think we're doing a pretty good job. I'm going to make sure he doesn't make the mistakes I did.

We will probably move. We wanted to make sure that the whole immigration thing was done with. Now that we already did that, we're planning on moving and finding a better place. It's hard because there's gangs everywhere– well, not everywhere, but it's really hard to find a place where it's like clean. Even if you do find a place where there's no gangs, there's also other issues, like drugs. There's always going to be another issue. I feel like if we do move from the neighborhood, it is going to make a big difference, especially for my little brother. For me, if I do move, I don't care what happens; I'm always going to come back and make sure to give because there's so much that I can still change, and I'm willing to do it. So I'm going to come back no matter what. I going to make sure I'm still going to be doing community work with them or whatever I can do–maybe not living there, but I'm going to come back.

> And next to my house, I have gangbanger neighbors. So my little brother's always playing on the sidewalk. A lot of times, their kids ask him to play with them, and a lot of the times, he's in the crowd with all of them, and I get mad at him. I tell him, "Don't do that, because you never know when another gang is going to come by and start shooting, and what if you're there? It's not good for you to hang around with those people."

Reflections

Zulema is on her way to graduating from college, yet when she was young, she found school boring. She felt that she was nothing more than a number and that the teachers didn't care about the students. She was also discouraged about the lack of a social security number. This kept her from setting higher educational goals at first and also from participating in programs sponsored by the schools. It was a source of anxiety for the entire family. Her older sister was a positive role model for her, and Zulema wants to give back to the community by becoming a mentor for young girls. She feels that they often get discouraged and look up to the wrong people. Zulema would like to go back into the public schools and let the teachers know how important it is for them to establish relationships with their students to show they care.

6

Alvaro

I met Alvaro through a community-based organization. He and I created a partnership between the community and university to implement his vision for a weekend festival, Tardes en el Zocalo. He wanted to replicate los *zocalos* in Mexico and their significance in creating community by bringing people out of their homes and into the central plaza to talk and play together. He believed that was missing. Alvaro Obregon is dreaming forward for his community.

Background

My name is Alvaro. I was born in 1966, and I work in the community at a community-based organization, but we're known for doing housing, although we do a lot of other things as well, like community organizing, work on education, work with youth–lots of different things in the community.

The organization's been here since 1990. It was founded by six Catholic churches in the community. Each one of them committed $5,000 to start off a new organization. There were a lot of things going on in the neighborhood. Part of the reason it was started was because there was a lot of disinvestment in the community, and although there were a lot of organizations in the community, some people felt like they wanted to be part of a new organization. So they got together and hired a community organizer. He worked and worked and worked and met with people for a whole year, and that formed what we know today as the Project.

If you look at the community, faith is at the center of everything. It's part of our life here. Our churches are the center of life of the community. There's a lot of other things going on as well, but really, the real center of everything is the churches. If you think about it, when you have a child, the first place you take them is to the church. You present them; you have them baptized. Every kid goes to school, but at the same time, I think from a very human standpoint, when people are in trouble, when people are having a difficult time with either their spouse or dealing with a certain issue or their kids, they don't go to the school principal–they go to the parish priest. That's what really brings people in on a very personal level. Whereas the school is very important, that's where your kids get educated, but at the end of the day, you don't necessarily go back to the school.

I think a lot of people would like to send their kids to a parochial school; however, it's difficult with the cost of tuition. I think they're both [public and parochial] needed in the community; I think people need that choice. People would like to send them to Catholic schools because people have that perception if you go to a Catholic school, you're going to be better off; you're not going to get into trouble or all of these other things in a community like ours. So from my standpoint, I think we need to support both, because both are important, vital, and crucial to our community. We need to have really strong schools at the end of the day. While parents go to work, you hand over your kids to the teachers, and they take care of them for five hours or whatever it is. So it's in our interest to have strong schools–all kinds.

My dad was born here in the United States. He was born in Texas, so he's probably a foreigner to some people. My father was very strongly in the Democratic Party. He was very close to the former mayor and very close to a lot of people from the machine back then. It was during the Depression, where a lot of people moved or tried to move to industrial areas. My grandfather was born in Texas too, and he moved up north and settled here, as many people did, and started living here. My dad was one of the first ones here and especially who worked with the Latino community, the Mexican community in particular. Last year, when I met the former mayor's son, I took a press clipping as an icebreaker of his dad and my dad and Mayor Wagner from New York. The caption underneath described a campaign to register thousands of new Mexican American voters, and so he was really involved in a lot of that. My mom looks at me, and she says to me, "Your dad would be proud. This is exactly what he wanted you to be."

My mom was from a little rancho called la Tinaja de Pastores. That's very close to a town smack dab in the middle of Mexico. My mom married my dad, and here's my mom: She lived in Mexico City for a while, but she's from this rural area. Here she is. She gets married; she goes to Mexico City, and my dad takes her over to the U.S. embassy and presents a letter. They pass them into the ambassador. They meet, talk, laugh, do all of these things, and two or three days later, my mom's a U.S. resident in the United States. So my mom never had to cross the border.

She found out he was twenty-six years older than her, but it didn't make a difference to my mom, because he was and remains the love of her life. She just always talks about him. Every time she has a chance, she talks about my dad. And so they came and settled here. Here's my mom—again, this woman from a rural place in Mexico. Yeah, she'd lived in Mexico City for a couple of years, so she knew the hustle and bustle of a big city, but now she's in a big city in a new country.

She did not speak any English. She didn't speak any English, and then she had me. When I was born, she and my dad went through a rough time for a while. They separated for a little bit, but as my mom always points out, he always took care of us. So even though they separated for a while, he would always come back and visit. He'd always be around. He never just picked up and left and was never around. He left because there were some things in his personal life that he needed to sort out. And so during this time, I was born, and my mom says my dad put a lot of his hopes and aspirations into me and cared for me a lot.

Probably around Mother's Day in 1970, it's one of the last times my mom saw my dad. He always kept in touch, and they were working things out. They were always trying to make things work, and they wanted to get back together like a married couple completely, move somewhere, and do something. My dad was willing to give everything up and move away and maybe go to Mexico City with its connections. He said, "We can go and live in Mexico." So he came over, and he gave her flowers and everything. They spent a little bit of time together, and then he left.

She didn't hear from him for a few days, and a few days turned into a couple weeks. So my mom was wondering what was going on, and there were no cell phones back then where she can track him down, no beepers. One day, she runs into somebody on the street she knows, and they start talking—"How have you been?" [and] this and that—and her friend says, "How come you didn't go to Jesse's funeral?" And it hits her like a ton of bricks. She didn't have a clue. She didn't have a clue that my dad had died, and my dad died in a car accident. He was crossing the street, and he got hit; you can imagine—my mom's world came crashing down. You know, here she is in a different country. It's not hers.

The love of her life—she finds out she'll never see him again; she'll never hold him again, and so that was really, really hard, as you can imagine, for my mom.

My mom says I took it very hard because I was used to my dad being around, because he always came around. He never left us, and one of the stories is that my mom remembers one night that I woke up, and I was talking. She turned on the light to see me. She said I was talking, standing up with my hands toward the door, and saying, "I want to go with you. I want to go with you." It scared the crap out of her. "You want to go where?" "I want to go with Daddy." And she completely freaked out. She obviously hugged me and tried to protect me, my mom being very religious, very spiritual, and, you know, she just said, "Jesse, you're where you're at now; leave me my kid." So I took it hard. I think it's so hard that I can't remember my dad. I can't remember what my dad looked like. I don't have those memories of him.

Educational Experiences

So at three, I started Head Start, and then when it was time to start regular school, I went over to the elementary school. I was a weird kid from the beginning. I had this thirst for knowledge. I wanted to learn, and I wanted to learn more about things. I remember being in the second grade, and my teacher, when she was done with the newspaper, would give it to me; I waited to get the newspaper so I can try to read. I mean, I didn't know half the words, because they were too sophisticated for me, but I wanted to read.

I was learning in English. What happened was that in second

> What happened was that in second or third grade, I started talking to my mom in English … I started asking for milk as opposed to *leche.* My mom was looking at me like, *Milk? What's milk?* So she started struggling, and she said, "Wait a minute, wait a minute, wait a minute. There's no way this is going to happen to you."

or third grade, I started talking to my mom in English because my babysitters were English speakers. My babysitters were from Kentucky. I started talking to my mom in English. I started asking for milk as opposed to *leche.* My mom was looking at me like, *Milk? What's milk?* So she started struggling, and she said, "Wait a minute, wait a minute, wait a minute. There's no way this is going to happen to you." So what she did—she took me out of the regular program and put me into the bilingual program. It was one of the best things she's ever done. When I was in the bilingual program, I started to be around Spanish speakers also—you know, people who speak to me during the day in

Spanish–and I started seeing my bilingual teacher, Mrs. Dixon, who had these pictures of the Mexican president and the Mexican flags. There was all these cultural things that, in the regular classroom, weren't there.

Mother's Impact

My mother, who spoke only Spanish, had the courage to go the school and talk to the principal and get me into another program. I spoke at an event last week, and I said my mom just turned seventy-five, and I introduced her as my hero because she is my hero. My mom did everything she could to raise me, and I think she did a decent job. She did all right. But she's a strong woman, and she modeled for me a lot. She modeled for me how to care for people, how to give of yourself, because my mom, growing up, gave everything of herself. And I don't think she knew that she did it. It wasn't conscious. She didn't say, "I'm going to go out there and help my brothers and sisters because I'm a good person, because this is my mission in life." She was just like, "This is what I should do because they're my brothers and my sisters. I should help them." She'd go and help them become legal–legalized.

She helped them; she helped them. I would go with my mom when I was a kid, and she would sign over her whole paycheck. Here's somebody– now, you can imagine–here's my mom, who didn't do too bad. She did okay when my dad was alive. Then, all of a sudden, she was in this world by herself. My mom worked in a factory. We were always at or slightly below the poverty level, but we always had enough. We always had food, always had clothes; I never felt like the poor kid. I never felt any of that. Even with that, even with the little money we had, my mother was always able to save money. And she was able to take her paycheck and go to the lawyer's office and sign over her whole paycheck so she can help her brothers and sisters become documented so that they don't have to cross the border illegally into this country. They came because they needed to work, and so my mom didn't want them to go through that, so my mom would help them.

All of those things, for me, modeled how you live your life: you give of yourself. Sometimes one of my weaknesses, my friends tell me, is that you don't give yourself any time. That's one of the things that I personally struggle with: balance. I go out. I get up and go to work; I'm involved in other things. Then it's nine o'clock at night, and I come home. I'm forty. I'm divorced. I would like to marry again, but I never find the time to go out and have fun and do these things, because I'm so used to doing things just in general. My mom did these things, whether it was doing helping her brothers or putting me into the bilingual program and saying, "Okay, kid, you're not going to lose your Spanish, because I don't have time to learn English."

At first with the bilingual program, I thought, *Do I have to go into this other program?* Then, all of a sudden, I found myself liking it. *Wow, this is pretty cool, hey.* I was learning about Mexican presidents. I was learning. I still was hearing English in school and outside of school, but I was learning this other thing. For me, it was a challenge, whereas some of my classmates were going in one direction to learn English, and I was going the other direction. I was like, "Wow, this is great! I can learn something new." So now I was learning how to write in Spanish. Now I was learning how to talk properly in Spanish. Now I was planning how to read in Spanish. And so that was a life-changing moment for me, one that I'm very thankful for. As I go to Mexico, people talk to me there, and even here, everybody assumes that I was born in Mexico because of my Spanish. I have no accent; I say the proper words. Within me, I still struggle sometimes. Sometimes I'm like, "Uh-oh, which word?" but when it comes out, it comes out fine. I think I was in bilingual for two years, but that was a great, great two years.

Life-Changing Experience

Also, one of my other life-changing experiences at the time, I think, I was in the second grade, when our music teacher walked in and played Louie Armstrong for us. I was just blown away. It was just "Louie Armstrong, wow! That sounds really cool." The class was over, and I walked up to the teacher, and I said to him, "Teacher, can I borrow your record?" He was surprised: "You want to borrow this Louie Armstrong record?" I think he was pleasantly surprised, so he handed it over to me, and I took it home, and that night the saints were marching in over and over and over and over and over again, but I just loved it.

It transformed something else, because here I was, this kid who grew up, who grew up listening to Mexican music at home. My mom loved singing; she loved singing. She doesn't sing as much anymore, but my mom's got a deep voice. She was always singing, so there was always Mexican music in our household. And then, growing up with my babysitters from Kentucky, I heard Hank Williams and George Jones. But then here's this guy Louie Armstrong, so all these musical doors were opening for me. A big regret is that I never learned how to play an instrument, but I don't think I had the discipline. I tried to, but I didn't. And so that was a life-changing experience as well for me because to this day, I love music. I love music from all parts of the world, and everything new to me is something I always want to hear. What's the newest thing—not the latest craze, but what's new and good? You look at my music collection, and there's huge Mexican, big classical, lots of English, but you've got significant music from Pakistan and the Middle East and India and like all of these things, things that I love hearing. So that was a transforming event, moment for me.

I think being part of three worlds as well has enabled me to fit in lots of places. I say "three worlds" because it's the Mexican world; it's the U.S. world; and it's this place somewhere in between for a lot of us who are born here with Mexican parents. Even though I'm second generation, I feel like I'm first generation because I grew up with my mom. I grew up with my mom, and we have a saying that we're not from here or from there. We're from this somewhere in the middle. We're not Americans; we're Americans because we're all Americans. We're not from the U.S.; we're not strictly from Mexico. We live in this weird place somewhere in between. So it's almost a third reality, a third place. It's helped me to adapt to a lot of other situations.

> I think being part of three worlds as well has enabled me to fit in lots of places. I say "three worlds" because it's the Mexican world; it's the US world; and it's this place somewhere in between for a lot of us who are born here with Mexican parents. Even though I'm second generation, I feel like I'm first generation because I grew up with my mom.

Gang Impact

So moving into the fifth grade back into other, regular classrooms was okay; that transition was okay. Moving over to the upper-grade center was the first time I was exposed to the different realities of my community. By that, I mean I remember being at the upper-grade center and there being one of our classmates who was shot—killed. He wasn't a friend of mine; I just knew him from sight, but it was the first time that it hit us that, like, "Wow, there's something going on in our community, that people kill each other."

That was the first time I really realized that kind of stuff. Before that, the gangs were just, the gangs were just, "Oh, I'll meet you after school at three behind the school," and they'd come, and you knew how many people were coming and go see. They'd come with a chain. If they came with a chain, it was like, "Woo, these guys are tough!" But rarely did you see a knife or anything like that. It was mostly them; they fought it out. The community was very mixed at the time. You had a lot of old ethnic white community who still lived there, Poles and Czechs, and then you had another group of Latinos—mostly Mexican, but you also had some Puerto Ricans.

I remember growing up and hearing about all these other gangs, but again, it wasn't like it is now. I remember the Lobos, and I remember the Latin Kings—I remember all of these, but it was mostly they formed to protect themselves against other communities who would pick on them or other people from other blocks who would pick on them, like the Czechs had their gang who fought against the Italian gang.

I always felt protected. Here's the thing: I had friends who were in the gang, in different gangs. I hung out with them—not on the street corners, but in school, I hung out with them. They were my friends. I never talked bad about them. But I was afraid of my mom. I wasn't afraid that she would hit me; I was afraid of letting her down. I was afraid of breaking her heart, that her only son would be a gang member.

> I had friends who were in the gang, in different gangs. I hung out with them—not on the street corners, but in school, I hung out with them. They were my friends. I never talked bad about them. But I was afraid of my mom. I wasn't afraid that she would hit me; I was afraid of letting her down. I was afraid of breaking her heart, that her only son would be a gang member.

She talked to me about gangs, telling me not to be in a gang. I mean, she understood as well that you can talk to them, just don't be one. I mean, to this day, I remember coming home a year ago, I think it was. We were coming home from something. It was late at night, and there was this gangbanger sitting in front of his house, and he's got one of those anklet things. He can't go beyond a certain radius, and my mom sees him, and she says, "Hey, how are you?" She starts talking to him, and he says hello; he gets up and gives her a kiss on the cheek, and my mom just starts telling him, "You be careful; take care of yourself. Don't get hurt; stay inside. May God bless you"—all of these things—and I was just like, "Wow." And maybe this guy liked getting my mom's blessing. I don't know; maybe his mom wasn't there. Maybe his mom wasn't part of his life like that. Maybe his mom was in Mexico. I don't know—sure, she'd probably have a fit. But I don't think she had to worry. I don't think she had to worry. I did okay.

Emerging Activist

I was still in high school when I became active in things, and there's a few things I remember starting to read about, hearing all of the news. Growing up, I remember hearing about Watergate–not that I understood it, but I read it. I knew that something was going on. Then I knew that Iran was happening and Jimmy Carter. One was the bombing of the barracks in Beirut, and then, too, something that just scared the living daylights out of me was the day after. That's when I started saying to myself, "I'm so young, and these crazy people want to blow up the world, or they're willing to blow up the world for their own purposes."

And to me, that was unacceptable, so I started becoming active around different things. I remember we'd have these discussions; I would say hi to my friends who are in gangs, but I'd go over, and me and my friends at the lunch table would have discussions about what was going on in the world about Beirut. No gangbanger cared about Beirut; he didn't care about the Soviet Union and the United States, the Cold War, or any of that. I remember Halloween came up, and my friend Gabriel came camouflaging, like bandages and everything. We're like, "What the heck are you supposed to be?" And he said, "I'm a marine in Beirut," and that was just like a shocker. First of all, it was bold, but that was his statement, saying we're doing something wrong in the Middle East. I'll never forget that, because it was such a shock to do something like that at that time. Nowadays, kids do all kinds of stuff. Back then, it was sort of like, "Whoa!" So I got involved with that, and the activity just grew. I went out, and I saw different things.

Facets of High School

My high school teachers–they encouraged me to think. I had a great time at the local high school because the teachers were really good. I look back now, and I sometimes say, "Wow, what a difference." We just connected. I felt like our teachers really cared. I don't know–I can't say the same now. I look at what's happening now. I know we've always had a high dropout rate. It'd be interesting to see if it's higher now than it was back then, or is it the same? But my teachers back then, like, they really, really cared. A lot of them were some of the first teachers when they opened the high school back in the late '70s, and they were actively involved with the kids.

Even the kids who were in trouble then–it was a different world. I don't remember there being the disciplinary problems that we have today. I mean, we didn't need metal detectors back then. I walk into the high school, and now you got to walk through a metal detector. I mean, it's like, wow, what a difference. But the school was great, because again, the teachers were awesome, and it's also a time when you were able to meet other kids from throughout the neighborhood. Because up until then, you go to elementary school, and you meet other kids that are right there in the four- or five-, six-block radius. Then, in high school, you suddenly meet kids from all over the community. That's great.

The one thing that was not great at the school were some of the initiatives to get a lot of the kids into college. I was a good student. I had honors English classes, so I was doing pretty good; I wasn't doing great. Junior year, I messed up; I messed up horribly. I missed a lot of classes. My mom didn't know it. I was hanging out with my friends: "Let's cut class. Let's go do something fun." I found myself, at the end of my junior year, saying, "Uh-oh. Unless I do something different, I'm not going to graduate with my friends," and this goes back to disappointing my mom. There's no way that I can go home and tell my mom that I will not graduate with my friends. So I enrolled in summer school at St. Rita's, kind of with my mom's help, 'cause I told her. My take on it was "Mom, I need a little help with school." Eventually, I had to tell her that I really needed to do this, you know. I enrolled. I obviously needed some money. I enrolled in summer school at St. Rita and then went to a tech school throughout my senior year. Here I was, going to the local high school during the day and the tech at night, because I needed to do everything possible to make up my junior year to be able to graduate.

And I busted my butt to be able to graduate in June of 1984. I did. I made it. But again, one of the weaknesses at the time was that the school system in a community like ours really looked at "Where's the cream of the crop? And let's get them into college." The problem was that only the cream of the crop went to college, and unless you had somebody who knew the process, you ended up lost somewhere. I ended up lost somewhere. Because how could my mom, who had to leave school in the second grade in Mexico, have any possible idea of what it takes to go to college in this country? Not only does she not speak the language, but it's a completely different world. She didn't even make it out of grade school. She didn't make it. She had to drop out. She had to help her mom take care of the rest of the kids. She was the oldest daughter. It was her turn to do all these things.

I didn't even take my ACTs. That's how much, at the time—that's how bad I think things were. I don't think anybody intentionally tried to fail kids. I just think people concentrated on the top class, the top students: "Let's get them in; we have

> I ended up lost somewhere. Because how could my mom, who had to leave school in the second grade in Mexico, have any possible idea of what it takes to go to college in this country? Not only does she not speak the language, but it's a completely different world.

some great ones." Some of them went on to Northwestern. Some of my friends went on to Northwestern, University of Chicago, and Berkeley, Stanford. We got smart kids, but I was one of those kids who was right below that. By the time I graduated, I was too busy just trying to graduate. I was trying to get out the door, walk through, because God forbid that my friends graduate. God forbid even that I would graduate in summer, in August, because my mother did not struggle and work so that I could be mailed a diploma.

The party is planned. I better walk down that aisle, walk across that stage, get a diploma in my hand, and show it to her with everybody else on schedule, and so I'm busy with that. And then here I am; I graduate. Then I'm like, "Wow, now what am I going to do?" I didn't take my ACT. I didn't apply to any college. Here I am; I can't disappoint Mom, so I got to do something. I decided to go to a trade school, and so I went to Coyne American Institute. Everybody was talking about computers. Everybody says it's the next big thing, so I got into that. So I got into computer programming, finished that. It was a one-year program. It was very intensive.

Postgraduation Reflections

I worked in school, worked to get all my stuff done, graduated, and then was like, "Okay, now what? Do I really want the computer programming? No. It would be nice to go on to college eventually. Ah, I'm too tired; I want to take a year off." So I decided to take a year off. So I decided to go work with my cousin in a factory because I needed to do something. And so it was August, and it was my first day. It was my first week. First couple days, I had to put my hand in this hot oil to get these scraps of metal out, and I remember taking them out and my hands just full of oil and these little cuts all over my hands. And I remember thinking, *Is this what I really want to do?* And I remember starting to evaluate that, and I'm starting to dump this oil out from this huge canister that's got all this metal on it, and it slips, and it comes crashing down on my finger. It's about a hundred pounds of steel coming down on my finger, and immediately, my finger bursts like a grape, and it starts shooting blood all over the place, and I'm like, *Okay, this is not what I want to do the rest of my life.* Of course, I bandaged it up, went to the doctor. I lasted a very short time at that place. So then I went to work in a print shop. That whole time: *Is this what I want to do with my life? No.* However, I was really involved. I was a social activist. So it gave me the freedom to do other things.

It gave me that freedom to do a lot of things, and I loved it. It was a great opportunity. Then the printing shop hit on hard times. One of the biggest clients pulled out. He was going to do his business elsewhere. So my boss was like, "Wow." This was going to really, really hurt us, almost to the point of maybe closing up shop. So he said to me–he gave me the option, and we had a heart-to-heart, and he said, "I don't know if I'm going to be able to survive this. It's up to you if you want to try to stay and tough it out or not." And I chose to leave, because I said, you know, in some weird way, maybe this is the time that I should go back to school. And so I said, "No, that's okay; I'll take off." So I took off and went to the local city college.

By this time, I was already burned out. Right out of high school and all of these other things–I was just trying to change the world around me and be actively, actively involved; I would have meetings downtown, and I didn't have money to jump on the train. I would walk there from my community. I would go right through the ghetto. I'd go right through ABLA homes. Kids would be out playing when I was going, but then at night, that was the tricky part–coming back at night. By that time, the real gangbangers come out and stuff like that. But I was, like, that crazy Mexican kid who's got enough guts to walk through this neighborhood at night, and it'd be all right. I did that, and at the end of all this, I was tired, and the world was changing. The Soviet Union, the wall fell–all of these things that were happening, and I was sort of burned out. All of these things were going on, and it was a good time to chill out and focus on my studies.

I said to myself, "I really like history, and I love Latin American history." A lot of my activism dealt with social-justice movements in Latin America–the things that were going on in Latin America. "Latin American studies–maybe that's what I should go into." So I went back to college, or I went into college and enrolled because I didn't need my ACT to get into the city colleges. So I get in. It was great: full-time, four classes. I had a great time.

I was living at home because in our community, you don't leave home until you get married. So as long as you're sixty and you're unmarried, you live at home. That's just the way it is. But yeah, I was still living at home. I was helping my mom out when I was working. It was just part of the thing you do.

Activism Reignited

So here I am, taking a break from all things I am doing, all of my activism, fighting for a just world. I get into the city college, and I take a full load. I'm hanging out around the library and see other Latinos there and start talking to them–a great group of people. There was a lot of them who were just about hanging out, and there was another group of them who would talk about those things like what we could do about Latinos in this world.

I became active with the Latino students there, and I kept on saying to myself, I had all that experience working in coalitions and groups for social justice and other areas. So I came with a wealth of experience that they didn't have. So I got there, and I was like, "You should do this; you should do that." I was challenging them to do more things, but I was the guy who was doing the pushing–you know, moving. And so they said, "You should be the next president. Elections are coming up." They insisted; they drafted me.

That was a great time because then we did a lot of great things there at Harold Washington. I mean, I started doing things. We had two scholarships, and during my tenure there as president, we went up to five scholarships.

I had my ideas how we can raise money, so we can give money to more Latino students so that they could pay for some classes so that they can go on. That was my idea. So whereas before, the students would have one fundraiser a year. We were given, I think it was, $800 for the whole year, and that was money to operate. What are you going to do with $800 to operate? You can't give scholarships with $800. We should raise more money, so I said, "Let's sell Mexican treats." We decided that was what we were going to do. I went to my friend from the bakery and said, "Hey, give me a deal. I'll buy bread every couple weeks or so from you." He's like, "Okay, cool." He gives me a deal, so I walk in with a big tray of a couple boxes of bread and start selling 'em.

"You know, we need coffee too. We should go and buy coffee." "Why you going to buy coffee? Somebody should give us coffee." "Who's going to give us coffee? We're students–what are we going to do?" "We could buy it out of our pocket and give it away. It either has to pay for itself, or somebody got to give it to us." I always go to this place called Starbucks. I wonder if they'll give us coffee. I'm not shy. I went over there, and I said, "Hey, we're from the organization of Latin American students, and we're trying to raise money every week. I want you to donate some Latin American coffee." It had to be Latin American because we're nationalist. So we got the pound of coffee and started selling it. It was such a hit that we decided we were going to do this every week. There we were every week, just selling and selling and selling.

And then I noticed African Americans had African American classes: history of Africa, and African American history. So I said what we should do is start a petition and a campaign to get Latin American classes there at the college. Everybody thought that was a great idea, and so there we were–boom. We started up petitions. Then we were getting signatures every day. We collected

And then I noticed African Americans had African American classes: history of Africa, and African American history. So I said what we should do is start a petition and a campaign to get Latin American classes there at the college. Everybody thought that was a great idea, and so there we were– boom. We started up petitions.

tons of signatures, and so we scheduled a meeting with the vice president, and you know, I was coming from an activist background, so I was ready for battle, and we sit down with him. "Well, how can we help you?" "Well, we're here because Latinos are going to be the largest minority in the city. You have African American history, but you don't have Latin American history or anything for Latino students, and we think that you should." And he looked at us, and he said okay. We were like, "What?" I was like, "But wait a minute–you're supposed to fight me on this." But the thing–what had happened, what I realized–was that we had done so many good things that we had made a name for ourselves.

It wasn't like we were in there to–our first action wasn't to go and march around the school in protest without having asked first. I'm very proud that at that time, I was able to take it to another level and start doing other things. By the end of the year, while I was president, we were able to put on all of our events. We were able get to all the scholarships, and we had $2,000 still left in our bank account at the school. This was the first time any student organization had done that, so I was proud that I was leaving something for the people who were following me. I was leaving them something. I'm proud that we, as a group, raised the bar pretty darn high. We were able to get the classes. To this day, it's one of the most popular classes.

Unfortunately, because I got so involved in the school and in the Latino affairs, my studies started suffering. The first year, when I was just a member, I was taking a full load. My second year became part-time, and then my third year, I became even more part-time. Because even then, I was helping the next generation, helping them think through things and help them do things. Then I got this part-time gig at Crate and Barrel, and that turned into a full-time job; next thing you know, I'm taking one class, and the next thing you know, I was out of college, and I never finished.

Lessons Learned

I think that what I've learned in the world that has been very helpful for me is there's nothing like practice. There's theory, and there's practice, and to me, the practice of being out there has really been important. I learned from books, but it's not until you're actually doing something do you really realize what that means. Even if the book is right on, it's still abstract until you've actually done it. That is why I recently returned to finish my studies at the university, and the awesome part about being in the ABS [Applied Behavioral Sciences] program is that I'm not talking about something abstract. It connects to my real life. It makes me think. The challenging part is how does this apply in your real life? You know, I remember the class that I took once I was finished with the regular ABS program, where you get credit for life experience. No, you don't just walk in there and say, "I've done this and this and this–give me credit." No. You've got to look at these things. You've got to look at these things, these subjects, and say, "How do these things apply to me? What did I learn from them?" That's very different and empowering.

For now, I think that working in the community is where I see myself in the short term, and I think in the long term, even if the day should come that I'm not working necessarily there, strictly in Pilsen, it would still be one of the places where I would focus a lot of my energy and work. I've always looked to find ways to bring more resources to the community and to the people I live and work with. Because I tell people, when they say, "Let's do a round of introductions," the way I introduce myself, I say, "My name is Alvaro. I was born and raised here in the community. I choose to live and work here because that's how I feel about my community. I'm very proud."

Reflections

Alvaro has been an activist and community leader for much of his life. His curiosity and determination have led him to take a practical approach to change: instead of simply talking about an issue, Alvaro articulates the problem, seeks a solution, and collaborates with others to implement change. This approach led to significant change at the city college, where he was responsible for strengthening the voice of its Latino students. Alvaro is committed to living in the community, where he can stay close to his mother and devote his energies to creating a healthy community; he is devoted to ending the violence and inequities by working with youth and developing programs to bring the community together. He currently works for a prominent city councilman and has an office downtown, but he says his favorite part of the week is when he can spend time back in the community, listening to the issues identified by his constituents.

7

Herminia

Herminia invited me to meet in her home in Little Village. There, we sat in the living room, surrounded by family photos and religious artifacts, talking for several hours about her family and how important it was for her to stay in the Mexican community. The cultural elements of the community are extremely significant for her, and she is rooted there. Her personal educational goals were not aligned with those her mother held for her, but education has driven the goals she has for her children.

Background

My name is Herminia. I have four children, and I have eight brothers and sisters. I've been living here for about twenty years in this area. I came here when I was eleven years old. Most of my relatives have moved from this neighborhood. I continue to be stubborn and live here. Back when I was a young kid, my mom and my brother were living here already. And so I was young; I had no decision back then. When I got married, this is the only place I knew, so I just basically decided to stay here.

What I like about here is that it's our neighborhood–it's our language; it's our people. There are things here that you will not find anywhere: the authenticity of the food, our authentic products from Mexico. The culture itself–it's just around here, around the corner. Here in the community, I can find people I can relate to, because we all come from the same place. That's important for me, also the language. I really want my kids to grow up being fluently bilingual, Spanish and English.

Two of my children go to private schools, and two of them go to public schools. The reason is that the two that go to public school have a disability. The public school system offers better services. My girls, one of them, went to public school until she was a fourth grader, and then I transferred her to a private school; I was concerned about her education in a school known for gang involvement.

The private school is different. There is a lot of parent involvement; there are stricter policies as regards everything from dressing to makeup. There's more communication between the school administration and the parents. The administration, staff, and teachers instill discipline, hard work, and values, especially values, to the students. That was not happening, at least not in the public school my daughter was attending before.

I went to public schools for three and a half years, from fifth grade to the middle of eighth grade. That's all the public education I had here. After these three and a half years, I went back to Mexico. I had one and a half years of secondary school in Mexico; then I came back here, and I obtained my GED. Years later, I went to a community college, then to Northeastern University, and now I am attending another university. I'm in the MBA cohort program there, offered at a community-based organization. I love it. But my education experience here in the city, as I can remember, was not welcoming in my first year because of the language barrier.

It was in 1978. First of all, the schools were not ready. If students did not understand English, teachers would take these kids out of the classrooms and put them in the halls so that a bilingual assistant could teach them. They would gather students from different classrooms and teach them all together at the end of the hall because of the language–because we could not understand what was being taught. That was the bilingual program in some schools.

I also had the opportunity to attend other schools here at that time. There was a school on Twenty-Fifth and Central Park. That school was, I think, better prepared–better teachers. One teacher from this particular school was a real good professional. She was very motivating; she cared about her students. Her class was a bilingual class; she really took personal interest in her students. She knew how to find her students' strengths. For example, she knew I liked reading, and she would challenge me with different readings, different levels. Although my English was very bad at that time, she would encourage me to write and read. She was always motivating me with words–words like

"That's so great. You're doing fine; you're doing great." Those were words I didn't hear at home.

I think not only did my mom not speak English, but she also never went to school. Education was not important for her, because she did not know about it. For her, it was more important to feed us and to provide us a place to sleep. I do not blame her for not being involved in my education. She couldn't react to something that she did not know. She grew up in a very little farm in Mexico—very, very poor, with no access to school whatsoever. I cannot blame her for not understanding my school achievements. I remember telling her, "Oh, Mom, I'm selected to go to this magnet school." And she'd say, "What's that?" "It's supposed to be a better school." She said, "I do not know about that, but I want you to be a good woman here at home—fix food, clean up. This is a woman's future." There was not much encouraging at home. There was no motivation.

She didn't want me to go, because she did not know what a magnet school was, but she was relying on what I was saying. She asked me, "Do you want to go?" "Yeah, it's a new school. It's supposed to be better." And she said, "Do you want to go?" And I said, "Yes, I want to go." And she said, "Go ahead." It was a great experience. It was a brand-new school, new classrooms; we had pianos in our classrooms. We had music. The school offered French as a second language. It was just awesome, and the teachers were great, too.

In Mexico

I was in eighth grade when my mom decides we have to go back to Mexico. My mom did not want to stay here. She didn't like the weather; she just wanted to go back to her roots and stay there. Going back to Mexico was hard—very hard. It was a very awful experience. I was getting used to, I was used to living here, having breakfast at school, having this environment where you have the teachers involved, and I was very involved in school. When I went back to Mexico, I couldn't go back to grammar school, and I couldn't go into high school, because I did not have an eighth-grade certificate. There was a lot of back and forth with the Mexican school system. They wouldn't take me at the high-school level, and I was too old to go to the elementary-grade level. They go from first grade to sixth grade. This was the point where I was just discouraged to continue with my education. What I did, because I wanted to go to high school, was that I bought books, and I studied myself at home. So I obtained my sixth-grade certificate, and then I went to high school one and a half years over there.

Earlier in Mexico, when I was a child, I did not have the opportunity to attend school; we were so poor. When I was six years old, I had to work along with my mom. We used to sell vegetables in the street. I remember my friends in the neighborhood passing by with their backpacks, and I always dreamed of attending school. They were attending school, and I was not; I could not. It was a trauma for me; I wanted to be someone. I did not want to spend my life selling vegetables in the street.

> I remember my friends in the neighborhood passing by with their backpacks, and I always dreamed of attending school. They were attending school, and I was not; I could not. It was a trauma for me; I wanted to be someone.

It was not until I received my bachelor's that my mother understood my school dreams. She told me she was sorry that she never pushed or motivated me. I said, "No, don't worry—what could you have done? You didn't know." For me, not having a traditional education became my inner strength. That's what motivates me. For me, education is something intangible that I have with me and nobody can take away. For me, education is about choices. It is not so much about money; it is having choices and just feeling capable of reaching my goals.

Being in school is hard work, but when I receive a good grade, when I see my teachers' dedication to their jobs, this compensates for the hard work. There's always something to learn, and that's what I enjoy.

Parental Involvement

There's some things I'm passionate about: education and special needs. I have two children with special needs, and I am aware of the hassles one has to go through to get the services they need. These two areas are important for me. Maybe someday something will come pop up for me in any of these areas.

Now I work as a business manager in a parish. Through my work, I'm trying to connect needs with resources; I see the need in our community. Parents are not involved in their child's education. I'm not sure they understand. These kids need guidance. Our parents are sometimes more interested in making money; these kids—a lot of our kids in our community are growing up alone. They're working just to make ends meet, to pay rent, to have food. On the other side, parents have become so dependent on the system—the school system. Parents rely too much on it. They are satisfied the kids go to school, and that's it. They don't look for after-school activities, for tutoring. They don't have a plan for the education of their children. It can be because they do not have the education themselves or because they do not know how the school systems work here in the U.S.

I think the school's responsibility is to inform the parents, but then the parents have to take the initiative too. It is their responsibility too. We need to educate them, the parents. We need to guide them. We need to provide the information in their hands. A lot of people, a lot of people out there don't understand this. They think we have the Internet. We have the computer. Our community's not ready. Many of our parents do not know how to use the Internet. What we're doing in our parish is trying to bring some resources to the community and let the community know: "Look, here are these additional resources for you and your kids."

We're trying to work with different not-for-profits to come and talk about what they do. For example, there's Metro for girls and Metro for boys; there's High Sight–different types of organizations that help tutor children, teenagers. We don't have them here in the community.

These organizations have their sites near downtown, outside of the neighborhood. If we had similar organizations here in the neighborhood, it would help the community so much–so much. We have the space in the church, but we don't have the volunteers; we don't have the professionals who are willing to come and do it in the neighborhood.

Private versus Public Education

I think that the church plays a very important role. My personal view as a Catholic–I think that if schools, private and public schools, could put more efforts on values, that would make a big difference. They could probably require some ethics courses as part of the curriculum.

It should come from all those: school, family, and community. I think we have to work together. Because sometimes you have values at home, but these values when children get to schools, public schools–the kids have pressure to things going on. Sometimes there's not enough discipline, enough control over these kids on what they are doing, what they're talking about. We all, as a society, should be combined. Of course, values come from family first. Values start in the family, because you're born there; you're raised there, in a family. But then these values have to be strengthened in school. I see it in my kids in the private, parochial schools; it's just so different.

In my personal experience, I thought private schools were for rich people. In Mexico, private education is for rich people even if it's church-based. You don't see private schools in low-income neighborhoods in Mexico.

When someone told me, "You should try Catholic schools," I said, "For what?" "They have a better program." I said, "If a kid is smart, the kid's smart." And this person told me, I remember, "It's not about being smart. It's about your daughter growing in an environment where they're going to cultivate her values. Aren't you concerned about that?" Then I said, "Yeah, that's my main concern." And she said, "Go to a Catholic school and see. Not all Catholics are good, but most of them are." During that time, our priest was promoting scholarships. He interviewed me. He knew my daughter because she attended religion classes; we were kind of involved in the parish.

My priest asked me, "What's your worry? Why can't you decide on bringing her to Catholic school?" I said, "I don't have the money to spend." He said, "It's not an expense; it's an investment in your daughter's life." At that time, I was working in a factory and not making enough money. He offered, "We'll pay half, and you pay half. How's that?" And I said, "We'll take it." First, I was afraid that we were not going to make it, and as time went by, I had to make a lot of changes. Like, we're not going to buy from J. C. Penny; we're going to buy from the thrift store. I'm going to go to Aldi and save, definitely. Then when my daughter graduated school, she applied to a Catholic high school. *That's expensive,* I thought. *Oh my God, not again!* But she had good grades, and she got a scholarship from High Sight and other scholarships; she also had a scholarship from the high school.

From her experience there, we know this is the way to go–Catholic education. She graduated last year and was accepted at University of Dayton; she's there. We had a talk, and I asked, "What are your plans?" She said, "I want to get my bachelor's and be a teacher." I said, "What else?" She said, "Why do you ask me what else?" I said there's more beyond a bachelor's. "Okay, Mom, I'll think about that." So then I thought, *Okay, I have to show her that having a bachelor's is good, but in today's world, maybe that's not enough.* She needs to go further; she was my inspiration to come back for an MBA. I want to go by example and say, "You can do it. So okay, I'm doing it. So you better do it. That's how I feel. If I can do it taking care of a family, working, then you have it easier. And you can't say you cannot."

When I was a parent at a public school, I was very lucky. My daughter had this teacher for two years. She was a very strict teacher. She was a very demanding Cuban teacher. We were always in contact; she was welcoming to me. The whole environment was not that welcoming, but my daughter's teacher and I had this connection. We were in frequent communication. When I mentioned to her that I wanted to change my daughter to a private school, she encouraged me to do it.

In a private school, there are less kids in each classroom; the teachers are attentive. Also, the public school administration during that time–the principal wasn't welcoming; the office staff wasn't either. One of the things that I've noticed in our community is that a lot of school personnel, even when they speak the Spanish language, they choose to speak in English, knowing that some parents are not understanding. That, for me, is disrespect. If you know the language, why do you talk in another language that parents are not understanding? It happened to me once where I was there in a public school office, and the lady was complaining about me, thinking I didn't understand English. Yes, in the office–the secretaries. I think that's one place

> One of the things that I've noticed in our community is that a lot of school personnel, even when they speak the Spanish language, they choose to speak in English, knowing that some parents are not understanding. That, for me, is disrespect. If you know the language, why do you talk in another language that parents are not understanding?

where parents might not feel welcomed; they don't know the language. It would be ideal, as parents come to the school offices, that the staff talk to them in Spanish. Make them feel welcome. Try to–do not discourage them by speaking a language they do not understand.

I have helped some parents with school processes. Some parents have come to me, especially with children with special needs. I have been to different IEP [individual education plan] meetings, helping some mothers understand the IEP process. It is so hard when you have a child with disabilities; it is like learning a career. The jargon, the process, everything, all the paperwork involved–it's hard. It's overwhelming.

Seventeen years ago, there was very limited information about autism–very limited. There was not enough in English, less in Spanish. There were no parents' groups–nothing around to know what to do. It was through pain and just wanting the best for my child. At some point in time, I knew I could not rely on anybody but on myself to be the advocate for my child. I needed to educate myself to be independent. I did research, reading, and I attended several seminars. What struck me at one of these seminars was their advice on how to manage IEP meetings; you dress up like a professional. For me, that was like, *Wow, I would never have thought that.*

I dream that my kids are able to have a successful career and come back to their community and help their community–if not this community, anywhere they go. That they always look back and don't forget where they come from. That they remember that anything they accomplished came with their family's help, came from the dreams of their parents. I dream that my kids will always be proud of who they are and where they've come from, that they keep their heritage, our customs, our language.

My dream is that someday we can offer programs in the parish for children or for youths where they can have something after school. Actually, we're trying to produce a CCD [religious handbook] for our program to reflect those values, to keep those values–their faith values–very strong so that that helps them in the future. It's hard out there. It is, especially because, like I said, the parents are not that involved. Then all the marketing they watch on TV. Everywhere these kids turn, there's an ad selling sex, drugs, violence, so it's just hard to keep them focused. They have to be real, they have to be strong, and they have to be good people so that they too can make a difference someday.

Community

We're thinking about moving, probably to the South–to the south states–because of the weather. But other than that, this is my community. I do feel aggravated when I hear the violence on the weekend. I've never let my kids play outside. I never do unless I'm outside. If I'm going to be outside, then my kids are outside. But if I'm not there, they're not out there.

Community is not just an address; it is relating to the people that live in the same area you do. I feel pain in my heart when I see people who suffer the same things I went through. Especially with my job at the parish, I see people who come and say, "My mom died in Mexico, and I can't go to Mexico. I am not legal; I don't have money." It is frustrating. And so we have people who come in with different problems. For example, probably a month ago, a person came. He was hungry, he was thirsty, and he had no money. When I asked what happened, he says, "Well, someone brought me from Mexico, and they left me here. I've been around for two weeks, and I don't know anybody in the city." I asked him, "What do you want?" He said, "I want to go to immigration and get deported. How do I do that?" I said to him, "Don't go do that, because it's not like old times, where you could go and say, 'I want to go.' You'll get a criminal background. Don't do that." I felt so sad because I could tell in that man's eyes he's not a criminal. He's not; he didn't hurt anybody. He was just looking for a better life. To see those things happen around the

> Community is not just an address; it is relating to the people that live in the same area you do. I feel pain in my heart when I see people who suffer the same things I went through.

community–it's just heartbreaking. In this specific case, we made calls to different parishioners. He ended up working with somebody–somebody who has a business.

I think this community has always been kind of not a permanent place to live. A lot of people come; they live here, and when they have a better financial situation, they leave from the area. But lately, there's people like me who won't leave. I've been here for twenty years. My husband and I met in Mexico; we got married, and since then, we've been living here. Being in touch with our culture is important for us. We find ethnic goods in our neighborhood; we never had a problem. We never had a problem with gangs or anything. I know they're here. I go past them, but they don't bother me, because their problems are between them. I don't see them hurting us. You can walk; they can be there. But the only thing I'm afraid, you know– what if they're shooting, and I'm passing by?

> We find ethnic goods in our neighborhood; we never had a problem. We never had a problem with gangs or anything. I know they're here. I go past them, but they don't bother me, because their problems are between them. I don't see them hurting us.

That's why I do not want my kids out there; that's my whole concern. Gangs have their own problems. God knows why. If there's not enough love and comfort at home, they're going to go out and look for it; there are some things the school cannot provide. They have gang prevention but not love. We need that human touch, love, and family. And that only family can provide. When we don't find love at home, maybe that's what we are looking for. Maybe that's what these kids are looking for, to be accepted or loved. Perhaps in a gang, they feel accepted or loved.

I think the support should start with the kids when they are very young–it has to start when they're young. There should be communication between parents and children–teachers, children, and parents. You might think that a child does not understand, but you'll be surprised how much they actually understand. Parents can start to talk about things that happen, even simple things. You can create confidence so that your child can come and talk to you. Many times, parents want to start the relationship with their child when the kid is ten years old, eleven years old. That's almost too late. For example, when I am with my youngest daughter, sometimes I don't want to listen to her childish conversations, but I listen to her. Her conversations will be changing as she grows up–the same with my oldest daughter. I need to give them the opportunity to know that Mommy is there and that we're going to talk; they can come to me anytime.

Defining Success

When my daughter went away to school, it was very hard. I didn't think it was going to be that hard; she has always been my right hand, helping me with the kids and tutoring them. It was very hard, but again, I always want her to know that I love her, and I want the best for her. If letting her go is what it takes, then I'm still here for her. If this is what she wants, then so be it. I was just glad she got accepted at Dayton; I know it's a good school. They have probably less than 5 percent minorities, but my daughter is so used to being in a not-so-diverse environment. She is open-minded; she's not afraid. That's the way I want her to be; that's what I expect. I expect her to be able to be academically and socially competitive in any type of environment.

She says that's her dream. She says she wants to someday come and teach in the community. When she came recently for Thanksgiving, she said maybe if not here, then in some other country. She is already thinking how to help, how to give back to the community. Since she was young, she was involved in the parish religious program. She was involved in tutoring; she was involved in different non-for-profits, helping kids with disabilities. She has those good intentions already. To see those values in her is something that has no price. Helping others just makes you feel good, I think. It is passionate, fulfilling, though sometimes financial issues are a constraint. And sometimes even my own family questions my decision to work for a not-for-profit. They're thinking, *You went to school–where's the money?* I say, "Well, being successful is not always about money. It depends how you see success."

I see success as just being happy doing the things I do, giving back, having a very peaceful life. That's how I see it. Of course, money–there's always the need for money. You're always in need, but money is not happiness. If it was happiness, you wouldn't see a Britney Spears suffering. She has all the money. Why is she not happy? There are many examples of people who are affluent yet have these drug problems, addictions. I just see myself as having a peaceful life and sharing with my family and my community. That's what success is for me.

I wish that more Latinos–not just Latinos but black and white people who have the opportunity to have an education–if they could think more about those that are left behind and just give back a little, it would make such a big difference to everybody's community.

Reflections

Herminia is very much rooted in her community and articulates how where you live is much more than simply an address. It is important to her to be surrounded by the Mexican culture and have access to the foods and other goods that are familiar. She was brought up by parents who did not have the opportunity to continue their education and, consequently, did not know how to encourage it for their children.

For Herminia, education has become important. While her mother expected her to learn the skills related to being a wife and mother, she always had different goals for herself. She did well in school and has been a strong advocate for her own children. The Catholic Church is a significant component of her life, and she considers herself fortunate that she was able to send two of her children to Catholic schools. She sometimes fears for the safety of her children but wants them to appreciate the community and experience the rewards of giving back.

Herminia articulates the importance of partnerships among family, school, and community and how when these elements are connected, they contribute to the ethics and success of their children and, consequently, the future.

8

Martha

I met Martha at the community medical center, a hub of activity in the heart of the community. She was sitting at a busy front desk, answering many questions at once. We found a quiet space where we could talk about her life and dreams. Martha is dreaming forward for her sons and the other children in the public schools.

Family Background

My name is Martha, but everyone calls me Marty. I was born here and just turned forty-six. I'm the executive administrative assistant and community liaison here at the community medical center.

Up to four years ago, I was strictly the executive administrative assistant, which meant I worked directly under our executive director. I started having more community contact in arranging for health fairs and staff to go out to other community-based agencies, schools, and other places where we were being invited, so I also took over the medical center health piece in the Fiesta del Sol, which happens every year at the end of July. I was offered the option of becoming the community liaison. I'm kind of juggling both things right now.

My mother was born in Mexico, and my father was born in Texas. When he got out of the army, he came straight to the city and settled here.

My parents met here. My dad was from Corpus Christie, Texas, and I guess it was too small for him. He wanted the big city. He had two brothers living here, so after the army, he just came here, and this is where he made his home. Well, my mom–she grew up in Mexico and lived there up to her twenties. She actually had six children in Mexico and came here because she had a sister here, and she started working. She brought only one child with her, and she actually got a divorce from her first husband; a couple years later, she met my dad and married. They used to go back to Mexico every year because her entire family was there. So they used to go back every year and visit her mom, who lived to be ninety-eight years old. So they used to go back every year.

Their first language was Spanish, and my mom never–all the years she was here in the United States–she never learned English, except for the bad words. She never really mastered the language, but she tried. She even had a private tutor, but it didn't work. I don't know what it was. She just did not master it, and she was a very intelligent woman, but maybe she didn't try hard enough. I don't know. But my dad spoke perfect English. In fact, he spoke some other languages also.

I try to tell people that I'm forty-six years old. I come from a time when children were seen and not heard. My mother spoke nothing but Spanish. My dad spoke to us in English. If he spoke to us in Spanish and we answered in English, it was okay. So we grew up speaking, I would say, more English than Spanish. It was more–the dialogue was more with my dad, and so English was stronger for us. For the older kids, of course, they all speak perfect Spanish. And my Spanish has gotten better since I've been here at the medical center, because I use it on a daily basis.

When I went to school, it was all English. We were the first Mexican family on our block when we bought the house, so it was all English. It was a Polish neighborhood back then, so it was all English. When my mom went to school for whatever reason, I had to translate, or she had to take one of my older siblings with her. It was always my job, and it was kind of rough for a quiet kid, because I was real quiet.

We really don't know Mexico. Even the older ones don't, because they left relatively young.

> My mother went to school but only up to first grade. Her mother's way of thinking–her mother raised them–was that girls don't need school, because you get married, and your job is to raise the baby, so my mother taught herself to read and write.

My mom's family–there's a couple of sisters left, and we have contact with them through phone or hear from them occasionally, but that's it. She spent the majority of the time she was in Mexico in Matamoros, and her mother lived in Matamoros. So yeah, when we were little, we used to go; we used to go visit my grandmother in Matamoros, which borders Brownsville, Texas.

My mother went to school but only up to first grade. Her mother's way of thinking—her mother raised them—was that girls don't need school, because you get married, and your job is to raise the baby, so my mother taught herself to read and write. She was real good at arithmetic, because actually, they used to have butcher stores, so they work the stores, and she was really good at that.

My grandmother came from a rich family. She was half Spanish, but she was disowned for marrying a poor Mexican, so he kind of left her to raise the household of babies. I'm not even sure how many there were, but I think it was more than ten. My grandmother made her living washing other people's laundry, and with her savings and my uncles' as they got older and did jobs, they were able to buy their first butcher store. So by the time my mother was a teenager, they owned three butcher stores and two trucks—two delivery trucks. They got on their feet by themselves. My grandmother's family was rich, but she was not entitled to any, even though it was not her fault, because back in those days, they used to kidnap the women—take them straight to the preacher and marry them. That's what happened to her. She had no control of that, but she was still quite disowned. It was my grandfather. He fell in love with her, took her on his horse, took her to the church, married her, and that was it.

For my mother, working was just more priority than going to school. For my father, it was the opposite. He had really high expectations, and going to school was the number-one rule. With my mother, it was "If you don't like school, get a job, but you can't be home doing nothing." That was the mentality.

Education

To me, education was more important. Going to school was real important, and I was reading at a young age. I loved school, and learning was real, real important to me. I saw my brothers and sisters were in school and working. I said, "I could do that." I never thought that you couldn't do anything, because my dad and my brothers always encouraged us. I was one of the three youngest, so we were considered the babies of the house. When I was growing up, everyone in my household worked. So I knew that was important. But I also saw my brothers going to school and working. So I thought, *Wow, that's how it's supposed to be!* So I've been working since I was fourteen—summer jobs or something.

We left for Houston when I was eleven years old, and I spent five years in Houston. When I came back here, they were just opening the local public high school. So I started public school there, which is my first experience in public school.

By the time I got to my senior year, I was told I wasn't going to be able to graduate, because I was missing one credit. They wouldn't give me another major, and I spent the first few weeks of school going to talk to my counselor; they were all too busy to talk to me. They weren't paying attention. Why can't I take another major? I had a friend that had been held back for missing one credit. She had to do a whole year over for one class. I'm not going to waste the whole year, you know.

What I did was, I was already eighteen, and I dropped out on a Thursday. I didn't tell my mother. I found a job in a factory, and on Tuesday, I was going to start work, so that Monday, I told my mother. And she was very upset. By then, my parents were divorced, so my dad was living in Miami. She was very upset that I hadn't told her that I was dropping out, but she was happy that I had a job. So I started working in a factory. And I stayed there for a year. I worked out in the suburbs. It was a company where they made the car kits. They put the car kits together—the model car kits and airplanes.

> What I did was, I was already eighteen, and I dropped out on a Thursday. I didn't tell my mother. I found a job in a factory, and on Tuesday, I was going to start work, so that Monday, I told my mother. And she was very upset.

The whole year I was there, I kept hearing since I was the youngest on the crew, "You have to go back to school; you have to go back to school. You're too smart to be here. You have to go back to school." There was this lady from Jamaica who said, "I have a daughter your age, and you know where she is right now? She's going to be a doctor." Her name was Linda. I still remember. She would keep on, and finally, I just said, "You know what? I do have to go back to school." What happened at the factory was that I received three promotions and raises. They had a layoff, and they kept me on even though I was one of the newest members. I kind of felt that that was really unfair, because I saw people get laid off that had been there years and years. But yet here I was, the new kid, and they were keeping me; I decided this kind of life is not me.

I thought it was unfair that those people who had been there so many years were getting laid off, so I decided to go back to school, and I started looking for a program. A friend of mine from high school had also left, because she had a child. She told me about a program where you could go, and you could get your GED, and you also get college credit and get a certificate. So I went back to that school, and I did all those things.

It was called City Professional College. It was downtown. I think it no longer exists. So I got my GED, and I got certified for typing sixty words a minute. I learned shorthand and typing, and you got secretarial skills. So from there, I got a fresh job and that sort of thing. And then I had a couple of jobs. I managed an auto-parts company. The owner spoke no English, so he needed somebody to help him work with the customers who all spoke English. He spoke nothing but Spanish, so I helped him manage that. By then, I was married, and I had a child, so I was able, actually, to take the baby with me to work.

While I was remodeling an apartment I was moving into, the painter asked me why I was working in this place. "You know, my mom works for the board of education. I think you could get a job there. They have an opening; you're real smart. You should apply." He took me to go meet his mom. I went to meet his mom, and she said, "Do you have a résumé?" I told her that "My stuff's all packed up; we're painting." She gave me a number to call, and I called the district office in this neighborhood. They asked me if I could come the next day for an interview. I had paint under my fingernails and everything. I went, and I was offered a position, but it was on a temporary basis, and with the board of education, there's a lot of rules and regulations, so there were a couple weeks where I had to actually just volunteer, but during that time, I was being trained.

It was to be a clerk, but with the Department of Early Childhood, and it was in the old district office. I was there, and it went very well. Then I was the bilingual school clerk. From there, I saw within the board of education, when you're a school clerk, there's really nowhere for you to go unless you went back to school to become a teacher or counselor or something. At that point in my life, I was going through a divorce. I had two small children, and it wasn't an option, going back to school. During the time that I worked at the board of education, I had taken classes–I had taken college courses. I went to two different city colleges. I took early childhood classes.

If I could have gone back to school, it would have been not to be a teacher, because I think it takes a real special person to be a teacher, but possibly a school counselor. When I was working as a school clerk, I was given a lot of other opportunities, like when we did testing, or if a teacher had to be called to talk to the principal, I would take over her classroom. I was given a lot of opportunities that the regular clerk was not, and I really enjoyed that interaction with the students from the community. I always have, so I related really well. That was the same area I grew up in, so I related really well to everyone, especially the kids, and so I did enjoy it.

I saw the issues and the problems they had, and I would use whatever information I could to help them. And that's how I made contact with the medical center. They were right across the street, so I became an advocate for the parents, because I had a lot of parents who didn't have access to health care. I would call the medical center, and I built a relationship. Even though they were right across the street, I didn't know who the operations manager was. We became friends on the phone, and once a child needed a wheelchair, I was able to obtain a wheelchair. Parents needed TB tests; I could send them over. Kids needed counseling; I could refer them, so that's how we built our relationship.

When an opening came at the medical center, my principal was leaving the school. And when new principals come into a school, they bring in usually new administration. Even though they like you, there may be someone they brought with them, so I thought, *Maybe it's time to go*. Plus, it was hard on the money that the board of education paid back then for clerks to raise two kids; it was really hard for me. So the medical center was offering a really good opportunity.

The school was doing a good job. It was a new school, built from the ground up. The administration was different from anything I had experienced. The teachers were young, and they weren't like the bell would ring and they would disappear. They were there for the kids, and they were willing to stay. You didn't see them coming for a paycheck. You saw a commitment–a real commitment. The principal was very innovative, and she wanted them to know the kids that they were working with, know the problems that the kids … faced on a daily basis.

There was a child that kept being brought to the office because he was unruly. You know, I started talking to him. He was living in the projects, because that was part of our territory. He hadn't eaten since the previous day at lunchtime. How are you going to sit in a classroom and your stomach's grumbling? You know, the teacher understood, but she was so busy with the other students she didn't have time to hear his story and find out why he's acting up, what he needed.

Shift in Public Schools

Well, we've gotten away from the basics in the public schools. Phonics–that's how I learned to read, and when they

> There was a child that kept being brought to the office because he was unruly. You know, I started talking to him. He was living in the projects, because that was part of our territory. He hadn't eaten since the previous day at lunchtime. How are you going to sit in a classroom and your stomach's grumbling?

took that and started implementing different programs, I think you saw a big difference. And it became that at home, you should learn manners. When I was growing up in school [a Catholic school in her early years], all those things were brought to you in that day. You were taught how you should talk to an adult and how you should respect an adult. And public school wasn't. They took away recess. They took away all those programs, and I think those were important, because a kid is just sitting there. You bring a child into a classroom and expect him to sit still for all those hours. It's hard.

I have a thirteen-year-old, but I have requested a transfer, and I am moving him to a charter school. Both children went to the same elementary school, but when my twenty-year-old started at that school in kindergarten, the structure was very strict. They didn't tolerate any gang violence. They didn't tolerate any rude behavior. The dress code was strictly enforced. In the last couple of years, I noticed that things were becoming a little lax, and I was hearing more issues. That's why I'm transferring my son. There's been more reports of gang violence. In fact, he was hit in the face. He walked into the bathroom, and a kid walked up to him and asked him to say a gang slogan; he said no and got hit in the face. He's thirteen. That's the age where gang recruitment is happening. They used to practice conflict resolution. I don't see that happening. I don't see those things happening anymore, and so I just felt my son needed a different environment.

He had to write an essay to get accepted at the charter school, and he just said that he needed an environment where a teacher would not be so overwhelmed that she could not answer his questions. He e-mailed it to me so that I could proof it, and I was going to fax it from here to the charter school. I said, "Who helped you with this?" because he used ten-dollar words, and it was pretty impressive. And he said he wrote something in there about me, too, which made me feel like crying. He wrote that "I don't need to do this for me, but my mom works hard to give me the best, so changing schools might be the best." If you're not involved in your child's life, you're not going to know.

My Children

Right now, all he wants to do is play the Xbox. We do talk about how they have to be in school. They have to be doing something. I don't care if it's clown college; that's the big joke. I don't care if it's clown college as long as you do something with your life. We work hard to be involved in these things—not because I want to be a part of this; I'm still the quiet kid. But I still feel real strongly about the injustice that I see. And so being a part of it and having done a part of it is important to me, and I'm hoping that they learn something. I would drag my kids everywhere, and so they've been exposed to a lot of stuff. They know that education, for me, is the biggest route. It is.

My older son just moved out. He always had a learning disability, which we didn't find, and that was another issue with the public school. How do you let something like that go so many years, and you just keep passing him with passing grades? He was there every day, and he doesn't want to go to school, because he doesn't think he's smart enough to go into college. So he's working right now–working for a big loan-brokerage firm. He's been there about a month and a half. He's doing relatively well, but I wish he would change his mind and take some kind of college courses, take something. I think that he will come around. It's just got to be on his own level and his own time, when he's ready. So I think he will. He knows how hard it is to work. He sees the long hours. If you don't want to be told what to do, then be your own boss. But you got to go to college, got to get the degree.

The older one had summer jobs. He had summer school. If he didn't have a summer job, he helped my brother. My brother has a vending-machine-type business, so he would help him in the summer. And the little one– actually, at Archer and Hamlin, there's a car dealership across the street. He went across the street to the car dealership and asked them if they needed someone to clean cars, and so they hired him. He is more of the man-of-the-house type. He's the kind that when he got five dollars, he'd look in the fridge. "You need tortillas? You need eggs? I'll go get it." So he does have more of that mentality, but I was afraid with him that work would become more important than school, because having money in your pocket feels good. That's what would scare me, but I'm hoping that he won't.

He does have go to college and get an education. Of course, doctor, lawyer, Indian chief–any of those would all be good. Clown, clown! And I've told him that. It doesn't matter. If you're a plumber, be the best plumber. If you want to be a mechanic, be the best mechanic. It doesn't matter if you want to be a doctor or lawyer. Just be the best. Of course, ideally, yes, a doctor would be real good, but that's my story.

Personal Development through Community Involvement

I grew up with two pictures my mom had hanging in the dining room. She had a picture of Martin Luther King, and she had a picture of John F. Kennedy. She really believed in what they represented. I think that's what we're about in my Pilsen Neighbors. That's what it is. It's about leading ordinary people do to extraordinary things.

You need to get people together, so the opportunity came for every organization within the Neighbors' organization to send leaders to leadership training. I was president of its board, and so I asked my director, "Do you think I can go?" and she goes, "I don't see why not—maybe that'd be good." I didn't know what to expect. That's a weeklong training, seven days—really intense seven days. I didn't get to travel far, but that was going to be my first chance to travel and be away from my children, because I've never been away from them. Seven whole days—I didn't know what to expect. But I came back, and it was pretty—it was really, really intense, really intense.

They make you really look inside yourself, find out your own interests. But it also brought out a religious aspect that I didn't expect, because we do our daily jobs, and we don't think about the religious aspect. But the spiritual aspect of what moves you is important because you have to believe in something greater than yourself to do this kind of work. And that was something that I wasn't expecting: I came back, and right after that, it was one thing after another, like one meeting, one public hearing, leading a group to Springfield, talk to legislators. You want me to do what? I didn't know you could knock on doors and people would receive you, and you could tell them, "Hey, what are we doing about this? How could our kids get four thousand dollars? Why do our schools get four thousand dollars, but over here in this area, they're getting seventeen thousand dollars?" You know, it opened your eyes to a lot of stuff.

I think I've always been passionate. I saw how my mom was treated because she didn't know English. It was so hard for her to communicate, how hard it was for other people, and it's always been real important to me to be fair. I just came from St. Louis a few weeks ago, where we had to talk to the African American Leadership Congregation. We had to talk about what's going on with the immigrant issues and why they should embrace it, how our two communities together can really

> I think I've always been passionate. I saw how my mom was treated because she didn't know English. It was so hard for her to communicate, how hard it was for other people, and it's always been real important to me to be fair.

make an impact. I had to explain to them, because they want to know our story. They want to know. I grew up being very grateful for that, because my parents raised us to be colorblind. Being colorblind is not an affliction; it is a blessing. My parents taught us that everybody is the same. Everybody should have the same chances. You should have a chance to own your house. You should have a chance to get the job you want. You should go where you want to go. No one should tell you where you can go and where you can't go, where you can sit and shouldn't sit. We had to explain that, and so I am passionate when I see injustice. Like I heard the other day on TV, as long as there's injustice, you can't be comfortable in your world. I can go home and close my door, but it's still going on.

Reflections

Martha grew up in a family with a mother who had little formal education and only spoke Spanish. The message she received throughout her childhood from her mother was that having a job was at least as important as pursuing an education. When she dropped out of school to take a job before graduating, she quickly realized that she had higher hopes for herself and returned to school. As her own children grew up, she ensured that education was a priority for them and that they were expected to pursue a college education. Martha worked in the public schools and was able to see firsthand that education was more than academics: teachers needed to address families as a whole and be a part of identifying resources that would strengthen the entire family. She has become a leader in her community and believes strongly that minority communities must work together to make a difference.

9

Ana

Ana was a student in the dual-enrollment program at the university. She took college classes on the weekend and talks about her experience at a community high school and how different it was from her elementary school. Her high school provided smaller schools within the larger campus and up-to-date resources that most public schools did not. Ana dreams forward to the day when all the public schools offer a quality education.

Family Background

My name is Ana, and I am seventeen years old. I live in the community where I have my parents, my siblings, my mom's parents. I pretty much have my whole close family living with me within the community, in the same house. On the second floor, there is eight of us: five siblings, my parents, and me. And then on the first floor is my grandmother, my aunt, my uncle, my cousin, and my grandpa. And then in the basement is my grandma, my aunt, and my uncle. We don't see each other every single day, because everybody works, but usually on the weekends, like on Sundays and Fridays, we gather around. We eat together on holidays. We don't have to go out anywhere. We just go downstairs or stay upstairs. We're pretty close.

My dad—he lived pretty much in the city in Mexico, so he was able to finish high school. My mom—unfortunately, she was the oldest woman in her family, so she dropped out in Mexico. It was like go to sixth grade, and then you go to high school. By that time, when she was in sixth grade, she needed to help out my grandma because my grandpa really wouldn't be a help. So she had to help out my grandma. She had to work like all the time, and she had to help take care of my aunt and my uncles. She was—she had a pretty hard, difficult life because she was always working, nothing for herself. At a young age, at the age of sixteen, she came to the United States to work. It was lucky for her.

She came with her sister-in-law and my cousin. It was still pretty difficult for her because she had no idea about this country or anything. To work, she knew how to work; it was just harder for her because there were two languages. It was different from Mexico. And then my dad—he was always very independent. He said he was the youngest one from the family. So he just came to the United States by himself, and he started working here. He would like to go out; he would go out. He would go to work. So he had it pretty good before he met my mom.

I want to go to Mexico and see my dad's family. My mom's family is here. I'd like to see his mom, visit her. She's very old, and she hasn't even seen my dad for maybe twenty years or so. I've never met her.

At home, we speak Spanish; everybody speaks Spanish. My cousin, my siblings, myself, and my mom's youngest sister—they know English. Some of my aunts get the hang of it. My grandma—she's not able to understand what we're talking about, but she kind of gets an idea. She does know how to say, "Thank you." I started off learning English when I was in third grade, because I was in an all-Spanish class and a little bilingual class. It was pretty hard because after fourth grade, it was all English class, which was pretty hard for me. So I've kind of been low in reading, but I was able to get better.

Education

I go to a high school within a larger high school, and I'm a junior there. The major focus is on math and science and technology. Instead of having three years of math and science, we have four years of math and science. And technology is used on a daily basis. We use the computers for everything. We were able to have an art program, I guess you could say. The supervisor lets us borrow a camera and lets us use the scanners, something the other schools didn't really have. I went there for starters because it was a community school. My parents feared, and so did I, going out of the community a little bit further, and this is a fifteen-minute walk, not that far. I also chose this school because I'm interested in math, and I thought that math would be like, that school would be a good school for me because it focuses on math, science, and technology. It's one of the four small schools on a larger campus.

It has its pros and its cons. For one, it's pretty good because we're small. We pretty much know each other throughout the school; we know the seniors, the juniors, the freshmen, the sophomores. We have uniforms, and the other schools don't have uniforms. I think it's a good idea because we don't have to worry about what to wear every day. But then again, it's not so good because many students from there come from a low income, so it becomes harder for them to be purchasing uniforms. The shirt is just fifteen dollars, and I think, for me, it's a bit too much. For students who have really, really low income, it's going to be harder for them.

When we're not in school, I usually stay home. I usually have College Bridge [dual enrollment between the university and the high school], so I come every Saturday. So I'm able to distract myself. When I get home, I have the Internet and whatever I need to do. I like reading. I usually read mystery books. R. L. Stine–he's my favorite author. I like reading books that talk about different cultures. At first, I never really liked them until I was in sixth grade. I started with the R. L. Stine books. My best friend told me about R. L. Stine, so I read the first book, which is *Halloween Night*. It was so awesome. I started reading more and then more. I was so interested in them. I've read about fifty books so far; I think I can relate to a lot to them. They're mysteries, and not only that, but it talks about a teenager's life in high school. The same thing that happened in the story could happen to me. I can relate it to real life. That's the part I like about the book.

I went to elementary school three blocks from the high school, and it was its second year functioning. I liked the students, and I liked the surroundings. They were also very, very strict with us. I remember this one time, I was in third grade, and I remember there was a principal meeting with the parents, and suddenly, the principal started blaming. Then one of the parents stood up to her and said, "It's not the kid's fault." The principal actually yelled back at the parent, saying, "It's your fault then, because you don't take care of your child." They just stood there because they didn't know what to do. They didn't have no action, like "I should report it" or something. I guess she

The parents did not always feel welcomed at school, because she would take care of them with a strong, mean look. It was every once in a while that she would smile. She talked bad things about us. I can pay no attention to her, but I feel that for my sisters and my brothers because they're there and they're the ones going through the drama.

apologized later on. The parents did not always feel welcomed at school, because she would take care of them with a strong, mean look. It was every once in a while that she would smile. She talked bad things about us. I can pay no attention to her, but I feel that for my sisters and my brothers because they're there, and they're the ones going through the drama.

I actually did get a good education there because I had a lot of experienced teachers. All the time, they were always able to help me. If I didn't understand something, they would help me how to do this and help me how to do that. The teachers were like if you didn't learn it, they would make you learn it. They would give us even more work than they planned if we don't understand it to the point we were able to understand it; they pretty much made me who I am. They would tell me their life experience, because they were a lot older than us. They would tell us, "All this happened in high school. This is not going to be it. It's not going to be like this in college." This started when I was little. When I was in third grade, they would say, "Stop and pray for high school, because this is going to happen." I felt pretty comfortable with them.

Leaving the Circle

One teacher stood out for me, and it would have to be my sixth-grade teacher, Miss Rosas. She was a very, very strict teacher. I really appreciate her because she made me think. She was one of the top teachers. She would yell at me. She would yell at everybody else. Because of that, she was able to get me off a track, because I was a straight-C student at the beginning of the year. By the end, I was an A, B student. I think that she made me; she turned my whole world away. She would be straight up. I remember once when she was telling me life is like a circle, and if it happens to this person, it could happen up you. But it's not going to happen as long as you're able to leave the circle and do it on your own. If you follow your parents' steps, it's going to happen to you. But it's you or your life, and if you don't want it happening to you, then get out of the circle, and do whatever you know is best for you.

> I remember once when she was telling me life is like a circle, and if it happens to this person, it could happen up you. But it's not going to happen as long as you're able to leave the circle and do it on your own.

That really made a difference for me. I was able to express myself to her, and she was able to help me out. And I still see her; she's still in the school. She still tells me I was doing pretty good, because I talk, usually talk to her about my grades. She tells me I'm doing pretty good, and she encourages me more. She's like, "Oh yeah, well, take this class and that class, and try your best."

Getting out of the circle maybe meant being different, I guess, with my peers, because they're like a circle. They're like my parents; they're related. I would just have to study, work, and get married. You would pretty much have to study and study and then work and then have family. I thought she made a difference, because my mom—she didn't even go to high school. My dad—he jumped out of high school, but he finished high school. My mom didn't make it through high school; my dad didn't make it through college. I'm going to make it through college. I'm not going to be like them, hang over and work in a restaurant. I want to become something.

It started off in the College Bridge program when I was a freshman, and then I had to get some practice ACT classes at a two-year city college. One of the teachers had told me about Bridge, and we asked her about that; she said it was like a program in which you could get college credit along with high-school credit and be able to get out of school early. So I was very interested. My sophomore year, I was talking to a counselor because I was interested in it, and so I applied. I didn't think I was going to get accepted until a counselor said, "Oh yeah, you got accepted. You're doing fine." The first class I took was U.S. history. The class that I'm taking right now is African art. I like College Bridge.

In the future, I would like to go to Illinois State University at Normal, because it's a teaching school, and I'm very interested in teaching. If not Illinois State, maybe I would like to go to Grinnell in Grinnell, Iowa, because when the speaker came, it sounded very interesting to me, and she told me it was one of the richest colleges in the nation. So I'm very interested in it because I also want to be able to teach a Spanish class or something. I would like to teach high-school students either math or science and maybe get involved as a bilingual teacher and, in the future, become a counselor.

Family Commitment

I do say I'm a role model for my five siblings, because they follow me with the things I do. We're pretty competitive, I guess you could say. I know the third child; she's pretty smart, too. She'll get in my face. The sister that's after me—she's smart; she's just very lazy. She doesn't do anything. So I tell her, "Come on—do your work. You can be even better than me." She'll be like, "Yeah, I know; I'm just lazy. I guess you might as well do it." They do see me as a role model, because

> I do say I'm a role model for my five siblings because they follow me with the things I do.

when they need something, I'm able to help them out. Sometimes I don't believe them, but I tell them, "I know from personal experience, because I've been the same age as you. I have friends that this happened to. I can tell you not exactly everything, but I can tell you what's wrong and what's bad."

If I went away, it's going to be such a hard time, because if I go away, it will be harder for them to be able to know what's going on. For my siblings, it's going to be harder for them; they come to me for every single little thing. Over the summer, I left for five days, and they were about to go crazy because "Where is she? Where is she? I need her!" I know my family needs me as much as I need them, and it's not just my parents; it's my grandparents and my aunts and my uncles. I'm the oldest one that's living here in the city, and they really like to see me. They told me they want to see me excel, and so I want to stay here, in a way. I love the city, and I love my family, so I really don't want to go away. But then maybe next year, if I go, for my parents, it'll be a great help for me, because I know what real life is going to be like, and I'm not always going to be with them.

> Over the summer, I left for five days, and they were about to go crazy because "Where is she? Where is she? I need her!" I know my family needs me as much as I need them, and it's not just my parents; it's my grandparents and my aunts and my uncles.

Relationship to Community

To me, a community is people being close to each other, sharing similar cultures and traditions. Families are part of the community. I don't see myself living outside the Latino community, but the community I live in—it's not so good. Gangs is a big issue. I think it would be better for me to leave that community and come back once in a while. For me, my family lives here. I don't think that's good. No, I wouldn't live here. I would probably come and visit once in a while but not live in the community. In my opinion, it's a bad community. It's not a bad community; it's just gangs are so tight.

My family stays maybe because they feel more comfortable here. We live in the city; we cross the street, and we're next to a store. We go everywhere, and the stores are there. We feel more comfortable here. They know their surroundings; they've been living here since they've come to the United States. The thing is, if they live out of town, they feel more uncomfortable, because they don't really know anybody. And here we pretty much know the neighbors and people who live around, so I guess they're more comfortable here.

I don't get involved in the community, but I do get involved in the school, and they talk about community. I get involved with the school things and get involved with the students that live in the community. I've done a couple of jobs over the past summers, and that involves the community too, because I'm not just helping people from this community. I'm helping people from the community next door. I'm able to try to help them unite with each other. Two years ago, we started out with a program that will help you out if you want to become a teacher. That influenced me to become a teacher, and . when I went to the program, they gave me a choice to go to another school in the community. I went a couple of blocks away from there, like a mile maybe. Right there, there were students from the other side of town that I never really paid attention to. That made me realize that students from this side were so totally different and how they were always separated; they're big rivals. One kind of gang, and the other one is another kind of gang, and they're big rivals. When I went to a little kid's house, I saw there was no difference between us whatsoever. So we would really help. I try to help them out, tell them that gangs are bad, tell them that there's no difference between me and that person and anybody else anywhere.

I think it's hard to solve the problem of the gangs, because they want to show who's better. I don't really know how to solve it, because no matter where you go, somebody's going to be better than somebody else. For example, today there was a fight because of gangs. It is a very big thing, because it's from two different perspectives: Who's better than who? And so until every single person takes a class or a lesson showing them everybody's the same, that might be good. Otherwise, I don't think–no program, nothing's going to be able to help them, because not everybody changes their opinion.

I think, for one, the parents can make a difference, because I believe the parents should have the big impact on the child. If they don't pay attention to the child, then the child's going to find someone else to pay attention to them, and unfortunately, it might be gangs. If a child doesn't feel loved by a person, they're going to go to somebody else. Sure, parents should work, but they should also spend time with the family, show them that they love them, and be careful who they're hanging out with. I think that's a

> I think, for one, the parents can make a difference, because I believe the parents should have the big impact on the child. If they don't pay attention to the child, then the child's going to find someone else to pay attention to them, and unfortunately, it might be gangs.

very big issue. They should know who their real friends are. Once they start hanging out with gangbangers, that could just be bad.

Improving the Schools

To make the schools better, I think they should get teachers that are able to teach better. Get better teachers, because with a couple of teachers that I had in the past, I didn't learn anything. So I think we should get more teachers that have more experience and teach very well. And not only that, they should get classes that are harder. Because in my personal experience, I don't think the classes I'm having so far are any harder. And I don't think those classes help us with college. They don't encourage us to go to college. If they do, it's like, "Oh my gosh, it's going to be easy." So I think they should get like a higher learning or something so we could be able to start understanding what college is going to be like. To me, a dedicated teacher would be like the ideal teacher, because I think if the teacher is dedicated, you are able to have more learning experience. They need to have their own patience. If a student passes by, they're going to help them out, talk to them. Try to make class harder so they can know what real life is like.

My hardest time in school was probably in my junior year, when I was in algebra, because I really didn't understand what one teacher was talking about. I'm getting better. I'm getting another math class, so that's pretty challenging for me right now, because it's more advanced than the class I'm supposed to be taking, but I think it's pretty good. I want to get more experience. Not only that, but also, my class of pop cultures is a great challenge, because the teacher, if you ask him a question, he'll respond to you with another question for you to think, and I've never really had that, and it actually makes me think. That's a good teacher, to me.

Reflections

Ana is very close to her family and is a role model for her siblings and cousins. Her parents had little formal education, but she was inspired by one teacher especially, who talked to her about breaking the circle formed by her family and friends. This meant taking personal responsibility for walking down a different path and setting her own goals. Ana understands why her family stays in the community, because it is comfortable with its cultural connections and close network. She is concerned, however, about the violence and predominance of gangs. She would like to become a teacher in order to help the youth of her community develop high expectations for themselves and experience a rigorous education.

10

Teresa

I talked to Teresa at the school where she was the community liaison. Much of our conversation took place in the hallways, where she was constantly on the move, helping everyone from teachers to students to parents. She exuded energy and passion for her work. Teresa is dreaming forward for her grandchildren and her community.

Background

My name is Teresa. I'm a mother of six and one that was stillborn, so I was pregnant seven times. I'm a wife for forty-seven years. I don't like the word *activist*, but if that's a term society recognizes, I've been a community activist since 1975. I like *community leader.* I like *organizer* because I am a leader, an organizer. I never get involved in an issue in which I don't feel very strongly about that issue. If I feel very strongly about it, I will not miss a meeting, and I will not take the second row. In other words, I put my heart to it, and people often find me in the front row. So I'm never by myself; I have followers. In other words, not followers, but I'm always part of a bigger team. And a leader has to have a following. And I never grab a camera or make a statement by myself, although if I'm interviewed, I know what I'm willing to take risks for. So it's real clear to me.

I've had a lot of education in the community, working with people, living with people. I've been in many discussion tables. I talked to a lot of people one on one, like in my work. I've always been a volunteer leader organizer. I have never made a living out of organizing; that is my heart and soul. It's about me; it's about my family; it's about the families that are neighbors, our fellow parishioners. It's about a community, so it's never really just about me. I'm always in touch with the grass roots. That's just where I've chosen to stay at this point in my life.

I'm an immigrant who really lived through a very, very tough time when there was no voices. And I was born in Mexico. I was born in Zacatecas, Mexico. My history just of where I was born makes me very proud, because I was born on the side of the road in a tent; at times, my parents used to live in train cars, boxcars. So my mother was pregnant when my father was working construction, and I was born on the side of the road in Zacatecas. Immediately, my parents moved to Jalisco, Mexico, so I grew up thinking I was from Jalisco, and there were such beautiful songs about the Mexican beautiful women from Jalisco.

In those days, our education came from the songs, and so my education about who I was and my self-esteem came from the songs of the beautiful women of Jalisco. It just told me that I was always proud to be a woman and that I felt beautiful. And that's important; that became important later in life, because my father would tell me, "Teresa, you were born on the side of the road. You were born in a tent." I didn't believe him, and I never followed the conversation. And I said, "Oh, he's joking." When I was little, I wasn't ready to accept or to deal with being born on the side of the road. I thought he was kidding.

> In those days our education came from the songs, and so my education about who I was and my self-esteem came from the songs of the beautiful women of Jalisco. It just told me that I was always proud to be a woman, and that I felt beautiful.

My father came in 1946. My father's uneducated. I was the first one to earn a degree. I was the first one to finish high school. My father didn't know how to read and write; neither did my mom. And my father, not being educated, not having any kind of background of knowledge other than what nature taught him, came undocumented

> My father came in 1946. My father's uneducated. I was the first one to earn a degree. I was the first one to finish high school. My father didn't know how to read and write; neither did my mom.

and stayed three years. And he earned his keep. He earned his keep here and was never deported in those three years.

You really like—you had to be the best you can be to survive. You really had to be like the best that God put on earth. You had to have a combination of very strong faith, and you had to be very strong physically, you know. As long as you have your very strong faith, you always want to do things. There isn't anything you can't do. So my father was always one of the best workers. But for him, not being educated and coming and staying in open ground in 1946 was unbelievable. For an uneducated, unskilled peasant to come and raise children in the United States—my hat goes off to him.

He raised us to be very, very strong. He didn't raise whiners, whining all the time: "Oh, this work is too hard. Oh, this and that." And he always made us proud by saying, always, "Anything you're going to accomplish or have in this world, let it be from the sweat of your brow." And of course, that was the only way to do it years ago—from the sweat of your brow. But even in this office, I still sweat. [laugh]

He brought us here in 1949. He had left home in 1946, so he left when I was four years old. For three years, I lived with my mom only. My younger brother was born after me, and there was also my older brother. So there were three of us, and we went to school in Texas. We lived just seven miles north of the Rio Grande. And we were undocumented; we got our visas in 1953. In those years, my father worked in the fields. For a year, he worked with this large, huge orchard owner's farm. And it was nothing but oranges and grapefruits. That's what the valley was about. The farmer had a little settlement of about twelve or thirteen homes, and that's where I met my husband. My husband's father and my father worked together for the same orchard owner. We had little homes: we had a two-room, one big room with wood floor. In Texas, you don't need insulation or drywall or anything, just a frame.

We came to the U.S. for the job—a real job where somebody pays you. Even if it's a backbreaking job; even if it was a job in Texas in 105-degree weather, picking cotton, people came. Picking cotton is very, very hard. It is very, very, very, very hard. Of all the jobs—and I have been in many fields; I worked in seven states in the country before I came here in 1966—picking cotton under the Texas sun is just something I would not like to go back to do. I'll go and tie up carrots, onions. I'll go back and do everything else. I'll go and be somebody's domestic worker, which I was also. When you're poor, you'll do anything. I think my story's a lot more different from immigrants today. Very, very different because the work was very, very hard. And you had no voice: you were open ground.

I've always been a happy camper. I was always grateful I could work. If they told us we were working thirteen hours, thank God we're working thirteen hours, because we know that in two more weeks, the harvest is gone, and we're going to have to look for another harvest. So you gave it all that you could when you could, where you could. And I'm very proud of our history, but it was so different because we really, really weren't complaining. Maybe because we were just grateful we could work. Because it was different here than it was in Mexico.

Experiences with Schooling

We didn't grow up knowing what education meant or gave you. The only education that I grew up with was the values that my parents taught me, and I remember my mother saying whenever we would interfere or interrupt a conversation or pass in front of other people, "Nina, have education. Say 'Excuse me.'" That was education—saying "Excuse me."

How do you become important? I really don't know. It wasn't a plan. It wasn't something that I heard from my father. I used to sign the report card; I used to sign my father's name. I didn't want the teacher to know he couldn't write. I myself never went to school when I was in Mexico.

There was no school. There was a church, and I used to go to church every afternoon. I loved going to church. I think I loved being around people. My mother said I loved going to church; it was the only social avenue I had. It was a very small town, and when I first attended school in Texas, I attended school with mostly Mexican Americans, third and fourth generation who didn't speak Spanish—first, because it was prohibited; you could not speak Spanish. Actually, if you spoke Spanish, you would be sent to the office, because in those days, they could paddle you with a paddle. You would be reprimanded for speaking Spanish. They would say, "Speak English, speak English; you are now in America."

Actually, if you spoke Spanish, you would be sent to the office, because in those days, they could paddle you with a paddle. You would be reprimanded for speaking Spanish. They would say, "Speak English, speak English; you are now in America."

I learned English in Texas. When it became part of the United States, everybody learned English, and how long has Texas been part of the United States? This is why all the Mexican Americans that I went to school with—there were more Mexican Americans then there were Anglos—did not speak Spanish. I'm talking third- and fourth-generation Mexican Americans. It wasn't even spoken at home. I'm talking about Mexican Americans who would bring the perfect-cut slice of cake to the teacher, like in the pictures. You don't see that anymore. Years ago, there was the perfect shiny apple and the perfect slice of cake. These were the Mexican Americans who were just like the Anglos. My friends and I were different, because in school, there were less than twenty undocumented recent immigrants–Mexican American immigrants. And I was one of them. I was seven when I started school. I didn't know how to read in English, and I didn't know how to read in Spanish, but I learned English. I had a very good report card. I loved going to school. I think I loved any avenue that would get me out of the house. I just loved learning. I learned from people. I learned from plants; I learn from everything that surrounds me.

And when I was in the fourth grade, I was writing letters back home for my father. I remember the greeting like it's today, because Mexicans–I don't know about other cultures–but Mexicans have the longest, most-beautiful, sometimes-boring greetings. They're beautiful. Nowadays, it would be, "Get to the point!" You know, you kind of learn the American way: "Get to the point!" But the greeting was beautiful. I used to write. I learned in English first, but then I made the transfer. I've never taken a Spanish class in my life–never, not even in college. And I'm pretty proud of my Spanish writing skills.

Actually, I went up to seventh grade. Then I was double promoted to ninth grade, and I dropped out. Supplies, you know–things like that. I was the spelling-bee winner for the junior high. I was a spelling-bee winner in a school where I had no roots at all. I rose to the top of the class, but I had no friends, because I was poor, and I looked poor. You can tell when somebody doesn't use shampoo; you can tell when somebody doesn't brush their teeth. You can tell when somebody doesn't have, you know, cream. So I kind of made the Mexican Americans look bad. I may have been their color; I may have been just as good looking as they were, but they looked better. And the Anglos, of course–we had nothing in common. Um, we had very much in common, I should say. We were classmates, but the interesting thing that I do not forget is the Mexican Americans would not ask me for the answers. Sometimes there was a kind of pride between us in our own cultures, but the Anglos did ask me for the answers! The Anglos will move forward, are more ready to put something aside even if it's for their benefit. But they asked me for the answers. I gave them answers, and they gave me pencils, and they gave me paper! Hey, you know, that's the American way. What's in it for you? What's in it for me?' And I learned it. Now, I learned that later in organizing, self-interest, how you can do things. What's in it for you, what's in it for me, and what can we do together?

Fight for Educational Equality

Why did education become important? I think it always was. The avenue just didn't present itself, because it wasn't time. My time came, and my time came here. I worked in a couple of factories. I stayed home for about five years to raise my boys. And in 1975, actually, my son was in high school, and that's when I started; I joined the fight for a new public high school. Everything I do in my life has to do with what I believe in, what I believe is an injustice. I don't have to read books to know what is not justice, what is unjust, what is not fair.

In the community then, my son was going to an elementary school that's old. Then he goes to upper-grade center, and then he goes to the public high school. The public high school only went up to tenth grade, and I didn't know what the school looked like. I never had to go to the school. In those days, you didn't pick up report cards. They were sent home. Parents' attendance–maybe they had meetings, but it wasn't like conferences or anything. But it's about your child. So my son comes home from the public high school in ninth grade. He had never, to my knowledge, been in trouble before, so I never really had to go to school–only the day I enrolled him. He comes in with a note, a pink slip, and he says, "Mom, I'm on PC," and I said, "What's that?" "That means parent conference. That means I can't go back until you go and have a conference." "Okay, I'll go and have a conference." It turns out that he had been cutting the class after lunch; it was open campus. And his way of cutting the class after lunch was that they would cut the class and sit outside in front of the school, in front of the doorsteps of the other homes. I asked the assistant principal, Jose Rodriguez, "Well, why does he do that? You're in charge. The school's in charge. I think I'm doing everything on my end. He comes to school every day, brings the homework. I really don't understand why you let him out there." He told me, "Well, you know they're sixteen years old, and they really should have inner discipline." I said, "Well, I don't think I would be comfortable in my classroom, looking out the window and seeing my student out there. I think I would say, 'You know, Herman, I'm waiting for you.'" His comeback was they're old enough to know what they're doing.

In 1974, I enrolled my fourth son at Head Start. Head Start touched– really touched–me. Someone said to me, "We'll enroll your son, but you have to come in one day a week and volunteer in the classroom." That was the condition of the program. I said sure I would come in; I was all ready to cooperate. At the end of the year, Miss Laredo, the school community representative, started seeing me. When you're the school community representative, you're like welcoming, and you look at parents' skills; I could speak English, which was a plus. There were a lot of people who could speak English, but it wasn't just the language. It was the personality of a confident person.

She said, "I want you to come to a Head Start meeting, Teresa. Could you come?" So that day, I felt like I was going to a special place, because I had been invited. I'd never been invited before. I groomed in a special way, just like going to church, and went to the meeting. I went to another meeting, and soon I knew what we were talking about. Our kids, right? Then Miss Laredo said, "Ms. Teresa, I want to invite you to a Neighbors Community Council meeting." She was on the board. And I said okay. She said, "I would like to have some parents there, and since you're involved in Head Start, I'd like for you to come." In those days, I used to iron and sew, embroider and crochet, and I had my older brother living with me, who was working. I had two men working at home, plus four boys and my little girl. I went to the board meeting at the Neighbors Community Council and took my embroidery. I guess it was a way to escape. "What if I don't know what they're doing?"–you know, but I'll know what I'm doing!

> She said, "I want you to come to a Head Start meeting, Teresa. Could you come?" So that day, I felt like I was going to a special place, because I had been invited. I'd never been invited before. I groomed in a special way, just like going to church.

I took my skills with me, and for a couple of meetings, I did my embroidery. I was listening, and pretty soon I kind of got it. This woman standing in the conference room at the school where the meetings were said, "Ms. Teresa, is this the first time you come here?" And I said, "Oh yes, my first time." I was proud, and she said, "You should come and visit the school. It's not really a good school." She said, "Just walk around the halls. Figure it out for yourself," and it got me thinking. I didn't take the walk, but I kept coming back to the Neighbors' meetings. There were, you know, meetings–not just board meetings but meetings on the high school. And it still hadn't clicked. And of course, an organizer's job is to identify leaders and have a one-on-one with you.

Father Donohue, who was a Jesuit seminarian, saw me and said, "Oh Teresa, how are you?" I said, "Oh, I'm real worried. I'm upset," because I had now gone to the school. He said, "Why don't you do something about it?" And I said, "What can I do?" I was in the mode of blaming others or at least complaining. I opened up with him and said, "What can I do? I'm not running the school; I'm just the mom." And he said, "Would you be willing to do something about it if you could?" I said, "If I could, I would." And he said, "I'll help you," and I said, "What could I do?" He told me that he was not going tell me what to do but that he would work with me if I was willing. He told me to find ten parents that think and feel the way you do. I did, because about five of them were already there!

We started having meetings at the public school. We were the Concerned Parents of the Public School. I led it. We started getting involved in the school. I've never been the parent or the person that leans on the other side totally, but I've always been the type of person that takes my responsibility very seriously. I wanted to work together with the ones that have the responsibility and the power. That's always been my stance. And I can never crucify somebody, although sometimes it would be necessary, but not in a way that demeans or puts down; it's got to be in the right context. We were pretty successful. But I realized we couldn't do too much about Froebel anymore. But it really, really did help me to say, "Here's what we need to create, and this is already in the works."

The fight for the new public high school was in the works already. The fight had begun. It lasted five years. That's enough time for me. I became the president of the construction committee. I knew nothing about construction. But you know what? It's about accountability. It's about meeting with the general contractor and the general contractor being accountable to a community, giving us a report about what phase they're in. It's the timeline: Are we going to hit the timeline? Are you on time? What's behind schedule? What can we do to help? It was a very interesting time. We formed a principal-selection committee and a teacher-selection committee. No other neighborhood or group in the board of education of the city had committees to select a principal.

This group never let go. This group was determined, insistent, convinced that there had to be a high school in the community. Why? Because it was a community of new immigrants that had larger families, and they were going to the old public school. I had learned, after my son went there and after the parent conference, that it was a condemned building, that it was an eyesore, not originally built for a high school, that it had a gym with holes in the wall. Anybody who went there can tell you this, because I saw them myself—holes in the wall on the third or fourth floor. The bathrooms were in the basement. In the basement, you would go in, and there's this hall and then dark, and to the right was girls' and boys' bathrooms. Because the discipline was so lax in this environment, it was just a depressing environment; the students would actually pull the wires off of the light switches to keep the

> When I saw the school, my inner voice said, "Your dad didn't cross the river and risk his life and your life for this. There's got to be something better."

bathrooms dark for fights–for fights. When I saw the school, my inner voice said, "Your dad didn't cross the river and risk his life and your life for this. There's got to be something better." And that's what pushed me. That's what pushed me.

Power–there is power in organizing. We say there is power in organized money, and there is power in organized numbers; we just organized numbers. We organized numbers and never let go. There were meetings and meetings and meetings and meetings. You can't let the issue get cold. You have to keep it warm; you've got to keep the people interested. It started with petitions; I had an archive of just newspaper clippings of those days from 1975 on. I kept as much as I could put my hands on. And it was just such an awesome, awesome fight–the march of a thousand people marching downtown. It was maybe similar to the marches today that are happening in immigration, but it was very, very focused.

The parents were the leaders. They were the ones making the decisions. Of course, it was in consultation with the church, because knowing that you have the church with you is something good. But it wasn't the church speaking. Now some churches are becoming the voice. They're not really letting the laypeople take the lead. That's a little bit in reverse and is not so good, because I believe in real grass roots. If I'm sitting with the parents, the people, the residents of this community who are there because they're affected, I will defer to them. That's why I believe in the grass roots; I believe in people. If we're going to work with people, then we let them take a lead in their destiny. We're not going to let them sink. Let's bring out their strengths.

The Dream Comes True

Let me tell you why the new school is a dream. To me, it's the dream of people, of parents. When you have all those people marching, when you have all those meetings, and so many people came through all those meetings, it is a dream. Because the dream is not a building, and the dream is not what it accomplished; the dream is that you actually had people have a say, people who had no political power. I mean, I wasn't even a voter then. I wasn't even a citizen. I was a permanent resident, but who cared? Of course, no one cared in our setting, but the city would. But there was power in our numbers, and the dream is that people acted on their values. That's the dream.

And the dream is that the school became the anchor to fight, to win other fights. And it is a dream. The new public school became a dream for this community in a way that we did not dream about. We wanted to have a high school for safety reasons and for reasons of equity that this neighborhood should receive a high school. So our kids could have a high school in our neighborhood. Safety was important; going across racial and gang boundaries was not a good thing for the kids. They would drop out. There was a 77 percent dropout rate. The Neighbors did a study at that time, and it was 77 percent at the old school in the community, because people either went to a private school, were sent back to Mexico, or dropped out at tenth grade. So in that sense, it accomplished having an avenue.

We were thinking education-wise, but we didn't know that in 1976, the Chicago 21 Plan [a comprehensive development plan to revitalize communities] was going to raze every building east of Ashland. We at the Neighbors organized almost the same people around this plan and came up with an alternate plan. I have a copy of the alternate plan. I was the president then, and I signed the alternate plan. We raised $25,000. Corporation Council raised $12,500, and the Neighbors raised $12,500 for the alternate plan. The alternate plan in itself never really became the plan, because we didn't have the vehicles yet like the development corporations.

We had the Development Corporation, which was, again, another education avenue. The Development Corporation was created by the Neighbors to bring in young men who were in gangs who did not finish high school to begin work in rehabbing buildings and to get them into the unions. That was the mission of the Development Corporation, and we launched it off on its own. It was started in the Neighbors by Ms. Reyes. Ms. Reyes was a member of the board; her daughter was a lead organizer when we bought the first building for one dollar. I was the president, and Ms. Reyes was the mom that carried the torch to have services for the special-needs adult population. So that's how it started in the Neighbors; we bought the first building. Once they had a board, we launched it off, because when you're organizing, you're not organizing to keep, to manage. We're not managers. We just organize it and get it off the ground. We're always working in education. We had some of the oldest schools and actually got all of the schools rehabbed. After the new public high school, all the schools got rehabbed.

The new public high school was just a torch that we came under. It was the one that touched us all. It was the issue that brought us together. But it's the issue that got us talking to each other. And it was the issue that said, "Well, now we need to celebrate. We're going to start the largest Mexican American festival in the Midwest." That wasn't their dream; it was just, "Let's celebrate." You know, let's have a fiesta because Mexicans are fiesta goers. We celebrate everything. That's how Fiesta del Sol got started and how the buildings got rehabbed.

We got hot lunches. They were serving sandwiches–cold sandwiches– in those days at school. Why? I don't know, but we actually got a hot-lunches program going in the community. We stopped the Chicago 21 Plan, and then there came the desegregation plan: "Okay, fourth graders, fourth to eighth grade are going to get on a bus, and they're going to go to *X* school in such-and-such neighborhood." We fought for a high school, so we could have all our kids together from one neighborhood. And now we're going to put them in a bus? We were very organized when it came to the desegregation plan, and it didn't work in the city anyway. But we were ready. We were ready. We also worked. You know what? I was in the middle of all those. That's why I can talk about it.

Continued Activism

I then worked in a special program called the Bilingual Education Home School Intervention Program. We worked part-time. There, we received a little bit of training and interviewing skills, parent-effectiveness training, and positive reinforcement—you know, working with parents of kindergarten children. We were going to be working in the home, but we were being trained and supervised. Every Monday, we reported our cases back. It was a very interesting program. So I had the luxury of learning from all those families that I worked with, that we visited for a year, once a week for one hour. And we actually took activities. These were parents of children who were experiencing difficulty adjusting to school. We were trained in identifying or helping the parent identify or feel comfortable with learning disabilities, and we also were the bridge to family therapy.

I learned a lot. I mean, I just will never forget, but I think I've really given back, and that's what makes me, because what I discovered about myself was just so beautiful that I want to share; that's what I want people to discover about themselves, and that's why I'm here. I taught for eight years, and it was such a wonderful experience. I just loved teaching.

I taught seventh and eighth grade. I love that age. I love that age because that's the age I never really went through. You know, I didn't; I didn't have that. I knew how I felt, and I have such a bond with my students—such a bond. I mean, I was what you call tough love. Once you have that setting, you don't have to be a policeman. We're in it together, you know? I would never embarrass them—never, never embarrass them, never call out their name. I would go and say quietly, "Do you need help? Do you know what page you're supposed to be on?" I loved it. But I was really needed in the office, because the principal always wanted me working with the community. She said, "You're a community leader. You should not lose that. I want you to work in the office with the parents. You are a born teacher."

I've had many opportunities to be the principal of the school. I work very closely with principals. Many times, they consult with me on an issue where they just need more input. The principal would say, "You're from this neighborhood; you're a community leader, a parent--all your kids came here. Don't lose that. You need to work with the parents." Okay, that's what I love doing. I know what being a principal is, and I could not be 24-7 just for the school. I feel the community needs me. I'm just part of finding good principals. So I work with the parents. If I didn't have that, I wouldn't be here.

I've been here a long time, and they trust me. I wear many hats, and sometimes wearing all of them on one issue helps. The trust and respect that I enjoy here is due to the fact that I don't waver. I don't care who I'm standing in front of. And they'll listen. They'll take it into account. So what's my relationship with the local school council? They trust; they trust my opinions.

Imparting Strong Values

I'll tell you what I hope for my grandchildren. I think I'm a little late in hoping, expanding my hopes, but I'll give you an example: I was working in a factory in 1968, and we had a neighbor. She is my age, and we had kids the same age. She said, "Well, I want Leo to go to college; I want Leo to be someone in life." I told her that what I learned from my father was to live off the sweat of your brow. Never take what doesn't belong to you, and remember, "I don't see you, but God sees you. I'm not going to be the one that judges you. It's going to be God that judges you, so you don't have to lie to me, because the one that can see you, you can't lie to." And he said respect older people. I mean, God gives you a cross—don't drop it. Don't drop it without really trying to carry it. I was still a seventh-grade dropout when I said this to her.

I said, "You know what my wish in life is? That my kids are people of good faith—people who respect others, who never steal from somebody else, and who never try to get away with things at work. And I want them to respect older people and have a love of children. That's what I want." If I had my wish, that's what I want. And I want them to finish high school. I do want them to do that. And I say to myself, "Why didn't you just wish that for me?" I wasn't ready. I didn't know I could wish for more. I knew that I had come a longer way than my father had, and so my kids finished high school. My kids are great people. Everywhere they are, they have good friends. They have strong values. They definitely live off the sweat of their brow.

My husband and I worked very hard—very, very hard—to raise our five boys in the community, where you can talk about having all the social problems in the world. And we worked very hard to help our kids, support them, have the open communication, fight in the neighborhood to have avenues, and I think my children reaped the benefit in the sense that they had to part with friends who did join gangs. I know that they went through the struggles of being in schools where there were fights, but they apparently never joined a gang.

I had one son, my oldest, who one day was talking to me—we used to sort of lie down in bed and kind of talk. We used to sing. I used to sing to them the songs that I sung in Texas!

He said, "You know what, Mom? Remember Jose? He got in an accident, and he got hurt; they slashed his throat, but he didn't die, because they came in time to help him. Well, our team was going to join the gang. Do you know I was going to join the Latin Counts?" I said, "No, I didn't know!" He said, "Yes. One day after work, after we all got paid, we were going to join, and this was a baseball team! And here I'm on the team with them, and I didn't know if I was going to go. I remember that day that my father said, 'I want you home for dinner this afternoon.'" When my husband spoke and said, "I want you for dinner," the kids couldn't say what they would say to me: "But I'm in the baseball team and have to go." He stayed home because they never quarreled with their father. "I want to see you for dinner tonight"–there was nothing special in that, and he just said that out of the blue. He said, "I think God spoke to my father, because that's the day we were all going to join the Latin Counts. Well, I didn't say no, but I couldn't go, so I was left out." I thought, *Oh my God!* He's the construction worker. He likes to work outside. He went to school. Actually, he took a class after high school. He went to a commercial high school. He took a class for business after that.

> He said, "I think God spoke to my father, because that's the day we were all going to join the Latin Counts. Well, I didn't say no, but I couldn't go, so I was left out."

But Alicia is another story. Alicia got pregnant when she was a junior in high school. She got pregnant, had a daughter. She was still living with us. Her boyfriend was a young man that went to the same school; we knew each other from being neighbors and going to church–you know, the moms. Anyway, she had her first daughter, and a year later, she has another daughter. She still hasn't moved in with her boyfriend. She's staying at home, and she had a Down's-syndrome baby; Gabriella has Down's syndrome. She is now– she'll be thirteen in July. Oh my God, she is such a blessing. Alicia has been a stay-at-home mom ever since Gabriella was born. She said, "I'm not going to have anyone take care of my daughter." She said, "Mom, I feel so bad I didn't finish high school." I said, "Alicia, don't worry about that. You are doing the most sacred job that God has given you. That is to be a mother. Never feel guilty about that."

So I have a daughter who got pregnant, dropped out of school, and I tell people, "You know what? I'm a person from the neighborhood, and I never strived to be different." Because that means that I know what I'm talking about. That means that it always makes me feel good not to stray away from the grass roots.

We could have left, could have strayed from the grass roots, but we chose not to. At one time, my husband's boss said to him, "You know, we have a house in the suburbs, and we have a church by the house. Right now, it's empty, and we're inviting you to move into the house by the church. We just want a family living there to mow the lawn, take care of the garden, and dust a little bit in the basement of the church. You have four boys, and we'll pay you two hundred fifty dollars a month." That was a lot of money in those days. You could buy a car for $250 a month. By then, I had discovered the Neighbors. I discovered myself. I discovered my roots. I discovered my potential. And do you know what we said? We said no! And I don't regret it. I don't regret it, because in this community, we found ourselves. In the suburbs, we might have had better schools; we might have had better opportunities, but maybe we wouldn't have discovered what we know, who we are. So I never regretted it. No, my family feels good here. So we've always had a choice. We've always had a choice.

Reflections

Teresa raised her family in the community, and even though she and her husband had opportunities to leave the community, they chose to stay. She was deeply influenced by her father, who brought her to the United States and instilled in her a strong set of values based on self-reliance and faith. She became involved in the community through the schools and became a change agent, as she was determined to advocate for equal opportunity and represent those who felt they had no voice. Teresa discovered the power of organizing and how beautiful it felt when parents had a voice and made a difference.

11

Fernando

I met Fernando at his office in the community. It was a busy place, and he worked right in the middle of it all. He wanted to talk about why he returned to the community after going away to college. Fernando is dreaming forward for his community and the hope that others will also choose to give back.

Background

My name is Fernando. I'm twenty-five years old, and I'm a community organizer. I'm a resident of the community on the near west side of the city. I've been here most of my life. I'm trying to organize churches to support the immigration reform going on nationally.

My parents are from Mexico, but they met here. They got married when they were older, but they came here for a better future, like everyone else. They came to support their family in Mexico; they would send money back to Mexico when they were here. My dad never went to school. He grew up in a small town, and he never had access to it. It just wasn't offered over there. My mom went through third grade, and she had to quit so she could help take care of family at home.

My mom's family—like, her brothers and sisters are here, but my dad's family is still in Mexico. They came to Pilsen because it's just part of the

Mexican community, and they had friends who moved into the area. They worked in factories. My dad understands English, but he doesn't really talk it, because at work, he's a masseuse. My mom took English classes, but she had a difficult time picking it up.

Early Education

Growing up in this community, it was tough. I guess it was tough because being the oldest, I always had to experience everything first. It was a little tough compared to my surroundings, all the things I had to deal with. In terms of violence and gangs, you always had to be careful who you talked to, where you walked to, and just to be safe, you have to know the streets where you walk. You can't walk through any street.

I started school at the Community Academy. It's a public school. I remember I never wanted to go to school. I always had stomach issues. I guess I was nervous. I don't know why. I was just nervous, and I would always get sick, supposedly. I just didn't like school. I kept going there until fourth grade. The teachers had a lot to do with it, I guess–the comfort level or the way they made you feel. I wasn't comfortable for some reason. Then I changed to the grammar school. Everything was a lot better there. I was challenged. Everything was a lot more challenging. It made school more interesting. I guess I was actually challenged by teachers in terms of just what they taught. I was able to pick it up better. I like the challenge. I like being pushed. I did well; I was picking up my grades. I was doing well. I guess the level of education they were teaching us and the way they taught it to us was what changed. It was different compared to my old school. And it was good. I felt like I was getting prepared, and I felt like teachers really cared about the students.

My parents came to school just to make the required conferences for report-card pickup, not really for anything else. They were just always busy, and my mom was working, so she couldn't go. My dad was always working too. But they couldn't really go to the meetings they had, the school board meetings and meetings with the teachers.

I would pick two after-school programs, art and some types of programs there. They were pretty fun. I enjoyed it. I guess it helped me stay out of a lot of trouble. I did it because I didn't want to be home, bored. My mom wasn't at home; she was working, and she would get out around four o'clock. We would just stay after school and do more. It was fun; I enjoyed it. It's something I feel like, hopefully, the kids still have.

I was a procrastinator. I was such a procrastinator. I always started homework around eight or nine. I always started late. I finished, but I should have done it earlier. I never really had help from my parents for homework and stuff. They weren't educated enough to help me with my homework after a certain grade. Sometimes, if I was having trouble, I went to school early, where I could do my homework, or I would stay late. But that wasn't all the time. In the morning, there was teachers there to help. In the morning, if you wanted to come in early and go over your homework, you could do it here. That helped a lot.

> I never really had help from my parents for homework and stuff. They weren't educated enough to help me with my homework after a certain grade.

Our parents will drop us in the morning when we went to school. They always—ever since I can remember—they would take us to school. They would drive us to school every single day. That helped. Coming back from school, they couldn't make it, so we would walk back. That wasn't a big deal. I guess I got used to it. I kind of took the same path every day to school. Like, *Okay, this is safe.* I always took the same way.

High-School Years

Then I went to the public high school, and unfortunately, it was a mistake. It was a mistake going there. I remember a teacher over at my grammar school saying, "Where are you going to high school?" "I'm going to the public high school." "You shouldn't go there, because you're going to be just a number." I'm like, "What?" I didn't get it. And when I got there, I was like, "Wow!" There was no real support from anyone. I was never challenged. I felt like I would have done better going from Orozco to college than from Juarez to college in terms of education. I did learn something, but in terms of the level that was taught, it wasn't that challenging.

There were always a lot of distractions, a lot of kids acting up and teachers having to deal with the kids. And it was really, really annoying. The teachers had a difficult time dealing with the kids. Disciplinary issues—they would always act up. And everyone else would say, "Come on—leave already. We want to learn." It was one of the big issues there. Another issue was sometimes teachers didn't care.

> There were always a lot of distractions, a lot of kids acting up and teachers having to deal with the kids. And it was really, really annoying. The teachers had a difficult time dealing with the kids. Disciplinary issues—they would always act up.

They wouldn't really care, like, "Okay, here, read this chapter, answer these questions, and turn them in at the end of the class." Okay, whatever–people would be talking, and we wouldn't really do anything. I was really disappointed with that. I'm like, "Wow, this teacher sucks." Just different situations with different teachers. Of course, there were some good teachers there, but it was pretty horrible; it was like, "Wow!"

There were lots of discipline problems with kids who kept coming to school but just causing trouble when they were there. They just wanted to go have fun. They thought it was fun, and they didn't have to do any work. It was a big issue. Some teachers dealt with it better than others. One teacher tried to come on straight. She would call security every single day. She was on them until they kicked them out of the class. They would take them to the office, and then the next day, they were right back in the class, doing the same thing. Eventually, they were kicked out. She was a good teacher. She was always pushing us. But other teachers were like, "Deal with it. Leave them in the classroom."

I enjoyed my friends and being with people in school. Getting education was okay; I have to do it. I had to go to college. I have no idea where I got it from. I'm going to college–that's it. And I always knew I was going to go to college. For eighth grade, I was voted most likely to succeed when I grow up. I guess people thought I was driven. They're like, "You're so smart." I'm like, "Okay, I'm not smart. I'm just doing my work. I enjoy being challenged, and I'm going to make something out of it. Why don't you make something out of yourself? You're just as smart as I am." It was just weird.

Teachers didn't see that I was motivated or I wanted to go to college or that stuff. But I did. I did want to go. No one ever tried to find out what I wanted. The teachers weren't challenging me, and they didn't see that I was passionate about school. And that's why I was never considered for the better classes. Counselors–I would just see them when we had to pick our classes at the end of the year. That was it. My senior year, there was a counselor, a college counselor–a brand-new college counselor. She was recently a University of Illinois graduate. Her name was Solis. She was there that year. And I guess I just wanted to talk to her. "I'm going to college–where can I go? What can I do?" She started helping me. She started really pushing me to like "Fill this out. You need to do this now; you need to do this." And my other counselor wasn't doing anything. She helped me fill out the application and everything. I actually applied late to University of Illinois. She wrote a letter telling them there was a family emergency in Mexico and I couldn't turn it in in time. She helped out a lot. I probably would have not actually got to University of Illinois if she wouldn't have helped me.

My parents knew I was going to college, but I didn't tell them I was going to apply to the University of Illinois. I really didn't tell them; I wasn't comfortable to tell them. They wouldn't be upset. I just wouldn't tell them. I was in my own little world, and I wouldn't tell them. I told them when I was accepted. They were happy.

Culture Shock of College

I didn't know what to expect when I got there. It was a culture shock—different cultures, different people. It was really, really different. I guess just the neighborhood and the area where I was living was so safe. I was like, "Wow!" It felt weird; it felt really weird being like that. I could be out at two or three in the morning. It felt really comfortable—a different setting, small town. Everything was a slower pace. Everything was less tense, more calm. Everything was more chill,

> I didn't know what to expect when I got there. It was a culture shock—different cultures, different people. It was really, really different. I guess just the neighborhood and the area where I was living was so safe. I was like, "Wow!"

more relaxed. Of course, the classes were tougher, and I wasn't ready for college in terms of the education I would be receiving.

Going to class—that was difficult. Coming in, I felt like it's high school again; I don't need to do anything. I need to show up and pay attention in class, and I'll pass. I had to literally learn to study. I just started reading and looked around me and thought, *What is everyone else doing?* And just tried to do the same. I had friends who are like, "Let's go study; let's go do this or that." I didn't study as much as I should have. I should have studied more. I had mediocre grades at best, Cs. I was doing okay. I could have done better.

I really didn't get to know the professors. I guess it was more up to the students to do the actual reaching out to the professors. It was a larger university, and it was 100-level classes where you had to take bigger classes—bigger, lecture-style classes—so you had to literally do it yourself. You had to go to the office hours. I guess it was up to me, and I didn't do it. I didn't know the importance of actually doing that. I wrote it down that it would have been really important. Wow, it would have made really a big difference—a big difference.

My sophomore year, I started tutoring at a local grammar school. It was a job. It was one of those work-study programs that they had. I started tutoring because one of my friends had done it before. I started getting to know the community there. It was a lot of fun. I really loved the kids and their families—the kids and their parents—and I was really interacting with them; it was great. It was a good experience with them. I was investing time into the community.

My junior year, a group of my friends wanted to set up a fraternity. I just went to the meeting; I don't think anything of it, but they started talking about it. The values were community-service based; we're founded on community-service values. And I guess that's how it started. I thought, *Okay, I'm in.* We started it: unity, honesty, integrity, and leadership. Those are the four values we follow, and I guess we did do it–wow. It took us a year to actually take it there and become a registered student organization. There you go. We started doing the requirements of the service hours we had to do, and then we went through the actual founder's process that was involved. We just did it. It took us a year, fourteen of us guys.

Integrating Community Service

I felt like I was really part of that community. I was a community-service chair for my fraternity. I started looking for stuff for guys to do. We started tutoring. We started up an annual Thanksgiving dinner and haunted house. The community actually came to our frat house. We set it all up for them and scared them. That was fun. That was so much fun. I miss that. Then Thanksgiving dinner–we did that with the Boys and Girls Club. We cooked the food, and we invited the families–the kids and their families. It was a lot of fun. They really enjoyed it. The organizations were involved too.

I would come home every weekend, unfortunately. My friends were like, "Why are you leaving again?" I shouldn't have done that. Just coming back, I was not a part of this community. I was just here for the weekend, and then I would leave. I was never really back home here in my community. My junior year, when I started the fraternity, was when I started getting more involved at school. And that's when I started becoming part of that community more and less of this one–less than I already was. But what else was I doing? We started interacting in the community more. My friends started becoming more involved with the community. We also started a soccer league at school with the Boys and Girls Club. There were trailer-park communities there and immigrant communities, so we would go pick them up from the trailer parks and just have a soccer league for the kids and then take them back. I was pretty much in charge of

> I would come home every weekend, unfortunately. My friends were like, "Why are you leaving again?" I shouldn't have done that. Just coming back, I was not a part of this community. I was just here for the weekend, and then I would leave.

the league. I was so overwhelmed. I had so much work to do. It was a lot of work but the most fun I ever had.

I didn't actually have much time to study, but I did really well that semester. It forced me to manage my time really well and really focus. So it was really, really, really good experience getting that involved and getting that focused.

Getting involved also taught me patience. I had to learn a lot of patience with those kids. I guess that and just interacting with the community– how to get involved more, how to service them. I started to understand what they needed. It came from the kids. And it just came from interacting with them, getting to know them, and asking them questions. One of the kids I was tutoring–I asked him, "What are you going to do with your life?" "I'm going to work at McDonald's like my mom." I said, "Wow, you're not going to do that! You're going to go to college, right?" I started talking to him about college and asking things like, "Do you want to become like an astronaut?" It really got to him, because I asked him a couple of months later, "What are you going to do?" "I'm going to go to college." That was cool.

Coming Home

I graduated. I had no job there, and I wasn't going to have any financial aid or anything. I had to come back. There were no real opportunities there to service the community. There's like two nonprofits there that service the communities. I had to come back. I've been living at home. Now I'm involved. I really feel like now that I'm more involved, it's my community.

I started doing a summer fellowship that I applied for. The description was "involvement in the community." I register people to vote; help get out the vote. It sounded interesting. It's helping the community; I'll try it out. And then I was placed here at this community organization.

Right now, what we need is interaction with the youth and crime prevention. One of my big issues with people who graduate from college from the neighborhood: they get out and succeed, and they don't come back. They don't give back. What are you guys doing? You need to come back and give back. We need more people involved and more professionals to become mentors, to start going to classes, talking to the kids and talking to them about

> Right now, what we need is interaction with the youth and crime prevention. One of my big issues with people who graduate from college from the neighborhood: they get out and succeed, and they don't come back. They don't give back.

college. They need to give them new and positive ideas and be positive role models, because unfortunately, they might not get it at home. That's what gangs do: give support and be there for them.

They say, "Okay, we'll support you, and we'll love you. Come and join us. You have to come early. You have to be violent for us and protect us." Like, wow. We need to really start focusing on giving them an alternative and being there for them. If we don't, it's going to stay the same. Honestly, it's going to stay the same if we don't start giving back to a community. That's one of the biggest challenges for a community. It just causes so many other issues. It would definitely help in terms of education and kids going off to college.

The schools can help; they definitely can, especially schools here in the community. The schools are getting better. The high school is getting a lot better. There's more support; they need more people, though, that actually care about the kids and the community, to be more attractive to the students. There is a new principal, and he really understands the students. I think he literally knows every student's name. It's like, "Wow." He sets the tone for everyone else. He's open to hearing, open to listening to teachers and students. That really sets the tone—just the way he deals with issues. That's good. And the kids are going to feel he cares, and they notice that. They're like, "Wow, the principal's changing stuff for us. He met with us. Now he's going to change this for us?"

It makes a difference. I guess teachers need to start caring more about students in terms of just education and knowing them personally, too. Especially in our community, a lot of kids feel like they don't have any support. I had support from my parents but not as much as I would have liked in terms of education. I can just imagine other kids who have less support than I had. And they really need that. They're not going to be encouraged to go to college. It's important for us, as professionals who already graduated from college, to give back and go back to those kids and talk to them about college. They'll make it. They'll know the options. They'll know they have options: college or gang. Have fun in college. It is a choice. To go to college, they need more love and support—and from the positive mentors. It'll be like, "All right, try this; do this. You'll have fun. You'll enjoy it. You'll learn a lot. You'll have a better life than the other side."

Choosing the gang, I feel it's very easy because that's all they know. Violence is all they know, and they feel like they have no other choice. That's why it's important to

Choosing the gang, I feel it's very easy because that's all they know. Violence is all they know, and they feel like they have no other choice. That's why it's important to get to the kids at a younger age, to talk to them about college and be a positive role model.

get to the kids at a younger age, to talk to them about college and be a positive role model. If you get to them at a younger age, they're not going to have to even choose between violence or education and college. And that's where I feel we're lacking in our own communities here. It'll definitely prevent it. It's a big issue. If you don't have the support, they turn to gangs, and they have support from gangs. It would definitely make a difference if we were able to get more professionals involved, kids from the community who graduated and made it out to come back and support the kids who are going through the same stuff they were probably going through when they were younger.

I'm going to start getting involved, just going to the local high school. I know they have a lot of support there. They support the grammar school well. Maybe going down the block or going to additional schools, talk to the teachers and bring them on board—something else I planned on doing with my fraternity. I was planning on getting them involved with the kids, going to the grammar schools and talking to the kids—the guys who graduated already—having them talk to the kids. Something that'll help.

Staying in the Community

I just love this area. It's so close to everything; it's the center of the city. I just love the way I grew up, the interaction with other kids in the community. It's changed so much from before, though. I feel there's less sense of a community now than before in terms of just neighbors interacting with each other, from what I see. There's less sense of that; they're more sheltered. They're more protective of themselves and trying to close themselves off from their neighbors. They don't really try to get to know their neighbors. For safety reasons, they say, "I can't go out; it's dangerous. I can't go out and talk to my neighbors." That's one of the issues: safety.

Also, one of the big issues that caused that was the gentrification and people moving out and new people coming in. That causes people in the community to think, *Okay, there are people that live here and are permanent versus people that are constantly coming in and out of the community.* That interaction's not going to be there. It changes the way the community is set up, but I am planning on staying. I really want to make a difference here. I see the violence and the crime and think, *Wow.* I'm getting tired of it already. Wow, I'm tired of it. I'm really just really tired of it. It's really frustrating. Oh, I don't want to deal with this anymore. Please, stop already.

I'm back because of that. One of the reasons I'm back, hopefully, is to prevent it, to stop it. It's not going to go away if we don't actually start being more involved. The violence is just going to shift somewhere else. Nothing's going to happen if we don't start interacting more and be more involved. It's going to shift; crime's going to start moving outward. For me, it's more about prevention and changing the structural way of things. And just trying to control the issues with cops–it's not going to make a difference. It hasn't. Crimes are still being committed.

I guess my big thing is just getting more professionals involved with the community, having them get involved with the kids. I feel like people feel like they're above getting involved: "Okay, we're at the top level with this up here. We'll talk about the issues, but we won't actually go out and get involved." Of course, that's not going to solve the issues. You have to be hands-on to better understand the issue. That'll definitely make a difference. It would make them more interactive with the students and teachers. They'll be like, "Wow, this is the issue; I see now. Okay, let's work on this." And that could make a difference if they start doing that.

Reflections

Fernando found ways to avoid school when he was young. He said that he felt uncomfortable and that teachers didn't seem to really care about their students. He knew he wanted to go to college, but no one at school picked up on that until he connected with one significant counselor who encouraged him to apply. Fernando left his community to attend college and found it difficult to make the transition academically; no one had prepared him for what he needed to do in order to succeed. He figured it out on his own and also became part of a fraternity that served the community. It was there that he began mentoring young people and realizing what a difference he could make. After college, he returned to the community and was overwhelmed by the violence and gangs. He is now working in the community and wants to make a difference.

Fernando believes strongly that not enough people come back to help once they have left. Communities will flourish when individuals who leave make the choice to return and dig in to help resolve ongoing issues. They can make a difference by bringing in additional resources and signaling their belief that the community is healthy.

12

Rocio

Rocio came to my office to talk about her experience of growing up in Mexico and speaking Spanish when she arrived in the city. She compares the school systems and how she felt little challenge in the schools. While at the university, she was a tutor in the Center for Academic Development, helping other ESL students. She is dreaming forward for her nieces and nephews and a more rigorous public school system.

Family Background

My name is Rocio, and I'm twenty-three years old. I was born here in the United States, in LA, but I grew up in Mexico, the state of Durango. I lived there until I was fourteen.

My parents would come here from Mexico and stay for a couple months and then go back. They're much used to living over there. My sister—she got married and moved here. When I finished middle school over there, I always had that thing that I wanted to come here. If I get a degree in Mexico, I'm going to have to move here anyway. The situation there, as you know—it's kind of bad. It's really bad, especially if you have a degree. You have a degree, you are really well prepared and everything, but you won't find a job. If you find one, it's really bad pay. I was like thirteen when I decided to come here.

My brother-in-law said, "If she wants to do that, she can come and live with us, and I'll make sure she does it. If she wants to get in this, I'll make sure she does it." That's how we kind of convinced my parents, and they let me come here. So it's me, my sister, my brother-in-law, my niece, and my nephew.

My brother-in-law, his English is just–I don't know how to say it correctly–it's just like whatever he learned in the streets, just to be able to communicate the basics with people. He came to the U.S. because their situation in Mexico was really hard. He comes from a very big family, and economically, they were doing really bad. His dad was here. I think there are eight or nine, and most of them are men. Their mom was over there, so most of them came here to help their family who stayed there. There was just one woman supporting eight kids. I have a lot of respect for her, because she raised all of them. Some of them started coming with the dad–most of them. They grew up, and they started coming here. They did a great job. They worked, and they supported the family there, and they didn't stop until they brought their mom here. They helped her fix her papers, and she moved over here, so they're all living here. Sometimes he asks my sister. Whenever they have meetings at the bank, he usually likes to take my sister. "Because," he says, "there's some things I'm not going to understand, and I need somebody else to help me out, understand the concepts and everything."

I was always curious. A lot of people told me I was way more mature for my age since I was five. I just saw what life was like over there, and I saw how most young people would do, like young women. They would go out to high school. They would finish there, get married, have their kids, and that was pretty much it. Then I saw the other end, where they would go out, have a degree, have a career, but they would always complain, "It's too bad. We don't get well paid. We have to go to the United States, because even if we go there and do a blue-collar job, we're going to have more money than we're making here with our career." I saw these things, and I see what people have done here so far. For some reason, I think I can do something else. I wanted to try. I always felt like I had to get out of there, for some reason, and see what's out there.

Learning English

My first language is Spanish, and I learned English here in the city when I came back. I started in high school; they put me in a bilingual program. I didn't learn much, because I was in a high school that was mostly Hispanics, so I didn't have much need to use English. The first year, they set it up where I had most of my classes in Spanish. And I had just one English class, one ESL class, and it was like two hours. Other than that, most of my classes were in Spanish except for gym; that was the only class I had totally in English. She was the only teacher I had that didn't speak Spanish at all. It worked kind of good, and you could tell, because in all my classes I have in Spanish, I have As, and gym was the only B on my report card.

When I was in high school, my sister and brother-in-law, with their education level—they didn't really understand. They would tell me, "If this is what they are telling you, I don't think you can work your way around it." I just kind of had to figure it out on my own, and actually, I wanted to do it that way. Of course, I would have to go and ask them for support if I needed something. For the most part, I was trying to do it myself first. I would give it a try and see if I could change things around. If I couldn't, I would have to go and talk to them. But in that sense, the advisers and all those teachers in high school kind of tried to help me understand how the whole system was. The way I saw it, even if I asked them, I don't think it was going make much of a difference, because it is something already established. And if they're requiring that much things, I don't think they can work their way around it.

> When I was in high school, my sister and brother-in-law, with their education level—they didn't really understand. They would tell me, "If this is what they are telling you, I don't think you can work your way around it." I just kind of had to figure it out on my own, and actually, I wanted to do it that way.

My sister and brother-in-law came to school only when they picked up my report cards. It was hard for him. He still says that. Up to this day, whenever he needs to see my teachers, he says, "Well, I do want to talk to them, but sometimes it's hard for me because I don't understand. I understand English to a certain point. But other than that, I have a lot of problems." That's how they found out the problem with gym; they didn't speak English. My brother-in-law saw my grades, and he saw that the only B I have was in gym. So he went and asked the teachers, "What is she doing wrong, because I see that all her classes she's getting As? What's the problem with the B? Is she not doing that well? What's the problem?" The teacher told him, "I don't know if it's sort of a tension problem or something, but sometimes I tell her things, and she does kind of like the opposite. When other girls kind of explain to her, then she kind of gets it, but when I first tell the instructions, she doesn't quite follow them. I don't know if it's like a tension issue or something going wrong with her because she doesn't understand." Then he says, "Don't you understand? She's in the bilingual program. Probably she doesn't understand the language." "Well, that would be possible." "No, that's what it is!" After that, it did change a little bit, but it didn't change much. I still had to go to my classmates to ask for the specific instructions. It would become even worse when I had driver's ed.

As I said, it was only one class in English, and most of my classes—the stuff that I was seeing in those, I already saw it in Mexico. I don't know how they figured out which classes I was supposed to be in, but for me, they were too basic. I think I was ready to take more of the advanced classes. Pretty much, it was just a review of what I already saw in middle school in Mexico.

I think my placement was based on my grades and what I had from Mexico; they took most of my credits, because I started here as a sophomore. The whole thing was kind of weird, because I was a sophomore, but I had more freshman classes. I don't know how they figured that one out. I know that in math, they placed me in the most basic one because my grades weren't that great in Mexico. So I placed in algebra and then worked my way up. But the other ones—I don't know how they figured those out. It made me feel bad because I just thought that I already saw this. I feel like I'm, in a certain way, wasting my time. I didn't feel that I was learning anything.

I talked to some of my teachers, and they said, "Unfortunately, we can't really work our way around this, because you have to meet requirements," which was something that threw me off. I never had that thing that you have to have so many years of this; that was really, really strange to me. They have electives; I could pick some classes. I was like, "Whoa, that's interesting." What did I pick?

I picked chemistry because you could pick for your science; you could either have physics or chemistry. I never liked physics, so I went to chemistry. And for me, that was very strange because I was very used to the system in Mexico, where you have to take both. There was no way around it. You had to take them. This is kind of fun; here I can avoid it if I want to.

Obstacles in the School System

School really wasn't what I thought it would be, because like I said, it was a like a review for me. I already saw this. I was doing chemistry, and I already saw this. I had this foreign-language requirement, and they placed me in Spanish—Spanish II, which was the same for kids who spoke Spanish, but they didn't know how to read and write it. I could read and write Spanish really, really good. My grammar and everything was really, really good. So I was sitting there learning how to change verbs from like present to past. It was like, *Oh my God, you have to be kidding*. It was good for the other kids—I mean, yes, it was for the other kids, because they could ask me to help with the work and everything, but for me, it wasn't doing anything.

I had to have one or two years of a foreign language. I asked, "Can you place me in something else?" They said, "Well, that's the only thing we have. We have Chinese, but that's only for Chinese speakers. We don't have a teacher who will teach from English to Chinese, and even if you have, it would be English and Chinese, and you don't speak either."

My adviser would say, "This is what you need to take," and then go into the system and see that I have some requirements that I still need to cover. The system was pretty bad, I would say. Hopefully they changed it by now, because a lot of people will be in the same position I was. But for me, the whole thing was really confusing, so I had to ask a lot of people, "How do I do this? How do I do that?" That's why, when I started here at the university, I would rather get a degree start and finish in some place instead of going to a community college and transfer. Because I just find the systems too confusing, and they change things overnight. Like one day, you can use this thing, and the next day, you know what? "We changed the requirements."

Moving on to College

After I graduated, I started looking for some schools, and then the ACT tests really threw me off because my points were really low. I took it the second year after I got here, so my scores were really bad except for math. That was the only thing that was kind of decent. So when I started applying for college, most of the universities will tell me that I have to go to community college and then transfer. From my previous experience in high school, I'm like, "No, if I'm going to do something, I'm going do it in the same place—start and finish there—because I don't want to go through the whole thing again of transferring credits."

So when I started applying for college, most of the universities will tell me that I have to go to community college and then transfer. From my previous experience in high school, I'm like, "No, if I'm going to do something, I'm going do it in the same place—start and finish there—because I don't want to go through the whole thing again of transferring credits."

That same teacher, Mr. Gonzales—he had contact with an admissions representative for the university. I think she went to the high school and probably did a presentation or something, because he gave me her business card. So I started looking for her. I called her; they sent me a package, and I sent them my application. I spoke to her in Spanish because he told me she speaks Spanish. The very first time I talked to her, I tried to learn English, and that's when she told me—it was really funny—"You know, you should take our English program. Your English is pretty bad." I'm like, "Excuse me?" and she goes like, "Oops, I make a mistake." And I'm like, "Why? I thought you were my friend." "I didn't mean any offense or anything." Then I said, "Now, wait a minute—tell me more about that English program." So that's how she told me about the ESL program they have here at the university.

I took the ESL program, and at first, I was a little disappointed because I thought I was going to place a little bit higher. But then I understood my problem, and I thought it was a really good placement system. First of all, I thought I was going to score higher, but then I went back, and it helped me a lot. I think if they had placed me higher, I wouldn't have made it the first quarter. I think my high school should have encouraged me—like probably placed me into more English classes, so that would challenge me, and I would have to learn it. In high school, I found my place in this very comfortable position where I didn't have to use English. I can do very well. I was doing excellent without using English. As I said, in all my classes, except for gym, I had As.

I was working part-time when I started at the university. Most of the time, I'd be working in the CAD [Center for Academic Development]. I'd be doing work study, but there was a time I actually got another weekend job. So it was like three jobs. And then I started to volunteer with a community organization, which was sort of like another part-time job, because I got elected secretary for that organization, which surprised me a lot, because I was really young. It was like the second year that I started going to their meetings, and they started getting to meet me. They were having elections for their board, and somebody said, "You know what? We should give Rocio an opportunity." And they were like, "Okay, would you like to join?" The day of the election, the other person that was running for the same position just got one vote. It's pretty much an organization that's people from my home state in Mexico. They raise funds, and they try to pull people over here. And it's really interesting the way they work and everything. They do work here, and they go back there, and they also try to help over there.

The organization already has eleven years, and each year, they have their celebration, like their anniversary. Then for that, they sometimes make workshops and things of that nature. They also educate people. Right now, they're working really hard trying to get legalization for immigrants, so they actually joined with other groups from other states in Mexico. They kind of did this network and then became an even bigger organization that would create an umbrella for all of them that will represent all of them. They're part of it, and I think the first march was here. When was it—last year, two years ago? They were one of the pioneers that started working on that.

This work has made me think about getting my master's degree. There was a career fair here with government agencies, and I talked to somebody in the U.S. Department of State. I told them I was going to get my bachelor's degree very soon, and they told me to apply. And I actually wanted to do it, because they told me that you have to do a test if you want to get into it. It's a long process, they told me. But first of all, you have to do a test. And after the test, you'll move on to interviews and all that stuff. The next test is in March. I really wanted to do it, but then I sat back and thought about it. I would like to be more prepared. I know that even though they said a bachelor's would be good, I would still like to go the extra mile and get a master's and be really prepared and more informed of what it's all about. I looked, and I saw a graduate program in public policy. Well, I think that fits, because I'll have more understanding of how the system works; I'm not going to be jumping into an empty pool. That's what I would like to do.

Advice for the Public Schools

If I could change the schools here, well, first of all, the English, the ESL program if they still have it. I understand it's hard; the students are really young when they first come from Mexico. They don't understand English, but they need to challenge them a little more. I feel the same way I did—most students have most of their classes in Spanish, and they feel just too comfortable, so they don't challenge themselves to use English; it takes them longer. I know that it takes practice to learn English, and a lot of students did. But if the school pushes a little bit more, maybe half and half, that will help a little bit more. That way, it will be—I don't want to say forced, but at least they will have to learn it. They will be exposed to it, because if we're not exposed, we don't use it. They say in English if you don't use it, you lose it, and most of those kids—most of those kids in that neighborhood speak Spanish even in the stores and everything, so they're not really much exposed to the language. So that would be my first change. Change school to force them to take more English classes.

And then the whole design of the curriculum. I don't know how they go about that, but I think there are some classes that I would bypass. The whole thing with science, that you can choose either or—for me, I had a problem with that. That means that if I want to, I can go to college without knowing any physics. I think it doesn't matter what discipline, you know; it's always useful to know something about that subject. If you are not going to teach both of them, at least join them and have one science class, but have a little bit of everything. I think that's very useful, and that would be another change that I will make. I will try to incorporate as many classes as I could. It was really very strange for me that they didn't offer geography. I was like, "Okay, there's Earth science and all that stuff, but what about geography?" We cover some geography, but you don't have something that gets the whole thing. Well, no wonder you got a lot of people, a lot of kids, are shown a map but they don't know what the United States is.

Sources of Inspiration

I would say most of the people I talk to for some reason will inspire me in one way or the other to move on and do things. Most people will think probably you got your influences from somebody who already did it, but I will also talk to somebody who didn't have the opportunity for x or y reason, and that motivates me to go on. Maybe the person didn't have the opportunity, but it still makes me want to go on. I did have two teachers in high school who really motivated me to go on. They made me see the reality. They said, "This is how it is here: A lot of people think it is a fairy tale. Ah, you're going to go there, and you're going to become rich and all that stuff. You might be able to do it, but it's a lot of work. And if you don't get prepared, it's going to get even harder."

> "This is how it is here: A lot of people think it is a fairy tale. Ah, you're going to go there, and you're going to become rich and all that stuff. You might be able to do it, but it's a lot of work. And if you don't get prepared, it's going to get even harder."

I have an internship now. Julian is my internship boss, and I think the work he has done–it's pretty much a big inspiration. You can see the determination, the motivation he has to do things, and how he transmits that to other people. Because he is a person who looks like he really cares about the people who work for him. He will stop by in the morning and just have a little conversation with you: "Hello, how are you? How was your commute today? Did you have a hard time getting here?" and stuff like that. It's a big motivation. I think he's sort of like a role model. The thing that's really good about him is that he's shown people that he really cares about them. At least he wants to know how you're doing and stuff like that. A lot of jobs that I've been to really didn't have that. It's really nice to work with him.

Advising Other Students

School was harder in Mexico; I think it's something culturally, even when they start in elementary. My niece—she's in eighth grade, and she's complaining about her homework. I was like, "You should be glad, because when I was your age and I was in your grade, I had much more homework than you do. That was a little bit more; it was harder than this is." At that age, you don't really think in the future how those things are going to help you. But it does help you.

I try to help my niece with her homework, and you know, sometimes she's very curious. That's something that I like about her. She will sometimes see me doing my homework, and she will say, "What are you doing?" So she's very curious; she'll start asking me things, so I try to explain and talk to her as much as I can about what I'm doing. Because she procrastinates about work a lot, and I used to do that. So I try to tell her, "You have to do it, because then you're going to be last minute doing your homework," and all that stuff.

In addition, my advice to other students is "It's just a matter of doing things for yourself." Because I see, especially, like, in my community, young kids—sometimes they do things like getting a degree or something to please their parents or for their parents to be proud of them and everything. But what they don't stop and think sometimes is that they should do it for themselves. Because I run into many kids, many who are in college, and they start the degree, but when they're about to finish, they decide this is not what they really wanted to do.

It's really weird, because my family—they have an interesting way of supporting me. Some families will say, "You can do it! You can do it!" Mine—they're more laid back. "Okay, let's see if you can do it." They're more challengers. I think they've been that way since I started in school, because I would do things, and sometimes they didn't surprise me with things. Like I see here with my niece, my nephew, my cousins even my friends, when they pick up their report card, if they got really good grades or if they got straight As, they'll say, "Let's go to the store. I'll get you this; I'll get you that." I never had that.

> It's really weird, because my family—they have an interesting way of supporting me. Some families will say, "You can do it! You can do it!" Mine—they're more laid back. "Okay, let's see if you can do it." They're more challengers.

Personally, at some point, if I have kids, I would not do that, because you don't know if they're learning. You don't know if they're just getting good grades for the prize or if they're doing it and they want to and they are learning it. I would get good grades, and my family would say, "Okay, well, that's good–keep going." That was pretty much it, so as I said, I started doing things for myself. And I started learning things for myself, because for me, getting good grades just meant not failing and not having to take the class over and not having to stay in the same grade. It didn't mean getting something at the end of the month. It's a different approach and, I think, for me, worked. I don't know if it'll work for everybody, but at least for me, it did.

Reflections

Rocio is curious and has an incredible amount of intrinsic motivation and determination. Her family supports her, but they do not have the same experiences and can only provide so much advice. They want to see her succeed, and she calls them "challengers," as they are not always sure of the outcomes; rather, they wait to see if she can do it. She would like to see the schools become more challenging and offer more instruction in English to native Spanish speakers. She found the public school curriculum less rigorous than the curriculum in Mexico. Rocio also had a difficult time adhering to the ever-changing requirements of the system.

Rocio's dream adds to the mosaic by advocating for a more-challenging and less-rigid public school system for all learners. She struggled with learning English and having teachers who did not understand her needs even when they were pointed out by family members who were also struggling with English.

13

Eliamar

Eliamar was interviewed in her store by Laura Bauer. She told her story surrounded by the artifacts that she has brought back from her trips to Mexico each year. She sells them to community residents who want to preserve their culture and also to those from outside the community who are just discovering the richness of the Mexican culture. She is dreaming forward toward the preservation of the Mexican culture in her community.

Family Background

My name's Eliamar. It's a Hebrew name. It means "God's love." I'm the oldest of five; I have three other sisters and a brother. My parents still live here. We've been here for forty-two years. My family came from the northern part of Mexico, called Nuevo Leon, which is just one hour away from Laredo, Texas. My sister and I were born in Mission, Texas. After I was three, we went back to Mexico until I was eight. I was in Mexico for a total of five years, and I learned English in Mexico. My father thought that English was the key thing when we came to the United States. We had to have good English as a second language, so he had a teacher come to our house and teach us English. The English teacher was British, and we couldn't get rid of some of the accents.

Because of the fact we were close to the border, we were too Americanized. The northern part of Mexico is a total different area from the rest of Mexico. I remember my father used to buy all our groceries in Laredo, Texas–clothes, shoes, everything. Bread, milk, fruit, vegetables–everything because we were just one hour away. He was so accustomed to living in the United States that he didn't think anything of crossing the border and going back to Mexico, where we used to live. It was very, very Americanized in my family.

My father used to work in different things, at first in the railroad. He would be traveling all the way from California to Flint, Michigan, and my mother did not want to follow him after she had the two kids. That's why she went back to Mexico when I was three. After that, he just started working in the fields, picking the crops. From that point on, after I was eight, when we came back, he found a job in a factory here. We came here to live, and then he found, in the city, a job.

My mother does not speak English to this date. She never wanted to learn. She just didn't–not wanted to, but it was very difficult for her to learn English. My mom is seventy-four, and she was here since she was twenty-one. She felt it was very difficult. She had gone to school, but she just could not keep it. She will understand everything, but she doesn't carry on a conversation, whereas my father did. My dad had been here since he was eighteen.

My mom only went to fourth grade and my dad to sixth grade in Mexico. They said that the best inheritance that any parent can give a child is education. Because they could give all the money they could get to the child, but with a bad business, the money would go away. But with the education, you can come out again and start over. And they were right. They never actually told us what we should go to study, but whatever we did, we did it with passion. And they told us to really do the best that we could and you will be successful in whatever you do, and that's basically it. And still to this point, my dad says the same thing. You do it with passion, and you will get whatever goals you have. He's eighty-two, and God, I can't believe this man. He walks I don't know how many miles, but I know it's ten square miles, blocks that he walks every single day twice a day, in the morning and evening. Yeah, he's got a lot of muscle tone, and he's always very, very active.

Living in the Community

I was ten years old when we came here, because we lived in Laredo, Texas, for two years. When we came to the city, we stayed in an apartment that my father rented. Later on, my parents bought a house next door to that building, and we bought the building, but it was many years. We're talking twenty, almost twenty-eight, years ago, and we bought the building that my mom was renting from the landlord. I've never moved from the building, so I know that place like the palm of my hand.

Because of the fact that my dad never drove, we were always going on buses, and the transportation here was key for them. Schools were close by. For them, education was very important. We went to Catholic school, grammar school, and then I graduated from St. Ann's High School. It was only two blocks away from us, so for them, that was very important. The other thing was that the transportation for my mom and dad to get to work was key. So he really never had the need to own a car, because everything was so very easily accessible with the transportation situation.

Ah, this is home for me, even though we were raised part of our lives in Mexico, but we were very young. My mom—she says, "I will never leave this community." She had a chance to get out of here. My sisters—we all fill different lifestyles: we all had education, and we're all professionals. One of my sisters did go to Houston, Texas, because of her husband, but my other sister—she teaches. She doesn't want to leave here either, because my sister lives next door to my mom. So it's just the whole family here, and my mom lives in between the two of us. This is just home. I felt very comfortable. I got my roots here, and I have a lot of memories. I feel very comfortable living in Pilsen.

> So it's just the whole family here, and my mom lives in between the two of us. This is just home. I felt very comfortable. I got my roots here, and I have a lot of memories. I feel very comfortable living in the community.

Early Memories

My dad bought me a car because I wanted to go out. I love dancing. I had been in the folklore dance since I was three years old in Mexico; I started in Mexico. My dad used to take me to the dances or the practices whenever we had to do this, because I was the oldest. But then I got to the point where I wanted to date. My dad said, "You're not going to go in the car with another boy. I know you." In the beginning, he used to take us to the dance halls on the bus whether it rained or snowed. That was a love for a daughter, really. He used to take us to these places and leave us there. He would go home and then go back at one o'clock in the morning to pick us up. There were no cell phones or anything. We just knew he was going to be there at one, and if you were dancing, he'd just sit down at a table. He never drank, smoked, or anything. He waited until we finished the dance, and then he would ask us if we were ready; we would go outside and take the bus again and go home, and we were happy. Yeah, I love my dad so much. For them, the family was very important. When we were younger and we wanted to go out, my dad would just take the whole family. We would go to the dance hall–my dad, my mom. I was the oldest–I must have been like sixteen–and from there on down. I'm eight years older than my youngest, so the little one was little. And sometimes they would not allow us to go in because of the little ones. My dad would always tell them, "I'm coming. Is this a family place, yes? Well, this is my family, and we're coming here to have a good time, and that's the end of that."

> And sometimes they would not allow us to go in because of the little ones. My dad would always tell them, "I'm coming. Is this a family place, yes? Well, this is my family, and we're coming here to have a good time, and that's the end of that."

He bought me a car, and I was so excited. From that point on, I'd tell him where I was going to go and what time I was coming back. If I was going to be late, I'd call him from whatever restaurant, using the public phone, so he wouldn't be worried. When we were coming home, the neighbors, as soon as they heard a car coming in through the alley where I was going to park, would check out for you so something wouldn't happen. We felt very safe to come home twelve thirty, one in the morning, because we knew someone was looking out for us. Somebody was waiting for us. So that's why we have not left the community, and we were the first family–one of the first families–that came into that block. Most of them–most of that area was Bohemian, German, Polish, Italian. And when we moved into that block, no one knew we were Mexican.

I graduated from high school, and after I graduated from high school, I went to the University of Illinois and got my master's in business administration. I became the director for Neighborhood Housing Services in the division which is right here in the community. I was there for several years. I was eight years as a director there. And then I left, and I opened up my business, but it was construction–a construction company. I always wanted to do that for some reason. I opened up a construction company. I had a partner, and my husband had his own thing going. He was working in a factory, and then he also had another construction company. But he had three people with him, working at his company with construction. He would do the construction during the day, and he would work at the factory during the evening. So it was eight hours of sleep, eight hours of work, and eight hours on the construction.

It was a lot of work, but we had a goal in mind; we knew what we wanted to do in life, and that was the only way we could do it. I had a real-estate license because I was doing real estate part-time prior to that. It all came together. We bought buildings, did the construction and rehab. We did the purchase and rehab type of loans, and then we would sell them. Then we began to do total rehabs, new construction. We did everything, but my partner got ill, and I decided I'm not going to be able to do it on my own. To find another partner is difficult. So I decided I was going to leave; I didn't know what I wanted to do. I just took a couple of months off, and I got a call from the Northern Trust Bank that they wanted to recruit me to their bank to design the mortgage-control program for low- and moderate-income communities; that was my major, my strength. I thought about it for about two or three weeks, because I wasn't sure I wanted to work for a bank. It was totally different from what I was doing. The bank was very good to me, and I was there ten years. I left it four years ago. While I was at the bank, I took a leave of absence for three months. My mother-in-law in Mexico was ill, and my husband wanted to be with her. So I took a leave of absence for three months. She was fine after a couple of weeks.

We came home and said now, "What'll we do? Let's take a trip." So that's what we did. For three months, we traveled through Mexico. We read so many books about Mexico and what it's all about, because every state is totally different, the culture of history and traditions. We opened up a map and traced the places we wanted to go to and routed ourselves out. And we drove for three months in Mexico. As we were going through Mexico, we were finding out that the further we went through the states into the country, the more beautiful things that they would do in reference to the arts. And that's how we became with the store.

> We read so many books about Mexico and what it's all about, because every state is totally different, the culture of history and traditions. We opened up a map and traced the places we wanted to go to and routed ourselves out. And we drove for three months in Mexico.

We bought a piece. I would not go away from a place without buying a piece. So I bought a piece of pottery, took it in, and finally, after I came home after the three months, I had a van load of merchandise. I didn't know what to do with it. I was boxing it, and I put it in the basement. My husband said, "What are we going to do with these things? I cannot display this at home, because it would look like a museum." So I went back to work, and when I went back to work, I thought, *Well, yeah, I'm going to display.* I was feeling very proud of Mexican culture; I was telling people about it. The more

I would talk about it, the more interest I would see, and people would want to buy the piece. I would go to the office and put that piece on my desk, and there was a lot of interest in the pieces I would take into the bank.

When we first started, it was a whole year working together without seeing each other. He had two jobs, and I had two jobs, and we never saw each other. The refrigerator was our communication source, where we'd put a little stamp in there, a little piece of paper: "I want to see you. I want to go to lunch or something with you." A lot of people don't understand that. You've got to go through sacrifices. Nothing is ever handed over to you free. You've got to work for it and achieve it. Put your goals and objectives in mind. Put them to work in a time frame, and things will happen. It's basically the way we do it.

Like I tell people: I take my life as a business also. If you just keep on working and you don't have a goal and objective for your life, for your personal life, you're not going to go anywhere. We saw that with my parents, and I see what they go through, because they were not prepared to retire the way they should have retired. And even though my parents invested money in properties also–they've got it in Mexico, and they've got it here–they were always thinking of their kids. What are we going to leave our kids?

After that, somebody mentioned, "Why don't you put up a store?" I thought, *Oh God, no. A store–it's just too much. Seven days a week–it's too much responsibility. I would never have a life of my own.* But I did talk to my husband; he had another business at that time, distributing Mexican food products. He was distributing to 175 stores. He was doing really well, but then in the last few months, the margins were just not there; there was more competition. So my husband sold his business, and he was off for a couple of months.

Basically, I told him, "What about a store?" "I don't know, Eli. You're going to tie yourself down. If we want to go someplace, we won't be able to do it." We decided to open up a showroom instead. That's how we started for just wholesale; we started upstairs on the second floor. We did the wholesale showroom, and that's the way he started doing it ten years ago. After a year of doing wholesale, this storefront became available. My husband didn't want to rent it out anymore. We owned the building, so he didn't want to rent it out. As we're here, we were selling rather quickly, and he was going much sooner to Mexico than what we had anticipated.

He was going like once a month just because we were bringing small amounts. We did the first semitrailer after the second year we were here. During that second year, we found out we were selling it in three months. We needed another semitrailer of merchandise because we were distributing; we were expanding to different parts of the country here in the United States. So we distribute now wholesale to different parts of the country. We stock different stores and restaurants. We work a lot with the developers who are building new construction for restaurants, and they call us in with all their decoration needs or tables. And then we'd just go and take the orders, and then we'd go to Mexico and bring them on our next trip. He needed help in doing the administration and everything, and he couldn't be doing it on his own, and I couldn't be doing the two jobs either, working here. I left the bank years ago and came to join him here full time, and now that's what we do. Two months we're here, and two months we're in Mexico. So we were able to do it, start it as a hobby, and now it's a full-blown business.

Seventy-five percent of our clients are non-Hispanic, non-Mexican; it's people from all over, different walks of life. A good probably 10 percent is just tourist, and 15 percent is just Mexican–different people from different ethnic groups. But the neighborhood–people from the neighborhood–we don't get them as much. First of all, because they can go to Mexico; they go quite often. Those who cannot go are the ones that I get here who are not able because their documentations are not in place. And they begin to kind of miss Mexico, so they come in here, and they talk to me about their stories and history.

It's really interesting because I learn so many things from different people. As a matter of fact, I even get to know some of our artists now from some of our clients. They tell me, "You should go to this state. They do this, and they do that, and this is the name. My uncle is an artist. He's an artisan doing his thing," and we go. Our mission–and that was something very important for us. Why are we going to be opening up the store–to make money? No, because you will never get wealthy out of the air. It's love for the arts. You kind of make enough to survive, and that is the truth. Secondly, one of our missions was trying to promote the Mexican history and tradition through the arts but, at the same time, opening up jobs for Mexican artists in Mexico.

> Secondly, one of our missions was trying to promote the Mexican history and tradition through the arts but, at the same time, opening up jobs for Mexican artists in Mexico.

The most important part for me was trying to promote and enhance the Mexican culture to the kids who were born here. I'm a product of it. So that they can learn a little bit more of our roots. So they can feel proud of who they are. A lot of times, they're caught in between two cultures, and they lose identity. And that's what was happening to me as I was growing up, because I had a lot of friends where if you said you were Mexican, you were looked at as somebody different.

Secondly, if I would be with my Mexican friends and I would speak English with them, "Oh my God, you have become so Americanized. You're not a friend of ours." Weird things would happen. There was that disconnection. It was not discrimination, because I never felt discriminated. It was just a matter that this was facts of life at that time. When I went to grammar school and high school, they were still teaching Polish. They were teaching Polish for the first two years that we were there in grammar school. We're talking in the early '60s. They just were teaching Polish, and my brother would be hit on the hands with a ruler by the nun because he would not be able to speak Polish. So we had a bitter, sour taste in our mouth sometimes from Catholic schools in this area because of that. They're very strong believers that you had to learn the Polish because this is a Polish community and a Polish church.

Schooling and Language

In Mexican schools, I don't want to say they're more productive, but they teach at a higher level, like the math, the history—everything. Over there in second grade, you will be learning things that you're learning over here in fourth grade. You learn much faster. You get out of school much earlier, and you get out of school at a much younger age. Over there, grammar school is only six years, and then from that point on, you have three years of high school. It's much shorter, but then they

> In Mexican schools, I don't want to say they're more productive, but they teach at a higher level, like the math, the history—everything. Over there in second grade, you will be learning things that you're learning over here in fourth grade.

compact all the information in those years. It's a little longer now. It used to be September to June. Now you're starting as early as September 15, and then you will go up to July 10. You only get about a month off vacation. It's like eleven months for the school year. I think the kids have it tough now because it's only one month off, and that's it.

When we moved to Texas, I was in third grade, and I was put into first grade because of the English, not because of the level of education. The thing is, I understood everybody, but nobody could understand me. I had a very hard accent in British with the British English added to the Spanish. So it was a combination of I don't know what language accent that I had. The teacher couldn't understand me, but then I would stay after school. I would go to summer school, so I made it up before we came here, where I was already at the level that I was supposed to be here. So I graduated, when I turned eighteen, from high school. So I made two years into one year basically to make up for that. They would test me because they didn't know what I was saying.

So they would give me a written test, and I would pass them. And that's how they found out I understood everything they were saying. When I got here and I went into fifth grade, I was already, with mathematical problems and everything, I was so much advanced. I came into fourth grade here. I went through the mathematical problems and all that, and they took me over to the fifth grade in a few months. So I was at the right level.

I'm not too much for bilingual classes, because I think they have to learn English at an earlier age. They need to have that in place, because this is where they're going to continue living, and this is where they're going to survive, basically. I think once they have English language in place, it's easier for them to learn Spanish, because it's spoken at home, and this way, they're not confused with the two languages as they're growing. Now all my nephews and nieces, by the time they are three, they're completely bilingual–completely. I mean, they go back and forth, but that's because my sister always speaks Spanish. That's the first language: Spanish. All my sisters and my brother–they speak Spanish to them as the first language. And they're adding words here and there as they're growing. Then they go back and forth, the Spanglish. And they're fine, and now sometimes they even try to teach my mother!

Changes in the Community

The other thing in here we've seen so many changes in the community. It used to be really good. I remember when we used to be up till twelve o'clock at night and still have everybody around on the block–you know, play on the street–and it was never a problem. Things got pretty bad. Unfortunately, families who come from Mexico to the United States–they have a misperception of coming to the United States, where it is a free country, and they misunderstand. Personally, I feel that they misunderstand the word *free* from having a responsibility as a citizen, whether you are legal or illegal, and things began to get really rowdy here.

Change began in the late '70s, early '80s. There was a lot of crime, graffiti, that type of thing, gangs. But then we got organized. As a matter of fact, when I was the director of NHS, we began to organize people, teaching them that there was a different way of living. We used to give workshops on home ownership. We used to let them know that they should take pride of that. One of the things that I always thought and always said to this day is when anyone comes to a community and buys a piece of property, you're not just buying the piece of property; you're buying the community, with its problems and successes. And if you see a problem, you better be a part of it to fix that problem, because you are a part of that community.

And with that, then we went along and opened up block clubs. We organized forty-nine block clubs at that time before I left NHS. We used to knock on doors. It's a different way of thinking for people who would come here and get home. I can understand that they were tired of going to work and coming home, and they wanted to relax. So they didn't have time or strength, basically, to deal with children or deal with problems that the family had, much less to deal with problems, then go to a meeting. We would go and knock on the doors, because I was living here and did not want to leave the community. I had the opportunity to leave and still do, and we just didn't want to do it. We had invested too much time in this community—too many things, too many parts of our lives had already rooted here. That's one of the things we did, and once we organized those block clubs, we talked about issues to the community. A lot of people were afraid to talk about gangs in a public meeting, but we gave them paper and pencils: "Write your problem; you don't even have to put your name down, and then we'll call in professional people to help us with that." Little by little, things began to change.

> We would go and knock on the doors, because I was living here and did not want to leave the community. I had the opportunity to leave and still do, and we just didn't want to do it.

We would call attorneys; we would call the city, the police department, FBI for drugs. What are our rights as citizens, and what can we do to alleviate this problem? So they can tell us, "These are the issues of concern, and this is what you can do to try to help us fix that problem also." And we did. We were able to close a lot of taverns, because a lot of that problem also existed in taverns. Now, there used to be a tavern every other block, and two in one block, and gangs would kind of center there. We wanted to make sure that everybody had the opportunity to come to these meetings, and if they didn't want to say anything, like I said, they'd go through the paper communication. But in every block, we used to get a president or a captain. There was, once a month, a meeting for the block meeting, and there was another meeting once a month for the Block Club Association. The Block Club Association was only for the people who were the captains, and they would take that information to the block club.

We had a system in place—basically, block club, captain, members, once-a-month meeting. The captain would attend the block-association meeting once a month, where we would take bigger problems. And little by little, people moved in and moved out and just disappeared. But it helped. Meanwhile, and now, I think the churches are working with that also, trying to eliminate some of the problems in Pilsen. Things have gotten much better.

The real-estate values, I remember—and I'm not kidding you—have gone up probably a good 400 or 500 percent higher in this community. You would buy your property in the '80s for $40,000 to $45,000—you know, for four units. Now you can't even touch it for $500,000. That's how bad it is. Good and bad.

It's good for the people who have been here for many years. They want to cash in, and then they can move somewhere else where it would be less expensive. It's bad for the people who stay, because real-estate value goes up, the insurance goes up, rent goes up, and there's displacement of people because you have to raise the rents. Secondly, senior citizens or people who are on a fixed income won't be able to afford to pay the taxes, especially if they have a single-family home. These people who are senior citizens right now are on a fixed income, and their income level is not more than $1,000 a month. So that's the sad part of it. Good for the people who are able to keep it up, because a lot of people have worked on getting ahead and doing a lot of things. That's fine, but it's like a catch-22; it's like a double sword.

Reflections

Eliamar feels passionate about her native country, Mexico. She has traveled extensively to become more educated about its history and culture. Through her store in the community, she hopes to create a deeper appreciation for Mexican arts across the city. In addition, she feels a commitment to her community; that is where her family lives, and she works hard to make a difference there. She has organized block clubs and fought to close taverns in order to curb the influence of gangs in the neighborhoods. Eliamar experienced schools in both Mexico and the United States and believes that they were more rigorous in Mexico. Her lack of English initially held her back when she started school in the city, but through testing, she demonstrated her true skill level.

Eliamar is committed to building a healthy community through partnerships with external agencies and encouraging residents to use their voices to make a difference.

14

Patricia

I interviewed Patricia in her office at the Wellness Center. She talked especially about the women she serves and is enthusiastic about their increased empowerment and developing capacity in their leadership skills. She dreams forward for her community and its continued development.

Family Background

My name is Patricia, and I'm thirty-seven years old. I was born March 14, which is why my name is Patricia, because it is three days before St. Patrick's Day. Presently, I am the director of a division in the Wellness Center. I've been in this role for, I think, going on my fourth year. I've been here for twelve years, and in my relationship with this agency, I've also gone and worked part time with other agencies part time and full time. So I've worked five years in the Humboldt Park neighborhood, and I've worked in Mujeres Latina as a volunteer. I've worked for the Domestic Violence Council for the Latinos in that community. I try to spread out my experiences so that when I come back to the community, I can give a better perspective and hopefully bring that knowledge back to the community.

My parents grew up in Mexico. They grew up in Central Mexico and Guadalajara Jalisco, and they immigrated here in the '60s. My mother and her family came in more due to a family conflict in Mexico. Her mother passed away, and my grandfather was incarcerated, so the family brought them here. My father came, I would say, about two years later to be with my mother. They met in Mexico; they were married here. They dated while they were in Mexico, and my father just followed her over here. I was born here; I'm the oldest of four, and I know my parents were always working.

My mother, when I started school, became a volunteer in the school. I was in Head Start, preschool—all the programs—and she would always be a teacher aide or parent aide. And I remember her presence always around. As I go back, I remember that my mother was always the one taking myself and my brothers and sisters through different activities, going to the museums, going to parades, going to art workshops at the Art Institute and just always being active. Whether in the library or the park district or whatever it was, we were always active. I remember my father always being the worker, always being out working, and work was priority. He would come back, and the message was "I'm working hard so you won't have to." So he was the provider. I also remember my mom taking on part-time work.

Language

When I was first born, for the first five years, the language spoken at home was Spanish. It wasn't until I entered school that I started hearing English. And we would live with my aunt, so it would be my mother and her brothers and sisters and my father and me. I was the only child for the first three years of my life. It was always Spanish, and as a matter of fact, my name started out as Poppy, and then it evolved into Patty. There was a change, and if I remember, first grade, I was monolingual English. So I think I was in bilingual preschool or Head Start; kindergarten, it was both, but in first grade, it was monolingual English.

I don't recall having difficulties language-wise. I think I kind of lost consciousness of the differential between the languages, because it was pretty much normal for me as long as I understand the Spanish, speak the Spanish and then the English here. It wasn't until high school that I noticed I was dominant in English, and I had forgotten my Spanish. I was put in the native-language Spanish course, and I found myself struggling there. What frustrated me was—and this was something inside of me that I guess motivated me to learn or to regain my Spanish—is when I had my monolingual English-speaking friends speaking Spanish, and they corrected me. I thought, *I should know this. I should be able to speak basic English or Spanish and not be corrected.* When I would speak to my mother, she goes, "No, you spoke Spanish first—everything." How did I lose it? I wasn't even conscious of the difference happening.

I was in public school for the first three years, and then in fourth grade, I was in Catholic school. It was always English, because I was transferred into the monolingual English speaking. Even other Mexican friends that I had, we would talk English. We understood the Spanish—we understood the Spanish fine—and when we talked with adults, it was Spanish. No problem—I can understand exactly everything. Reading and writing was something foreign to me, because it was all English—read and write in English but not so much in Spanish.

My father spoke Spanish, and my mother began to integrate English, because then she started going to school. She went to English classes at several high schools. My mother, as I remember—always my mother working first and then working and going to school, night school. She obtained her high-school diploma. Then she went to the college for education, and I do remember her doing homework with me. I would be her flash-card holder. One of the earliest is the periodic table, where I would have the letter or the word,

> My mother, as I remember—always my mother working first and then working and going to school, night school. She obtained her high-school diploma. Then she went to the college for education, and I do remember her doing homework with me.

and I would be the one sitting there and testing her. But I guess that was a good thing, in a way, because it was in my head now too. I was in third or fourth grade, where I was just holding the cards and doing some recognition with her.

I also remember the family conflict—my father working, and my mother studying at night—and I would remember my father arguing with her, stating, "You're neglecting the children." But it wasn't true. It was just nitpicking, fighting, as I look back. But I always gave my mother—and I do give her—credit for being strong enough to keep going, stand her grounds and stay firm, and continue to go further.

My mom, on one hand, has her personality trait of stubbornness. No one is going to tell her anything different when she has her goal. The other thing is, I think she wanted something for herself, an opportunity. If she came to the United States, she came for opportunity, and that was hers. In the beginning, she was taking my father around to the English classes. They were going to go to school, and my father just stopped. My father has a sixth-grade education, and he was working since he was young. He was always working in Mexico, in the streets, like selling candy or gum. But he was discouraged, and he stopped. He always learned a little, because he would ask us, "How do you spell this?" and we would tell him, and he would write. He wasn't going to class, but indirectly, he would ask us, and we would show him. And then my mother kept going.

Language wasn't a barrier for my mother, because I think she was picking up the English just going around. And her younger sisters were in high school here as well, so they would come and speak English. My mother was the type who would throw herself into it and just practice and try, and she would do it. I remember that.

School Is First

Starting in the fourth grade, we went into Catholic schools. I remember my parents saying that's a better school. My experience in the public schools— it was large classes, large classrooms. I remember it was a larger population because of the assemblies. It was more bigger. Honestly, I don't know if it was me, but I remember being very outspoken with my mother taking me out of the public school. There are certain incidents that I do remember: I would hold my ground and go, "No, I disagree." I would also disagree with teachers. And I remember one time, the last year I was there—I don't know if this had something to do with it—I remember I had a parent-teacher conference because I got into an argument with a substitute teacher. I was very outspoken and headstrong, I think, is what they were saying.

That stopped when I went to the Catholic school. It really—that stopped. I don't know if my parents thought that if they paid for something, it would produce better results. I knew they were smaller classes and more attention. I was in Catholic school through high school. I graduated from elementary school and then went to the high school where all my aunts had gone prior to me. I had three aunts who had gone to that school, so there was no choice for me; I graduated from that high school.

Education, I can honestly say, from both my parents, different reasons, but at least for both my parents, it was very important to us. It was no question or doubt that we were not going to go to school. It was to go to school, finish, and we were always to bring As. There was no—at least from my experience— there was no reason that I should come with anything less. And as we go forward, it was always: "Be the overachiever and do good, and practice and practice, and aim high. And you're going to graduate, and then you're going to keep going, going, going, going." And like I said, they both have different perspectives, different reasons, but the bottom line, they would agree, is school's first.

My mother was like, "You're going to school to get a career and better yourself and learn more and explore different and new things in life." My father's rationale: "You go to school so you're not in a factory. So you find better work, not hard-labor work." But I think my father didn't see that school also brought a different way of thinking, or different perspectives, or a different view. It's not black and white, concrete. My father's more with holding onto the Mexican culture and tradition, where my mother has assimilated and acculturated into the American lifestyle. That's what I mean; their perspectives are different—one stayed firm to their roots, and the other one let go of their roots and went forward.

> But I think my father didn't see that school also brought a different way of thinking, or different perspectives, or a different view. It's not black and white, concrete. My father's more with holding onto the Mexican culture and tradition, where my mother has assimilated and acculturated into the American lifestyle.

Different Expectations and Outcomes

So that's what it was, because my father was still, as we were growing, "You do as you're told." My mother was the one you reasoned with. You were able to say, "I disagree," and you would reason. She didn't have her parents, and I think that was the other thing. Her mother had passed away, so she didn't have that mother role model where her father would work and she was a caretaker. I don't think she truly had a model of being a Mexican woman and wife and everything, because her mother was sick. Yes, she was the caretaker, which is probably another reason she wanted to do something for herself versus for others. Her childhood was taking care of the household and stuff like that.

The expectations were overwhelming at times. It became overwhelming when I would come home with a B. As an example, I came home with a B once the first quarter from school in geometry, but then I got an A. My father would always go, "Why'd you get that B? What are you going to do about that?" And I go, "You can't do anything about it." That's when it became overwhelming. And he would just see the negative. That's when it became overwhelming. But other than that, it was the expectation of me. I guess I was okay with it until I wanted also a social life. I was the oldest one; I was a groundbreaker, but I was the oldest female. I even remember at seventeen, if I wanted to go to a dance, my argument to my mother was "I bring the grades; I'm a good kid. I follow the rules, I do the chores, and I meet curfew." I remember that argument, but it was an argument literally with my rationale as to why I should. Then I remember into that full emotional drama that I got what I was wanting. I won the argument there. Yes. I won the argument there on that one.

I was not involved in the community. I think it was partly overprotectiveness, as not to get into deviant behavior, gang behavior, or just get in trouble. We had strict curfews. I remember as a child, seven o'clock, in the house. Even in the summer, seven o'clock, in the house. You could not cross the street. You could not be without the fence boundaries. You had to always be in eye view, or they would bring things we could use in the backyard. Swings—no, you don't have to go to the park unaccompanied; we have the swings here. If we wanted to go, it would be my aunts accompanying us until I was older to walk alone.

It wasn't until my senior year that I had this big sister/little sister; I was paired with a freshman who lived in another community. When I came to visit her for the first time, it was a whole new world for me. It was a curious world for me. I had never known it existed. That's how much overprotective my parents were that I had no, no idea, no knowledge that other communities existed. I mean, I knew more when I was in high school, but I never knew the concentration of Latino, Mexican population in these communities. So that's what just opened my eyes in a different way of living and a different way of expressing or living the culture.

It was all new to me, so I was just absorbing it all; I can see where it was crowded. I just noticed that was a negative, if anything. It was crowded; it was noisy. It was people just sitting in front of their steps. Not that I didn't get that in my neighborhood, but where I grew up with, there was Lithuanians and Polish that I was exposed to; it wasn't just all Mexican the block I grew up in, and I think we moved as it was becoming more predominately Mexican. In Archer Heights, it wasn't all Mexican. It was more Caucasian and an older population. And there were no kids around. It was quiet. And when I came over here, it was just very noisy, very crowded, very busy.

We kept moving, I think, because of the crime. I remember the one incident, how my father was riding his bicycle, and someone just came and pushed him and took the bike. So that—it was crime; that was the one. We didn't move far. It was just down street. But it was just far enough to be one of the first Mexican families in the community and in the block. So that I do remember—we were one of the first ones there.

I came back from visiting one community, asking more questions, more curious, and wanting to know. So I became more verbal and more interested in learning about Mexico, how it was when they were growing up, and foods. And I do remember coming back, asking them why we don't do this. Why don't we do that? Why don't we eat this? Why do we eat a lot of macaroni and cheese, hot dogs, and all that? And why is it that we don't have beans and rice every day with our meal? Growing up, I remember my mom cooking more, but as we got older and we moved, my mom cooked less, and it was more prepackaged foods. We do have beans and stuff but not as much as I saw when I came to the other nearby community. It was a lot.

And then there were a lot of connections that made sense. Like, "Oh, that's why our family does this or the meats; when we go for picnics, it's not peanut-butter-and-jelly sandwiches." One time, when we were little, my mom made sardine sandwiches, and it was the worst! It started making some better connections on some level for myself. It made connections for the little that we did or what she maintained, and there was always a pride, but it was never the whole tradition and behaviors, the behaviors that I saw over here or even the roles. And there were just a lot of questions: "Well, why aren't you like the mom that cooks breakfast, lunch, and dinner, whatever we want, and is folding our clothes and everything? Why do you make us do this?"

College and Culture

I went to the university and lived at home. I had no choice. It wasn't an option. I know when I was talking about my options, it had to be economical, and it wasn't away from home. It had to be where I commute but always came back home. I believe my father wanted me to go to a community college, and I had been accepted here at the university; my mother was pushing, "No, the university." My father's, "No," because it was more economical to go to the city college. And I remember that debate. And what helped was that I did get the academic scholarship to go to the university, so of course, my father: "Well, if it's paid, you go there." I'm like, "Okay." That wasn't a debate; we were going to college. The biggest debate for my father was financing it. That was it. It was the money, not so much whether or not you were going ... Did we have the money to finance it? That was the bigger debate.

> I went to the university and lived at home. I had no choice. It wasn't an option. I know when I was talking about my options, it had to be economical, and it wasn't away from home. It had to be where I commute but always came back home.

It was hard going to college and living at home. It was hard because being the oldest, being the first, I think there wasn't very much known.

Although my mother was the first to go to college, she was going to night school, but she understood studying. She understood papers and syllabus. My father did not. However, I think it was so hard because I was still expected to, even though my mother understood, "Come down here, and eat with the family. Come be with the family. Be with the family." I go, "I need to study." Even my birthday celebration–I'm going out with my friends; it still felt weird. "No, you have to be with the family and take care of your brothers and sisters and help me do this while I do that." I was still part of the family, still had my role to fulfill within the family while going to school.

On the flip side, it gave me more freedom in school that I've never truly had. When I was in school, it was new to me. If I go to school, I go to school; if I don't, I don't. And no one's really going to yell at me. So I do remember, even my first year of college, going through withdrawing from classes when I knew I was doing bad. I learned you could withdraw after a certain point, and that's okay! I was like, "Wow." So I discovered a new social freedom that I had more autonomy over what I wanted to do, and it was separate from my parents. I kept them distant.

They had a social center, and I found myself being more out there–like, "Wow!" I was meeting people, just being very observant, and liking the atmosphere of freedom. I can socialize, and no one knows. And then I started a little bit engaging. "Well, I'm in a social club, so I have to stay late at the university; I'm going to sleep over in my friend's dorm," when I was just going out and socializing. It worked; it worked.

But then, after a while, I had to get serious in deciding where I wanted to go. I was in prenursing to start off, but I found myself taking more Latin American history, as I was learning more about my family, myself, and other Latin countries and Latin cultures, and I was just amazed. I had no idea. It was another open door, and it was more exploring. I learned more about the city. I learned more about different immigration issues, and I learned about different entries into the country and started learning more about social issues. It was in a class, and I remember where we talked about entitlement. It was clear to me that as a minority community, we're not entitled because we're minorities; we're entitled because we're people, and as people, we should have equal access to health care, and we should have equal access to education. That's where a lot of discovery for me came as differences. No, it's not a race card or ethnicity card; it's a person card. So that kind of thinking started evolving and developing for myself as well.

I also remember those classes helping me dig into my family. With one class, I can either come to class and do all the coursework, or I can use a semester to really do a genogram. Given the choice, I did the genogram.

I started learning more about my family, and I started discovering that my mother and mother's side completely are very quiet about their past, and that I was finding curious. Even when I would ask my father, he'll be like, "Don't bring that up." "Don't bring what up? What's with my grandfather, and what's going on?" The family secrets were coming out, and my probing and probing and probing. And I was like, "Wow," because it was interesting. I approached my mom three times of how my grandfather passed away, and each three times were different stories. Okay, so there's something there. So that's when we noticed people don't speak about my grandfather and what happened. So that's very interesting, how school really helped me really get to know my family and the community and my ethnicity and stuff.

I did the traditional Mexican thing, and I got married. One big mistake, I can actually say, is I was one semester from getting my bachelor's. I was married with the thought, *I'll go back*. It took two years for me to go back and obtain it; I took a class a semester until I finished my degree. I never knew how ingrained school was in me. I was very disappointed in myself. I had to learn to forgive myself for that, but that's when I started realizing that my parents really ingrained education where it's second nature and it's in everything. Even

> I did the traditional Mexican thing, and I got married. One big mistake, I can actually say, is I was one semester from getting my bachelor's. I was married with the thought, I'll go back. It took two years for me to go back and obtain it; I took a class a semester until I finished my degree.

indicators as to when things are not doing well, and I'll explain that. And after that, I went straight into my master's, because there was no way I was not going to finish. I wasn't wasting time anymore.

After my first semester in my master's program, I received a C, and that just did it. A C? I am not a C student. But that C opened my eyes to really reflect that my marriage wasn't doing well, and that was impacting me. And that's what I mean: education's really ingrained in our lives.

And it was. It was interesting to me–like a C. Now that I look back, it was that C that made me start reflections to "Why did I get this C? What's going on?" And it stemmed back to my marriage. The more I was into school, I realized that it was a similar thing that my mother and my father were going through. My ex-husband wasn't sure what he wanted to do yet. And I was just like, "Wow," so I stopped school to take care of my personal life. I ended up divorced, and then I just channeled everything back into school. And I haven't stopped. I just want to keep going.

Moving On

I was already back in the community, and it was 2002; it was just a whole brand-new life for myself. I was back living with my parents. I was back in school, finishing, and I was working here full time. And then, as I obtained the master's in social work, I became a supervisor, and within nine months, I became director. Then my next goal was my license. While I was getting my master's, I had my alcohol- and drug-counselor certificate. So I'm just used to having two or three projects at the same time in my life that just kept going. And then, being in the position new, I realized soon, when budgets started coming across my desk and decisions and staff turnover, I got myself kind of confused or lost. I even asked a mentor, and he suggested, "Why don't you take class in business here and a business class there?" And it was like, that makes sense just to orientate myself.

I remember Robert coming to one of our administrative meetings, and he came and talked about the class of the master's in business administration at his university. *Oh! That's my mother's college! My mother!* So it wasn't foreign. I know where they're at. I know that building. So I'm like, "Okay." It was a cohort. I liked the idea, and I also liked the price. The kicker was when my CEO was like, "Yes, you should go; you should go." Then he said to me, "Some people are just too busy to go back." I guess my mother's characteristic kicked in, and I said, "Oh, you want to see?" That same day, basically, I got on the phone right after the meeting. I'm already doing the online application for NLU, and I'm just going, "What else do I need to do?" Within a month, I was in. I remember December 17; I received my acceptance, and I was in. I'm like, "Great." I just kept going.

I had a mentor, but I don't even think this individual knew he was a mentor. It was important–very important–because I needed to see someone, a Latino, reach a high position. He was the division director at the neighborhood office at the Circle, and he used to give trainings. I liked the training, so okay, I'll learn. But it was important to set myself a goal. If I wanted to continue in this field, I don't want to be an intake worker. I want to get to his level. And then, indirectly, I just followed where he went.

From there, he went to another higher level. And now he's the regional director for the state. That's why I say I don't think he knew he was a mentor. I would go to him every so often for chitchat. I saw how he was able to excel, and I would ask him, "So how'd you do it?" Or I would even go back to him: "How do you stand people just coming and complaining? And now that you're higher, you've got a bigger scope of people going to you." It was really good because I felt myself just get discouraged with bureaucracy; your eyes widen, and your knowledge widens, and then you get hit with bureaucracy and politics. When you get discouraged, I would go, and he would reframe it for me. He had the life experience. He had the professional experience–something I haven't had–so I think he had a different perspective based on experience to reframe my thoughts of discouragement. He goes, "Well, you're just having difficulty working with that type of style. Or you're having difficulty; it is not so much you per se, but it's a system, it's a process, and look at it this way." It was very important for me not to get so discouraged and frustrated and go somewhere else. He helped me stay on track within the field that I liked in addition to setting goals and was very supportive. I would go, "Would you write a recommendation?" And he would write a recommendation. I thought it was important. Not just my parents–I guess they gave me the passion and the knowhow you need to go for school. But this other person helped me with the encouragement and the knowledge to just keep me going. My parents were there to always push me, but this other person just pulled me.

Mentoring

I have tried to mentor others, and what others have told me is that I don't know the meaning of the word *no*. They always wonder how I do it. And I tell them, "I don't know how I do it. I just know it has to get done, and you do it. You find a way." There's been those directly under me that I've known, I've mentored, and I've pushed to go back to school. I've sat there with them in front of a computer, getting their transcripts. I've paid for people to get their transcripts. I go, "You need to go, go, go, go." If they talk to me, I will give them the time. I'll be like, "We'll fix it this way; just go, finish. It's your last semester, last class." And they would be nervous: "Well, it's in the middle of the day." "Well, take your lunch; we'll work your hours with your accrued time, or we'll work your vacation. But you need to finish." And once they're finished, or even before they're finished, I would laugh and smile because I don't need to make extra pressure, but I ask, "Where are you going to go for your master's?"

And for those employees, the direct line staff, when I bump into them, I let them know that I'm in an MBA class. I let them know I'm not afraid. I don't keep that to myself. I let people know I'm in school. I let people know. I know what it is to work and go to school. I'm still in it. There is no *no*. So I

There's been those directly under me that I've known, I've mentored, and I've pushed to go back to school. I've sat there with them in front of a computer, getting their transcripts. I've paid for people to get their transcripts. I go, "You need to go, go, go, go."

don't want to hear excuses. Let's work it through. It could be done. So I've done that already. And for those that are stuck, I go, "Well, go get your education. There's no way you're going to be able to move out of this pay scale; if you love this career, you have to go back." Or once they have it, I go, "What certificates are you going to get? Are you going to go for your CADC? Are you going to go for your license? We can give you supervision and get your license." I think whether people want it or not, I'll give encouragement to continue.

I tell them, "Just keep going." I am honest, and I say it takes sacrifice. It takes sacrifice, but it pays off. I believe it pays off. And then my assistant, who's leaving me to go to nursing school, was going on vacation right now. And they called her, saying the orientation's the nineteenth. And she's like, "But I'll be in Singapore." I told her, "You sacrifice now. You become a nurse; you can go anywhere in the country once you're making your money. So sacrifice now; enjoy the world later." I did tell her, and she goes, "Yeah, I guess." She was not happy. But I told her, "If you do the sacrifice now, once you're in there, you will gain a lot of money." I told her my sister's a nurse, and she's gained money because she's bilingual, too. And I told her, "There's the option of traveling nurse. I know you moved your flight, but I would recommend you move it one more time, because this is important."

Love of Community

I love community. It gets me close to the people at a different level. It's not as uptight, the way I see it, as structured and rigid as, for example, in my field, the inpatient hospital. I've always enjoyed community work. I've been in other communities, and I feel I'm able to connect with people on a different level with the community. In a sense, I feel that personal connection can make a direct impact and a direct connection versus if I were to go and be in an inpatient hospital; I can't make a good connection with a person, because it's in and it's out. Here, in the community, if I needed to go to a person's home to help them, I'd do a home visit. I'll be in their home; I'll meet their families, and I'll see them as a whole unit, not just the individual but the family.

To see where they live makes it real for me, so when I'm giving guidance to those recovering from mental illness or distress, I can

I know a lot of Latinos and Mexicans who say, "You're the professional–give me the answer." I said, "No, you have it. I just have to help you figure it out." And I like the unconventional community setting because if I want to get out of the office and take a walk and talk, I can do that.

keep a full context of where they're at. And when I do give guidance, I try not to be unrealistic about things that they can't do. That's what I see myself as—a guide. I know a lot of Latinos and Mexicans who say, "You're the professional—give me the answer." I said, "No, you have it. I just have to help you figure it out." And I like the unconventional community setting because if I want to get out of the office and take a walk and talk, I can do that. If I want to say, "Let's meet at the coffee shop and talk for your session," I can do that. I learn the rules that govern our profession, and I know how to maneuver with them within the community setting, which I like. I do like that—walking down the block and saying, "Hey, how you doing?"

Here, it's not that you can't touch—you're careful, but it's more you blend in better that people just can't tell you apart even though the way we dress. I don't dress in a suit, or I try not to. I like to blend in so we're just the same, same level, and I like that. I like being able to go to the store and just chitchat with someone there and come back.

I like the community feel. I still see myself in the community. I see myself hopefully giving back more to the community. I want to do more of community partnerships, helping one another or breaking down barriers that keep us apart. I want to bring us more together. Even within our Latino communities, I want to see more partnership and collaboration. I remember even in college, Puerto Ricans can't get along with Mexicans, and I think that's one of the reasons why I went to Humboldt Park, and I just couldn't see it. I couldn't tell—what are they talking about? Is it more superficial, or is it substance? What is it? That's what I would want to see even within the Latino or Mexican community. You see those rivalries. I would like to see less of that, and let's join together. And it may be idealistic, but I've seen it in little pieces.

I know as a director, one of the things I did want to see for the community is an increase in the quality of care. I wanted to change programming so that the Latinos or Mexicans and anyone who came to this clinic will get similar quality care as if they would go to a community-based organization, whether it be in record keeping or clinician. I wanted better-quality care. When I took the position, one of the first things I did was I had to go and do an open look and an honest look at every program, and I opened communication. Even within our own agency, there were barriers and noncommunication I didn't understand. One of my first things was "No, there's not going to be, within the same division, arguing and infighting." I was the one saying, "No, you're not the cream of the cream. Look at your charting. Your deficits are here and here; your improvements are here. You're good at this." And to the other ones, I go, "No, you're very good at this. Yes, you need to develop there, but don't see yourself here. We're all the same." And that took three years to do. It took three years to do that.

And right now, that's my message: "We're a team. We're one team. We will all gather together and help this one team that needs help, but we will all do this with each other." And it took three years and a lot of drama, just a lot of drama. It's just overwhelming at one point, where I thought, *Is this really worth it?* But no, you stick to it. And now I can see, like, we're moving, and we're working more as a team. There's some lingering nitpicking where people want to say, "Well, I want to know who was the one who made the mistake." I go, "You know what? Let's not spend energy on this. Let's focus on the solution, and let's move on." And it was just even last week's meeting that I had to do that still. I said, "No, we're going to move on. We're solution-focused; let's move on." Because the moment you start blaming, it falls apart. But I'm happy to say that that was one of my first tasks. The other one was making it hopefully cheery. It takes a lot of work, and the biggest work is attitude. That is the biggest. Not the paper and pen—people might say it's the paper or pen. But no, it's the attitude that's the hardest to break through.

I had to learn this. Ever since I took the position, I've seen my growth. I've seen my professional growth and my personal growth in the position. And I actually was talking in the clinical group about how we are young. Demographically, Latinos are a young population. So therefore, we don't have much life experience or professional experience in certain fields. So without mentors, we're young; we don't know. And I told them if we're to compete on a level where people have professional and life experience, they should take notice. I told them to take a step back. When you're in a state meeting, what demographic age do you fit in? And who are the players there? And they're like, "Well, their fifties." "Yes, and we're in our late twenties, early to midthirties. We're young for the supervisor. For our position, we're young, and you have to acknowledge that." And I told them, "We have to develop our professional knowledge."

I told them that's probably another reason why I wanted to know the business aspect of it. So when they're speaking in terms of productivity and outcomes and research and development, I understand what they're talking on, and it's not foreign; I'm not just sitting there with a smile, saying, "What is going on here? I don't understand." But I told them because we're young, we should still go and learn and learn and learn so we can be able to understand what's happening. It just doesn't go around us, but we're part of that cycle.

So now I really am passionate about the community and increasing it. I think it stems from that one class of learning that we're human. It's not an entitlement based on race. Because we're here and we're people, we should be on that same level there. And I want it for the community.

Reflections

For Patricia, education has had a significant impact on her development. Her parents expected her to be a high achiever. Her mother attended college, and even though her father did not pursue higher education, he wanted that opportunity for his children. She grew up in an environment where a trip to the park was considered dangerous; her parents bought playground equipment for their yard to help protect their children, and they moved based on their perception of the local crime. Once she went to the university, her world opened up, and she wanted to learn more about Latin America and her own genealogy. She began to reflect on how she would need to break from traditional family patterns in order to realize her own dreams through continued education.

Patricia articulates how important it is, especially in the young Latino community, to have a mentor who can share experience and expertise. She acts as a mentor herself and pushes her staff to be the best it can be. She is committed to staying in the community, being a part of its development, and advocating for equal services and resources. She will contribute to the development of a healthy community, one that respects its heritage but also knows how to move forward.

15

Francisco

I interviewed Francisco at his school in the community. He was able to find a quiet space where we could talk away from the whirlwind of activity all around us. His school is a model of innovative educational practice with high expectations. He dreams of the day when more children have the opportunity and resources to meet such high expectations.

Family Background

My name is Francisco, and I'm currently the principal of a community-based high school in the city. I'm not a native; I came here when I was thirteen from LA, California. Both my parents are Columbian, and I spent a lot of my childhood traveling between the two countries, the United States and Columbia. At thirteen, my parents finally decided that they wanted to not be so ambulant and settle down somewhere, and I had cousins here. On my mother's side, we had her sister here. So we decided to settle in the city. That's when I was thirteen, and ever since, I've been here. I went to high school here and also did my university studies here.

My parents moved to the States for the opportunity they knew existed for their children. Life in Latin America's pretty tough. I think they just wanted to make a better life for themselves and their children. My parents never went to formal education of any sort. They were autodidactic; they taught themselves. For me, what was great was my parents were self-learned, meaning that whatever they knew, they taught themselves. And I could see they learned, that they were learned people. You didn't need formal education to achieve that. So that in itself is very powerful, because I saw it. It even influenced me, because I then started to teach myself, and school, for me, was kind of just the background. But what was really important was what I was learning from my personal motivation. And I think every day, my parents were having that type of approach to learning. You do learn because you want to learn. You want to learn things that are important to you.

Spanish was the language in our home. You know, I learned English essentially on the playground in LA. It's kind of interesting; I've always felt like I was kind of navigating between two languages. I just learned from friends and school, but at home, it was always Spanish.

I have a younger sister. We grew up speaking Spanish. That is my native language. It will always be my native language; English will always be the second language. It was so important to me to maintain my first language that I actually studied it in college. And that was my focus, so I could retain that part of my culture. I wanted to really understand. I majored in Spanish literature, and I really wanted to get to know my language and also the linguistics. So I got to learn a little bit about how the language comes together. I even took it even further. I wasn't even satisfied with that. I became a Spanish teacher as well, for my profession, exactly again for the same reason of being able to retain my language.

Then I stopped to work in a Latino community to continue to develop my linguistic skills and my language. So always, and even now with my children, I'm trying to cultivate our language. And it's very difficult, very challenging. That's something I'm still trying to work out with my wife. What are we going to do as far as our children learning Spanish? Because about 98 percent of second-generation students do not grow up with the native language. My wife's native language is not Spanish, but you can speak to her like a native speaker. Aside from the accent, you wouldn't know that she didn't grow up speaking Spanish. So we're really into developing our language heritage.

Sacrifices for Education

Education was important to my parents for their children. I think they equated education with financial security and what comes from that. So for them, they knew that being able to send me to a university was important;

I actually went to boarding school as well. And for them, they knew I would have more success in life if I went through the formal education, even though, like I said, it was always something at home that education was the number-one thing. Everything that we did—everything we talked about over the dinner table or any outing we did—there was some educational component in there.

My father worked in an aluminum company. He was kind of a forklift operator, and my mother—she's tried different things. She's a seamstress, and so she's really good with that and could work on her own with odd jobs here and there. Now my father's a waiter. It was a lot of sacrifice for them to send me to school, especially at a very young age, losing the support of me. I mean, even at thirteen, I could help my parents fend for themselves, help them navigate society with language that I knew. So they lost that. It was a big sacrifice; they were on their own, essentially. Even to this day, our relationship isn't as strong after that, because after boarding school, I went to college, and I lived on the college campus and didn't see my parents that often. So it's now that I have my own family that we're just coming together again around my children.

> It was a lot of sacrifice for them to send me to school, especially at a very young age, losing the support of me. I mean, even at thirteen, I could help my parents fend for themselves, help them navigate society with language that I knew. So they lost that. It was a big sacrifice; they were on their own, essentially.

Being away from my family, it was tough. It was very tough. I saw the other children. I felt like they had more support, even more financial support, and I was always on my own, alone. And I spent a lot of time being alone. So even during college, I went off and traveled to Europe and Latin America. But I was alone. I felt those experiences of being alone and becoming self-sufficient empowered me to be able to do that and be resilient. Again, I always did those things for the sake of my own education. What would keep me going and always striving and always wanting? It sounds funny maybe, but it was ideas, I think—just things that were always on my mind that I wanted to understand. It sounds idealistic or utopic, like an idea. Like an idea, but really, it was definitely—I never thought I would, even though my parents cultivated education, get a job, become self-sufficient. I never thought I would actually have a job. I always thought I would be in academia, that I would always be a student or in some way involved in university life.

Impact of Family

Essentially, my parents, I think, are the ones who motivated me. I saw them struggle. I asked them the same questions: "What drives you? What keeps you going?" It's not financial success, because they were very limited in that way. They would always respond to me that they thought it was an odd question. They would never question that. For them, it was just living and surviving. And when I ask those questions, and I always ask those questions when I travel. I'm in a little community somewhere: "What keeps you guys going? What is it that you're driving toward? What are you building?" But I would say, like my parents, who because of their sacrifices, how self-learned they were, how hardworking they were. That's, I think, the motivation for me. Of course, there's a whole host of people, my teachers growing up, but I feel the strongest about my parents.

My sister has a different life. She's also very keen on education. I always could tell my sister was smarter, faster, and more curious than I was. Even though she was younger, I could see that she had talents, like musical talents. She was first violinist, first flutist, could write better. So she also, for some reason, picked up on education as being like the way to move on. I played the big-brother role, like the good brother was always successful in school, the whole comparison with the brother. I felt like sometimes my sister rebelled against that: "I don't want all the attention around academics. I want to be my own person." But she's very successful in her own right. Even though I strayed toward academia, she's also a teacher, and she has other goals, hardworking. Even my current job, where, on occasion, I can work eleven- or twelve-hour days for weeks on end, I feel like the work ethic that was instilled in me enabled me to do this job. I see it in my sister as well, always just working toward some higher calling or something to help others, especially.

Solutions for Schools

Because I felt like I got a really good education, great teachers, lot of support, I felt like maybe many of the kids I worked with weren't getting full exposure,

So becoming a principal, I felt like I could have a greater say as to providing kids with the very best education, especially around the belief that they ought to really be successful. At the core of my beliefs are that any kid–they ought to be really successful.

the full attention that they needed. So becoming a principal, I felt like I could have a greater say as to providing kids with the very best education, especially around the belief that they ought to really be successful. At the core of my beliefs are that any kid–they ought to be really successful. It's only the adults–I personally believe that it's only the adults in their lives where the limitations lie. Whether it's the parents and the teachers and community members–all those components can work together to support a child that could be successful. And I mean that in a really, really sincere way. And I think in society, there's an idea that there's the laborers, the academics, the doctors. That's kind of a fallacy: there's a role, and you're born into it. You're born into your role in life.

Unfortunately, because a lot of kids don't have the role models in their lives maybe to go beyond the limitations of what they see here, they don't strive for that. And maybe the adults in their lives don't even believe it as well. So a lot of my work here is around changing beliefs about what kids can do, essentially showing, through academic performance, kids can do a lot more, be very successful. So when I found out there could be a school like this one and there was someone who really had that same belief system, it was like, "Wow, this is where I need to be." So I did everything possible, and I was pretty quick. For one year, I was a teacher. I was a teacher one year, and the next year, I was already assistant principal. But it was quick; there was an urgency to me to have a greater say in kids' lives.

You lose kids. High school especially is kind of the last place in one's upbringing where you can have adults who can intervene and have a strong impact in your lives. After that, you really don't have that support. So for me, I needed to get in and do the same thing becoming a teacher. I went through an alternative program, just like I went through an alternative program for the principalship. Like from one day to the next, I was a teacher. I was just thrust into a classroom. I applied, and like a week later, I was in the classroom, teaching. I did that for six years and then the same thing as a principal. I was in the classroom one day, and two months later, I was an administrator in a high school. It was quick. But there's always been an urgency with me, because, you know, one year, one year in a child's life, especially in schooling, is critical.

You know, I think we have a good team of adults, teachers, and community members. I felt like together, in that capacity, there have been a lot of cases where we've been able to intervene. I personally have had an impact one on one with a student. I don't really see that necessarily, just me working collaboratively with my colleagues here, working like that. As a staff, we sit and talk about individual students, and we have good conversations about where the kid is socially, emotionally, and academically. Then we kind of hone in on that student and the family to get that kid on track; we've grown a lot. We've changed a lot, and I think some of the stuff that we do as a school now–definitely, I'd like to say kids are getting a better education and getting at becoming better, getting to the point where they can be successful in college. That's always how we see how successful we are, especially with College Bridge [dual-enrollment program with local colleges], and that's some really great data. For kids struggling in college, we need to do something to get them to perform better.

What makes us different here is the ability to be collaborative, to look at students' performance and hone in on individual students. I think that individualization, the attention that we give students here and, of course, the parent engagement and seeking out the community members is key. Like the university is a great partner that really we feel strongly believes in our mission. So really seeking out those partnerships, and we have a partnership with the Boys and Girls Club. Amazingly, they opened up their building to us, their programming. More adults can become instrumental in working with students.

We really want people to change their beliefs around what schools do and what their purpose is. That's why we've been involved in bringing a clinic to the school and building a public library near our school. As an entity, that really helps improve the community, and it goes obviously hand in hand with education but also provides services

> We really want people to change their beliefs around what schools do and what their purpose is.

and empowers people. We keep late hours as well. We close around six thirty, seven because we have programming after school. Community members know that we offer GED, ESL. We know the high school's also in session at that time. We are open longer hours. We kind of serve as a community resource center, in a way.

Reaching Out

So we're establishing schools where the doors are open and not just open between nine and three and everything shuts down, everyone goes home, and there's no continuity with the work that goes on in school and what goes on in the community. I've been partners with the local church. When I came here, I said, "Who's going to be my greatest ally?" I went to the churches around, and we did great work.

At some point, we were going to have classrooms in people's homes, like in their living rooms. We would invite the pastor, the librarian, the principal. We would set up in people's homes and have school. After kids got out of school here, we'd go into their homes, and we'd invite everyone in the community to a certain home, and everyone would come, and we would have a lesson, a model of what teaching could look like in the home. So it's stuff like that. We'd go into someone's home, and we'd look at the living space; we'd say, "This is what you can do in order to make this a safe place for learning." And so we would just bring some school stuff, like a chalkboard or a lot of books, and we would have classes on literacy—how a mother or father can learn to sit down and read a book. That's something you might think is easy to do, but what do you do with a book and a five-year-old? And how do you ask questions? How do you ask your child a question? How do you check for comprehension? How do you get the child interested in learning? How to build a home library? Stuff like that—like, wow. We would have classes on safety in the community, everything, on domestic violence. We would take a few teachers with us as at the same time, and community members as well. We would just go block by block.

We would obviously establish communication, like who was going to host it that week. And then we would call. We got a list of everyone in the school who lives on that street, and then we would call; we'd just call: "You're invited to this home on this day; we'd like to see you." I started getting really fancy by having invitations I would make on my computer, just to make it more formal, like we're inviting, because our parents, our community members need that. A formal invitation on nice Crane's stationary; it's nice. I always felt like our community—they deserve more. That's why I love taking our kids out and exposing them to universities and other opportunities. They deserve more. They need to be exposed to more.

I don't think the parents felt that it was intrusive. They saw; they saw the need, I think. Who was going to deny improving someone's education? There's nothing wrong. Even opening somebody's home—obviously, that could be intrusive, but it was around education and empowering people to read and write. It was very easy to open the doors.

Getting the parents to come to our school was another reason for reaching out. We knew how difficult it was to make parents feel comfortable coming into a school. We were very strategic. Before each hosting of the community meeting in someone's home, we would prep by having a community meeting here. We get a lot of people here; set a topic; and around the topic, we would bring someone to talk about it, whether it was literacy or empowering men or whatever. We would have this huge community meeting here, and we would say, "We're going to follow up this conversation in someone's home next week." More and more, people started coming to our large gatherings. That's how we would get people to host the events. We have amazing attendance when it comes to report-card pickup. Ninety-nine percent of the parents come out in both the elementary and the high school.

Ongoing Challenges

The biggest challenge is really on how to, in a very meaningful way, manage a child's education. If you leave it to these huge entities, students easily go and stray away from their education and their own personal growth. By having schools who pay attention to the entire spectrum of what a child goes through, from their emotions to attention to what happens at home to what happens in the future college-wise, you will make a difference. The school must have a good sense to support all those components. It's not a one-sided thing where schooling is just about being here from nine to three or whatever, and we just hope and cross our fingers that the kid comes back again. We have a lot to gain from what happens between three and the next day at nine. There's a lot of stuff that happens. Learning really goes on outside of school–the real learning where kids are applying what they're learning in school, having a handle on that, and being able to be strategic and understanding about what youth go through. We're just at the tip of the iceberg at understanding adolescence and really making a difference. This is a critical time for learning. I think you have a critical time early on between zero and three or four and then adolescence. That's it for schooling– then college. These are critical moments–high school, early education as well. We need to do what's right for kids, if that entails getting rid of a year of high school or having students here year-round. It's not necessarily what every community should do as far as high-school students, but for this community, it works.

> By having schools who pay attention to the entire spectrum of what a child goes through, from their emotions to attention to what happens at home to what happens in the future college-wise, you will make a difference.

Reflections

Francisco grew up with parents who had little formal education but who were continuously learning. They sacrificed to ensure their children would have a good formal education. When Francisco left for college, they lost one of their strongest resources. He is a firm believer that when it comes to education, the school is a core component of the community but that it must work in partnership with the larger community. He and his staff take a holistic approach to working with students and include their parents and community members as they take education out of the school and into homes. His approach ensures that the school does not work in isolation; it works in conjunction with all the other parts of a student's life.

16

Estela

I interviewed Estela at her desk in the middle of a busy community organization. She talked passionately about her work with women and is dreaming forward especially for the women in her community and their continued empowerment.

Family Background

My name is Estela, and I work for a social-service agency that has been around thirty to thirty-five years. I am thirty-two, and I was born in Mexico. I was brought here at the age of four, turning five when I arrived here at the States. My uncle owned a building here in the area; he was the first one actually to arrive in the community. After him, basically, the rest of his siblings followed, and my dad was one of them. My uncle and my grandparents lived in the city, and they moved into this community. They realized a lot of Mexicans were moving further this way, and so he bought a building, and after he did that, his brothers followed. Interestingly, they're no longer here; they left after a few years living in the area. They moved into the suburbs, and the only ones who ended up staying was my parents and us.

My parents are from Mexico, and they had very minimal education—if anything, a couple years. They mostly worked to help support the family.

When we came here, education is one of the reasons why they brought us to the States; they figured that would be the way we would have more opportunities in this country. People would tell them that; people would go back to Mexico after they immigrated and then come back. One of the reasons was there were more job opportunities, employment. But in addition to that, education, so they brought us here in hope that we would be able to have some of that.

I think when they came here, they realized that would be the way for us to really find better employment opportunities. From the very start, they kind of instilled that in us. They really were there behind us to make sure we were doing okay in school, and we were attending school. They took that pretty seriously. Even though they didn't quite understand the whole system, for some reason, they figured it was important. And so I remember them being very strict in terms of making sure that we would make it to school on time and that we would be there. My mom couldn't actually be there, because she had to take care of eight kids. That was pretty difficult for her to do. I remember her trying to learn English. She was actually going to classes, and that also was very difficult. She went for a little bit, and then she left because she needed to focus on us. It was in the nearby community center, which is still here. I remember her trying to read newspapers. She understands it, I think, more than she speaks it. I think that's the case for a lot of people who are trying to learn English. It's always a lot easier for them to understand.

Early Education

I started school in the first grade. When I arrived, it was a little bit late for me to go into school. They had already started, so I ended up starting from the first grade. My mom says that she remembers me being the only one very excited about school. If I can recall back, I just like the learning. The learning experience, knowledge, and just knowing, to me, was very important. And it continues to be important.

When I arrived, I didn't really speak English, so that was one of the huge challenges that I encountered. It was a little difficult for me to sort of integrate into the

> When I arrived, I didn't really speak English, so that was one of the huge challenges that I encountered. It was a little difficult for me to sort of integrate into the school, because when I was back in Mexico, I had no previous schooling, so it was the first. In addition to it being my first experience in school, it was just like the whole transition into another country.

school, because when I was back in Mexico, I had no previous schooling, so it was the first. In addition to it being my first experience in school, it was just like the whole transition into another country. That definitely made it difficult at first. I can still recall the first year, kind of struggling. But little by little, it got better, up until I was in the third grade, and I started to learn more of the English language; I started in bilingual education.

I had pretty good teachers the first couple of years. I sure did, and they definitely made it a lot easier for me. But I know it was a struggle, especially when it came to take the testing. I remember having additional help and having to meet with this teacher aide, where they would teach me Spanish. And then in the classroom, I would be in an all-English class. It was interesting, but I somehow picked up on both. Well, the first few classes was all Spanish, and then in the second grade, they started to incorporate the English, and then I guess they were helping us in transitioning into that, into an all-English class. That's where I was pulled to the side. I do remember clearly that they do teach me Spanish, how to write and how to read. I think it's about the third grade where I was fully integrated into an English class.

I think it was my eighth-grade teacher that I thought was great. She was just great overall, really committed to all the students. And she really pushed us. I remember her incorporating additional tutoring for us where it would help us improve our reading level. I remember I was so inspired by her and reading so much that year that my test scores tremendously, like, increased from one year to next. That led for me to be the top scorer from the whole eighth-grade class. At that point, there was a program out of the university, and it was two of us that were actually selected because we scored so highly and we were doing so great in our classes. We were A students. They were giving a scholarship at that time. It was between both of us, and I was selected. So at that point, I knew where I was heading. That happened in the eighth grade. I received a scholarship to attend. And I think a lot of my college choice had to do with money and the university giving me the scholarship. I kind of didn't so much have to worry about that, even though I applied to other schools, but I think that the money really drove me.

My older brother—when he arrived, he must have been eighteen or nineteen, so he started working with my dad. That's how they were able to sort of sustain the family, because one income wasn't going to be enough. And my mom was staying at home, taking care of us, so it was actually both of them who were providing for the family. He didn't really go to school. The rest of them did but up only until high school. For some reason, they all stopped there.

High School

In high school, they're not the best counselors. I remember I didn't have that great of an experience with my counselor. For some reason, even though I scored really high on the eighth-grade test, in the placement test at Juarez, for some reason, I didn't test that high. So I was placed in regular classes. And from the start, I knew that wasn't challenging enough for me. I went to my counselor, and I requested

> I don't feel like I'm learning enough; they're not challenging enough for me, and also, there were some students that can be a real problem sometimes.

to be placed in honor classes. And she wasn't the most supportive. I can remember she said, "You should stay in regular classes during the first year and figure it out. Maybe you'll do good in regular classes." I don't know. I don't feel like I'm learning enough; they're not challenging enough for me, and also, there were some students that can be a real problem sometimes.

I didn't realize that the teacher would focus on them so much instead of really fully teaching. A lot of the assignments that were given, I guess, came pretty easy to me. I wanted more, and so I went to my teachers after I proved myself the first semester: I aced all my classes. I remember a couple of teachers approached me as well: "You know, we can definitely give you a letter of recommendation." That was one of the requirements for me to be transferred to honor classes. So I went ahead and did that. I got straight As, and there were a couple of teachers that were supporting me, were right behind me. So that's how I ended up the second semester in my freshman year; I was transferred.

The students there were more quiet; we were more focused. I mean, we had a pretty good class. It was about twenty of us, and actually, I still keep in touch with a lot of them. We all ended up in college, and a lot of us are now getting our master's. So yeah, I still keep in touch with them. We were really— we're pretty competitive among ourselves, yes. And I think it would have been a lot different had I been in the regular classes. It's pretty fortunate. That was at the time a reality, and I think it still is. There's a big issue right now with that.

One teacher stood out; her name is Miss Krisale, and she really pushed us. She was actually my psychology teacher. At that point, I knew where I was heading to. Probably until then, I wanted to be a teacher. I was involved in different clubs. One of them was the teacher club, Future Teachers, and I became the president. I almost applied for the E-Apple Award they give out. So right when I was about to apply, during that time, I took the psychology class, and I said, "This is what I want to do." I remember her clearly telling us that–she was just very supportive, "You can do anything that you want. As a matter of fact, there is so much need for individuals like you that are bilingual, that are especially in the area and the different areas and the different fields. Especially in that, and it's like there's a lot more research that needs to be done." Unfortunately, that's not my strength either, too clinical. Yes. She was the one. She was an inspiration.

Actually, one of the reasons why things were not great at the time: a lot of things were going on in the neighborhood. Still a lot of things go on, but I think it used to be a lot worse when I was growing up—a lot of crime, a lot of gang activity. I wasn't very far from the school, about three or four blocks, but it was pretty scary. I think it was a little worse, though, for boys than it was for girls, because most of the gangs tend to be predominantly male. There are girls, though, that are also involved, but I think that boys tend to be more recruited into that. But I remember my mom again being there and making sure. She would stand outside the house. I guess we were like about four blocks away. She would stand outside and make sure that we were going straight and we were not trying to go into the side streets or anything like that.

My dad actually wanted to move—move out of the city. He wanted to move to Texas. But my brothers and sisters tried to develop friendships here and have their jobs, so that made it a lot harder. They were not so much willing to move out. And it's interesting, though, because a lot of my other uncles—they moved into the suburbs, and that was one of the reasons why they say they did it. They were really concerned about their kids becoming involved in any gang activity, and fortunately, they're doing well right now.

College and Beyond

They were pretty excited that I would be the first one to go to college, and a little scared. Actually, I have to say that they were scared, especially me being a woman. They were very concerned, and they really wanted me to stay in the area too. The whole experience—they're not familiar with it. They don't know what the whole college experience entails. They knew that I would definitely get a degree and that would open doors in terms of finding a better job or doing something that I really enjoy doing. But at the same time, they were like, "Hmm, what exactly does that mean? Is it the same as high school? How different is it?"

They definitely had a lot of questions in that regard. Me staying late in college–that was kind of not very common to them. They would ask, "Why do you have to stay until nine or ten?" When in high school, I would be home by like three, so a lot of changes. I did live at home. I did, and then my senior year, I decided to study abroad. I really wanted that experience. I wanted to go away. I wanted to go to a different college, but again, because I had the scholarship, I think that drove me to staying there. Of course, I didn't have other siblings that had done that. I'm the first one. It was a little scary too, for me, being the first one. Even though they supported me as much as they could, they didn't really have a lot of the answers to a lot of questions I had. Had another sibling gone before me, I would have gone to that sibling and asked, "So how do I go about doing this?" I had to figure it out on my own.

I was not completely prepared for college. Even though I took honor classes, and that was very helpful, I realized that I would encounter other challenges there. It was definitely on a different page, new learning experiences, especially the first year. I think after the first year, everything kind of ran smooth. I did well. The first year, just the whole experience was just so different. I was more on my own, where in high school, it's different. You're still within the constraint of the same building. But there in the university, it's a pretty big university, so I had to find myself around. And fortunately, both my friends from high school ended up there, so at the beginning, we kind of supported each other. We'll major in different things, so we kind of went our own way. We reconnected after.

I applied to study abroad my senior year because I wanted that whole experience of going away, because I never did that. I found out about the program. This was actually after I had completed pretty much all the major requirements. Basically, I just ended up taking all Spanish courses, and they kind of came kind of easy to me. In Spanish, I had enough credits to have a minor in Spanish, but I was also minoring in sociology. So I ended up for just a semester there, and I graduated in four years and a half after I started.

I intentionally wanted to go to Spain, not only because I knew the language, but I know that we have our roots back in that country. So I wanted to become more familiarized with the customs, traditions, and I can see where we have a lot of influence from Spain, but also the going away and experiencing being away from home and that kind of thing. When I came back, I came back and started my internship right after that, I believe. I did my internship here at Mujeres, and a couple of positions opened up after; I applied, and here I am, going on nine years in December.

I went on for my master's degree because I value education so much, and I like the school experience. I think that along with the work, the personal experience is very fulfilling. It makes you grow so much. You're just a professional. I knew all the time that I was not going to stop there. It's interesting–I told my family, and I still do, "One day, you're going to call me doctor. I'm not sure when that's going to happen, but you will. I have that in mind." That's what I wanted to do. And so it was–it must have been five or six years in between. It was a matter of deciding when I was going to do it. Unfortunately, we're not in a very high-paying field, but that still has not discouraged me at all.

Working in the Community

Here at Mujeres, I transitioned from another program, and now I'm coordinating the leadership program. There's so many needs that I see in the community, and it's just so rewarding, hearing back from the women. We mostly work with women. I hear it from them, and I see the change that they go through as they come and receive our services. And it's so fulfilling it makes me want to continue to stay here, but unfortunately, I have to eventually move on. I still see myself being connected to the agency even after that, and that tends to be the case for a lot of workers here. They come back. They're still involved; they still somehow help out when they can. I think it's the environment here. We connect very well; we work very well with one another, and just the work that we do–it's just so rewarding. It's incredible. Sometimes I can't explain it with words; it's more of a feeling. I know we all impact a lot of the people that come through our doors.

What I do is run the Latina Leadership Program. So it's leadership development for women. It's interesting, because initially, one of the things that really gets their attention is when I promote the program: I speak about the program, and I talk about how it's going to increase their level of self-esteem. They are going to feel a lot more confident, and so that's one of the reasons why they decide to participate, not so much because of the word *leadership*. As a matter of fact, a lot of them

> I speak about the program, and I talk about how it's going to increase their level of self-esteem. They are going to feel a lot more confident, and so that's one of the reasons why they decide to participate, not so much because of the word *leadership*.

don't initially see a connection between them and the whole leadership. So it's not until they begin to participate, and we start the program.

The program started about twenty years ago, so it's been around for quite a bit of time. A lot of the women who come to the program have already participated in the rest of the programs. It's sort of the last step where they're on a different level, where they've probably already dealt with a lot of the crises they initially came with. So now they're really thinking about themselves and how they can continue to develop and go on and establish and pursue their goals. It's a motivator for them, the program. It really touches at the level where, because of their self-esteem, a lot of them don't go on and pursue or make changes.

Usually, they come first either to our domestic-violence program or sexual assault or parent support, because they are struggling with their kids, their behavior. They don't know how to deal with it. That was the program where I started. Actually, I've gone through three programs. I started with the domestic violence and then the parents' support. I was a counselor there for about three or four years. And then to Latino leadership. It's a fascinating program. It really is. They've dealt with a lot of crisis, like receiving individual or group counseling. Then they come to my program, where they're ready to take on basically anything. It's just a matter of them finding that space to speak about things they want, their needs. They feel empowered, and that's one of the objectives of the program: to re-empower women.

The program is divided into two phases. Each phase is fifteen weeks. The first phase has to do a lot more with the personal development and getting to know one's worth and, again, pushing self-esteem—becoming aware of their sexuality, their rights. A lot of them are not very aware of that. There's a huge focus on the culture and how that impacts who we are, our formation, and all that. A lot of them actually, when we reach that point of discussion, a lot of them, it's just an eye-opener for them to see how much that has really impacted their development, how they've grown as women. They talk about sexuality, establishing goals, developing other skills, such as communication, problem solving, negotiation—so that's part of the first phase.

And then they transition into the second one, which has a lot to do with what's around them, what's going on. They become more familiar with the government, the function of the government, and how laws impact us and how we can also, on the other end, be more involved in and advocate for ourselves. And we talk about community: What are the problems that our community is being faced with, and how [can they] become involved in the process of changing? And then it should actually be divided into another part: how to begin their own group, how they can facilitate meetings, how they can prepare agendas. Basically, it's trying to get women to feel that they can do something so their communities can change through informational groups. And then the third part has to do with being ready for job search. A lot of them come in without having a résumé or understanding the whole interview process.

A lot of them go back to school–go on to pursue a GED or go back and take English classes. We've had women who went on and started their business. There's a couple in the community that opened up their business after they completed the phases. Some of them have come back to school. I had one come recently, and she was one of the first ones to take the training. She was telling me how when she came, she didn't know English; she didn't have a high-school diploma. And so she started taking English classes that led to her getting her GED. After her GED, she enrolled in college, and now she recently finished her master's in social work. And she started off here!

> You talk about the culture–not so much a culture but, rather, some of the ideas that we learn as we're growing up. Like you either become a mom, or you pursue school.

They feel confident that they can really take on anything. You talk about the culture–not so much a culture but, rather, some of the ideas that we learn as we're growing up. Like you either become a mom, or you pursue school. And so a lot them share that. It is so true, and so when we have those discussions, we're like, "Who says we can't?" And how many women have done it? It's a matter of balancing your life.

Community Challenges

There are many challenges in the community. One is the whole immigration issue where a lot of them are stuck because of their status, unfortunately. That is where a lot of the women get stuck. They really do. As much as they would like to further their education, a lot of them get a little discouraged. Because of that, they ask, "What if I do this and prepare myself? I'm really committing to this, and then I'm going to reach a point where I can't move forward because of my legal status here." Education–it's pretty low, at least with people we serve. Like I said, I myself have seen how a lot of women have gone back or are currently enrolled in English or GED classes.

And some of this has been happening in the public schools. I'm not sure how to word this; I think their primary focus is education and the students there, but I think they should be definitely offering more services to the parents of these kids. They're able to reach out to them through the students. I think they're not really giving it the importance they should. We've collaborated with schools in the area. Another component of the leadership program is the mother-daughter program, basically where we offer the same training but to moms and daughters.

There's a huge, huge focus on how to build a healthy relationship through communication, through negotiation, so that's the big emphasis that we placed in those groups. So we've come out to some of the schools with this program. It hasn't come from administration; it has come from one of the community-based programs. We've either reached out, or somebody who's coordinating programs for parents—they're the ones that reach out to us. Sometimes they don't last long, and then they lose the connection or the relationship with the agency. I'm sure it has to do with what's going on in the school—maybe funding, or they don't feel the support. But an emphasis on programs for the parents, I think, would be very helpful.

I would love to stay in the community. It's going through a lot of changes, and it's becoming a lot more diverse, which is good. I like that. I would like to stay, but I don't think that's going to happen. I have to negotiate with my boyfriend. I've been with him for eight years now, and he does not want to stay here. He actually grew up in a nearby community but now lives in the South; I mean really way south. He's on the opposite end of me. I don't think he feels that connection with the community, not the way I do. I grew up here, and I've seen how the community has gone through so many changes. I would love to actually buy an apartment and keep it.

Reflections

Estela learned to be her own advocate in high school, when she was initially denied access to the honors classes. She wasn't challenged in the regular classes and was concerned that too much time was spent on students who created problems in class. Her parents wanted her to go to college, but since they had little formal education, they were not able to give her the practical advice that would have been helpful. Despite that, she continued to be resourceful and spent one semester studying in Spain. She is committed to the community and helping women achieve their true potential. She wants to see more women continue their education and learn to use their voice and become leaders.

17

Dolly

I interviewed Dolly in my office after work one evening. She was very excited about working on her MBA degree and wanted to talk about the power of determination and believing in yourself. She is dreaming forward to the day when high expectations and support systems are in place for all of the community.

Background

I was born in 1981. My parents originally came from Mexico. My dad came to the U.S. when he was eighteen years old, and then he ended up going back to Mexico, and he thought he was going to end up staying there. He got married to my mom and then realized things weren't going to work out for them in Mexico, so he decided to come back over here, and then he eventually brought my mom here. So they formed their lives here in Pilsen.

I know my dad—at first, he was in Texas when he originally started working. I know that my dad's aunt—she was one of the people that kind of convinced my dad, "Hey, your life will be much easier if you go to the U.S.," and that's the reason he was in Texas. And then she came—she came here to the city. And eventually, my dad's entire family started following her. And our whole family ended up over here. She actually was a businessperson. She opened up a few bars in the community. So it was just convenient for the entire family. We were just–the entire family was just close to each other. My aunts and uncles–for a large period of time, we lived on the same block. We were neighbors. We lived right next to each other in the same building.

I think that was very important. Especially since, in Mexico, it's all about family. You tend to mingle with each other and be involved in each other's lives. And I think that's what they wanted. They wanted a little bit of Mexico here. They wanted to be living next to each other whenever something came up, just having the ease of going up the stairs to other person's apartment and talking to them. It was just more convenient until much later,

> Especially since, in Mexico, it's all about family. You tend to mingle with each other and be involved in each other's lives. And I think that's what they wanted. They wanted a little bit of Mexico here.

after our families grew, and our families decided to buy houses. People just started separating and moving into other areas, but even then, a lot of my family moved, and a lot of them lived across the street from each other, two blocks away. They're still living close to each other.

They saw in Mexico, it was difficult to be able to provide for family, and so that was something that was important to them. I know that's the main reason why my dad came over here. And he found himself a pretty decent job, and he was earning–according to him, he was earning a good amount of money. And his whole plan was "I'm going to save up, save up, save up," because inside, he still had it in him that he wanted to go back to Mexico. They even had the opportunity where my parents were living in a building here, and the landlord was looking to sell, and this was probably in the '80s, and they approached my parents: "Are you interested in buying the building?" And my parents said no. And now my dad and my mom kind of hit their heads, because they were selling it for $29,000. It was a good deal. My parents had the money. They say they had the money, but they were saving up to go back to Mexico. Their plans were to save enough money, build our dream home in Mexico, and live there, because that's really where we belong. My mom–even to this day, she says that when she first came here, it was very difficult for her because it was mainly my dad's family that lives here in the city. My mom's family was still in Mexico. She said it was painful for her. She would cry a lot of the time. My dad would be out working; she'd be by herself. And to her, her dreams were "I want to go back and be with my entire family."

She–and that was another thing, because my parents came to this country illegally. So it took my mom eight years to finally be able to go over there. Actually, it took her eight years to go over there; she risked it because she didn't have her papers. And I remember that because I was six or seven years old, and it was my older sister and myself that were going with her to Mexico. We flew over there, but my mom—obviously, she didn't want us to know what their legal status was, because to her, that wasn't important for us to know. She just wanted us to see where they grew up, meet our grandparents, meet the rest of our family. And then I remember once, she said, "Okay, you guys, you're going to stay here. You're going to go back to the U.S. with your aunt." My mom would say, "I'm going to leave earlier," but we never even questioned it. We didn't know why that was. It wasn't until later that we found out that my mom was coming back illegally, and that's the reason why she didn't want us to go with her, because she wanted one of my family members who did have her residency to bring us back over here. It's interesting. More than anything, my mom suffered. And she's the one who said it more than my dad. My dad really doesn't talk about his experiences that much, but I know that's what was difficult for my mom from the beginning.

They've been here—my dad's been here since he was eighteen, and now he's sixty-four. You've lived your entire life here. If they have to, they'll find their way to communicate, and they know words here and there, but they do not speak English at all.

Language and Early Education

The language we spoke at home was Spanish until I was four years old. Actually, I was three years old when my mom put me in this Head Start program, and it was there that I started learning English. Then, when I went to preschool after that, I was always in a bilingual classroom. I was in a bilingual classroom, and I went to a bilingual school, Ruben Salazar, from preschool all the way to third grade. All of my classes were both English and Spanish.

Because the school was bilingual, everybody was in the same classrooms, because the school went up to third grade. Once you hit third grade, you had to start looking for another school. And one school at the time was known for having fourth grade to eighth grade, so it was convenient for us to transfer. They had a busing program, so we could jump on the bus and get to school safely without my parents worrying. So when I first started there at fourth grade, I was put in a bilingual classroom. And that's when I noticed kind of the difference, because I would notice that other kids were just in English-speaking classrooms, and they would kind of look down on the kids that were speaking English and Spanish that were in bilingual classrooms. They kind of saw us like dumb kids: "They don't know how to talk. There's something wrong with them or something."

Yeah, they were just like us; they were native Spanish speakers, but they had the English-speaking classroom. The teachers didn't talk to them in Spanish, and because of that, we were looked down upon.

I know at first, you do feel kind of like, "Why?" Because I felt like I could speak English perfectly well. Even when I was at my grammar school, a lot of our class time was English. It's just that we were known to be a bilingual school. I noticed that when I transferred, well, I really don't feel any different from anybody else. Whatever, however they want to look at me, that's up to them. Until the following year, fifth grade, when they evaluate you based on how you are doing, and if they see that you're advanced enough in English, they'll transfer you into an English-speaking classroom.

Fifth grade comes, and I was in an English-speaking classroom, and I kind of felt like, "Wow, I kind of got out of that." Like I kind of criticized myself because of what the other kids would say. It was like I wanted to be in an English-speaking classroom. And I even recall trying to speak more English, less Spanish; that's better. You want to fit in and be a part of what everybody else does—something I never did. A lot of my friends still stayed in bilingual classrooms, and they stayed from fourth grade all the way to eighth grade. I never treated anybody the way other kids would treat them or treated me when I was in fourth grade. I never saw the point to that. And it's amazing because I was always involved in school or something in the community, and when I was in Salcedo sixth grade, we had student council, and I decided to run for secretary. And I remember every year—and I lost every year that I ran: sixth grade, seventh grade, and eighth grade. But every year that I would run, I would always have the votes from the bilingual classrooms: "We're voting for you, Dolly." I would say, "Okay, good."

My mom was always a stay-at-home mom. My dad would always be the breadwinner, so my mom would always be involved. I'm the second oldest, so it was very hard for her to be involved in a lot of things I was involved with, and a part of me tells her, and I know she feels bad. At Salcedo, they would have Student of the Month once a year, and every year, I would be Student of the Year. And they would invite your parents, and my parents would never be able to make it—my dad because he was working and my mom because she was taking care of one of my younger siblings. It was hard because she never learned how to drive, so that was another issue. As a kid, I probably didn't understand that. I would brood. I knew she wasn't going to be able to make it.

> Yeah, they were just like us; they were native Spanish speakers, but they had the English-speaking classroom. The teachers didn't talk to them in Spanish, and because of that, we were looked down upon.

I'm going to be here–fine, take the award home. They would have honor rolls, and I would always be on the honor rolls. Every time there was some sort of award, I was always given an award or something. And so they weren't able to be a part of that, and I told them.

Holding onto Spanish

When I would go home, I would talk Spanish because the only language that they spoke was Spanish. But then I noticed myself that my Spanish was starting to get bad, because I wasn't practicing it as much. I would only practice it with my parents, and I would notice that I would forget a word or something. I would just say it in English. So I communicate half Spanish–Spanglish–to my parents.

My dad–he really didn't pay too much attention to it. My mom–and I think it's because of my grandmother, my mom's mom–she was always the type of person that in Spanish, never got any type of education, but her vocabulary was just really good. And she'd always teach all of my aunts, uncles, "This is the way you say things. This is the proper way to say things. You don't say it that way in Spanish." So my mom would be, "Why are you saying that? You don't say that word that way." And she would laugh: "I can't believe you're talking that way." And so it would annoy me, but I would ignore her. *Oh, what does my mom know? She doesn't understand what we're going through. My lifestyle is completely different from what her lifestyle was back in Mexico. She doesn't understand.* So for a very long time, my Spanish was getting worse and worse by the minute. And I learned how to read and write in Spanish when I was in my bilingual school. So I knew how to read it; I knew how to write it, but then even picking up a paper once, my mom put me to the test. She said, "Here–Spanish newspaper. Read that to me," and I couldn't read it. I could read it, but I was stumbling, and I was stopping a lot. It was not fluent at all.

She wanted to make sure I didn't lose my Spanish. She would compare me to one of the neighbors, because her daughters went to all-English schools. They were in a Catholic school, but the mother always taught them Spanish at home. Their Spanish was wonderful, and my mom was very close friends with the neighbor. "You know what? So and so can speak it very well, and they didn't even go to bilingual school, so I don't understand why you can't speak it well." I would still ignore her. *What does my mom know, blah blah blah?*

Once I got to high school, I had friends who grew up here in the community. And I also have friends who have grown up in other parts of the city. And one of my friends, because my name is Dolly, comes up with "Are you white, or are you Mexican? You look dark." One of my friends told me,

"Dolly, I've never heard you speak Spanish. Do you speak Spanish?" I think that's when it kind of hit. I had been trying to be American, to Americanize myself. Just talk English. I don't speak Spanish, and people don't think I can speak Spanish. That was kind of offensive to me. I told them, "No, I know how to speak Spanish; I just speak English, too. I don't understand what the problem is."

And then at that point, our family was a little bit better off. We were starting to go to Mexico more often, because by that point, by the late '80s, my mom managed to get her residency, so it was better for us. So my mom's youngest brother, who lived in Mexico, is only about five years older than me. All my cousins always looked up to my uncle. He's our age, but he's still my uncle, and he's doing all this. He was going to school and everything, and he would sound so well educated, and he was an inspiration to us.

He would talk to us. He would tell us of his experiences in school over there and would compare them to ours over here. And he would recommend a book: "You should read this book. This book is really good." But this book would be in Spanish, and I said, "You know what? Give me the book, and I'll read it." I was in high school, and I took the book, and I struggled. A lot of those words–I did not know what they meant, and to me, it was like a reality check. *This is what you've become. You're losing your Spanish. This isn't good.* So I pick up the book, I start reading them, and this author had several other books. When my mom would go to Mexico, I would ask her to bring me these books. I want these books. I started reading them.

Eventually, while I was in high school, toward my senior year, I found a job in Pilsen at a real-estate agency. Everybody spoke Spanish, and I thought, *These people grew up here; they speak Spanish, and they speak it very well.* And that was another inspiration to me. I was involved with a lot of people who were born here, spoke Spanish. I started picking up the Spanish newspapers, and I would read it all the time. Eventually, it got to the point where at church, I've become a reader at church, and I read in Spanish because I wanted to make sure that my Spanish was better. And to this day, I'm not going to lose my Spanish ever again. And I try to pick up on vocabulary and everything at work. That's what I love, because a lot of people that work here come directly from Mexico. And their Spanish is wonderful, and so a lot of times, I'll ask them to correct me if I'm saying something wrong. A lot of our employees can't speak English, so I'll conduct orientation in Spanish completely with them. I love that.

I think my older sister and I–we went through the same phase of "What's the problem? We don't need to talk Spanish." But then, I think, we had the same type of experience in the long run, where we really do need our Spanish. And then my parents–since they don't speak any English, a lot of the time, they would go to the store, and they would see someone that would look Spanish-speaking, and they would ask, "Can you help me?" And then when they would say, "Sorry, I don't speak any Spanish," my parents would come home, and they would be so disappointed, and they would be like, "I hope you guys don't turn out that way, because this is who you are, and losing a part of who you are–it's not worth it." So that's something that they would always instill in us. It got to a point where we all speak Spanish–some of us better than others, but we all try to be very competitive with one another when it comes to certain things. "I can read better than you." My brother would be like, "No, I pick up this thing. I can read it better than you."

I'm married now, and we speak both English and Spanish. My husband's experience has been similar to mine, but his parents decided at one point, when he was fifteen, that they were going to move to Mexico. So they took the entire family to Mexico, but then they realized they weren't going to make it over there. Then they decided to come back, so they were only there for a little bit–less than a year. But he said he struggled, and the teachers knew that he couldn't communicate in Spanish. So they kind of had a deal going with the teacher: "I'll teach a class in English." And the teacher was fine with it, so my husband was like the equivalent of freshman here in high school, teaching people how to speak English over there. But his Spanish is terrible; it's really, really bad.

At home, sometimes we're Spanglish. We'll speak in Spanish, and we'll speak in English; we'll go both ways. Something we have talked about– once we have kids, we want them to learn Spanish first.

It's something, for sure, we both want to do, and both our parents, my in-laws, they stress that a lot too. My mother-in-law does not know English. My father-in-law does, but he's the type of person that feels the same way my parents do. You–this is a part of you; you should learn how to speak Spanish, too. And we feel that they would have more opportunities down the line being bilingual.

Educational Expectations

Educationally, I remember struggling in at least one class every year– at least when I was in high school, freshman-year English. It happened to be my very first class of the day, and since I grew up here, I had a commute. I had to take two buses from here all the way to the high school; I didn't want to go to the local high school. It was known in my community, still is known, for–a lot of kids in the neighborhood do go there, a lot of them are good. But some of them get involved in gangs, and my mom didn't want that. My mom said, "You're not going to go there. I want you to be somewhere where I know you would be better off."

My dad didn't even go to school at all, didn't even know how to read or write when he came here. He managed to learn when he was about thirty-something years old, and I was in fourth grade. I remember coming home and him saying, "You have homework. You got to learn how to write your name." I remember my dad sitting me on his lap and feeling like, *Wow, my dad knows how to write my name out.* I felt like I could look up to my dad. *Wow, he knows how to write; he knows how to do all this stuff.* Now I come to know that he was learning with me; he struggled, but he knew that he needed to read and write.

Even now, my parents—my dad didn't read and write, and even now, his writing is not the greatest; he picked up something he loved to do. What he loves to read are kids' history books on Mexico. So every time we'd go to the library, he'd be like, "Bring me this book on Benito Juarez. Bring me this book on Zapata." And all these historic people from Mexico—that's what he reads. So you ask him anything on the history of Mexico, and he'll know it. My mom—like I mentioned to you, my grandmother was a person who always went, "Speak right; there's no reason why you shouldn't be." So my mom always had that. My mom only went up to the third grade. Even though she went to the third grade, she was fifteen in Mexico. It was known in their family that school was not the thing. They would say, "We need you to work, because we need the family to survive, and that's the way we'll be able to survive: by having our kids work."

I remember my dad coming home from work, and you could see he was filthy because of the type of job that he had, and he would sit my older sister and I on his lap. He would look at us, and he would tell us, "Do you want to look like me?" And then we were like six, seven years old. We would look at him and be, "What do you mean?" "Do you want to look like me? Do you want to come home looking like me?" I can tell now, looking back, he probably had a very frustrating day at work. And my sister and I are like, "No, we don't want to look like you." "That's right; you're in a country where you can go to school." Then he would ask us, "What do you want to be when you grow up?" And my older sister would say, "I want to be a lawyer. I want to be a lawyer." He'd ask me, "What do you want to be? A doctor?" I didn't know. "Good, then you need to go to school." And he talks in Spanish, and he'd tell us—because my dad's known for his vulgar language, but he'd make it clear: "You need to go to school; there's no option. There's no other way. You're going to go to school, and that's it." Even when it came to talking about boys and boyfriends, my parents would be like, "Nope, it's not going to happen". My dad's like, "You're going to have a boyfriend once you graduate from college."

He knew older cousins of ours–as soon as they got a boyfriend, they had a kid, so that was his thing. And he'd always compare us to our cousins. He'd be like, "You need to stop hanging around with them." So he kind of, little by little, started moving us away from going to family parties, because he didn't want us to hang out with our cousins–who were gangbangers, who, at the age of thirteen, they were affiliated with a lot of people who went to Juarez–because as I've mentioned, a lot of them didn't even go to high school. Knowing the history of kids that went to Juarez, they didn't want to take that risk with us. And my cousins–one of them was thirteen and just had her first baby at fifteen. A lot of them were real young. And my parents just wanted, I think, move you away from family–that's not the best thing to do, but in order to make sure you're successful, that's what we're going to do in the meantime. So for a very long time and even now, we're closer to my mom's side of the family, even though they live all over the country–California, Texas, everywhere else. We're closer to them than we are to my dad's side of the family. I think that has a lot to do with it. Because my parents were like, "See what they're doing? You don't want to do that. See what they're involved in? You don't want to do that." When I was in high school, I lost my cousin due to gang violence. So once we are growing up, everything that my parents would tell us, "Yeah, they're right," because we would see it. Yeah, there's consequences. Those are not the consequences we want to deal with.

It didn't scare me, because our parents always told us–my mom had this saying in Spanish: "Tell me who you hang out with, and I'll tell you who you are." My mom's like, "If you're going to hang out with them, you know what that might lead to. But if you don't hang out with them and you keep your head on straight, you keep your goals in mind, you'll be able to do that." So even growing up here, I lost a lot of my friends. Because I would talk to my friends the way my mom would talk to me. We'd talk about school, and I remember a few of my friends would be like, "Oh yeah, what do you want to do when you grow up?" My friend–I want to do this, and I still had the doctor thing in mind.

Little by little, my mom would tell us–as we were growing up, she would see our friends, and she would see what direction they were heading into. She would see their sibling, their older siblings too. And she would see what she wanted from us. And she's done it with all of us. When she would see that we were hanging around with someone that was probably not good for us, she'd be like, "You need to stop hanging around with them." We–I remember myself kind of getting upset: "What do you mean? It's just my friend; I'm not going to." But then, little by little, you start growing up and noticing things and thinking maybe it's not a good idea. And all my friends, once I was in eighth grade and high school, I noticed I stopped hanging around with them.

I started noticing, little by little, they're starting to hang around with the gangs from this area. It doesn't look right. And little by little, we just started moving away from each other.

And a lot of them still live there; I see them because my mom still lives in the same house. We ended up buying a house when I was in sixth grade, on Eighteenth Street, and that's one of the reasons they haven't moved—because they bought a house there. They love living in the community, because my mom says, "I feel like I'm living in Mexico. I have everything there that I need." And they're still there, and even three years ago, when I was still living with my parents, you know, a lot of the girls that I hang out with have two or three kids now. They didn't finish high school, and we talk about it. My mother's like, "See who you were hanging out with?" And I'm like, "Yeah." "That's exactly what I didn't want for you. It hurt me because I didn't want to take you away from your friends, but I saw that that wasn't—they weren't the right people to be with."

Path to College

Once all of us actually got to college, we realized we weren't able to compete at the same level as everybody else; we were struggling. And like I mentioned, I was always on the honor roll, always doing good in school. I realized the education I was getting wasn't good enough. I didn't realize it while I was in high school; I didn't realize it. I thought, *Hey, I'm doing good.* I was taking honors classes. *There's not that many kids that take honors classes. I must be pretty good.* Once it came to college, I had to take three classes that were not for credit, because I didn't place into the classes I was supposed to, and I had to catch up. We would all, and it's happened to all of us thus far.

We've told my mom there's a sign here. Maybe something's going on in the schools. Curie's known to be a vocational, technical school. So pretty much they were—I feel now, they were setting us up: "We realize you're not going to college; we might as well train you to do a decent job once you graduate." Once I kind of looked back, and I saw that I kind of felt they actually thought I wasn't going to go to college, but I did. But great, they taught me all these skills, because I learned a lot of computer software and everything that was good. But I wasn't strong in other areas, like math and even English and writing. I need to improve that. From those experiences, my mom now feels that my younger sister needs to—she wants her in a prep school, a college prep school. So I think that she wants to make sure that she's well prepared and that my sister's not struggling the way we were when we went to college.

The high school wasn't encouraging. It was my parents. It was those conversations when we were, like I mentioned, when my dad would sit us on his lap: "You're going to go to college; there's no way out of it." I even recall graduating from eighth grade, and graduating from eighth grade was a big deal in the Mexican community. You're graduating eighth grade, and your parents don't even go to school–and you're graduating eighth grade. So I remember walking across the stage when I was getting my diploma, and the vice principal–like, she hugged me and said, "I'm so proud of you, and I can't wait for you to come back with your high-school diploma." I looked at her, and I said, "It's not going to be my high-school diploma. It's going to be my college diploma." I knew. I knew. I was like, "A high-school diploma's not going to get me anywhere. I need to get my bachelor's degree." Even then, I was thinking about–I was a sophomore in high school, and I was already inquiring with a lot of universities.

My older sister went to a community college first, and then she went to the university. Like I mentioned, I was involved in a lot of community organizations. I was volunteering in a lot of places, so I had a lot of influential people in my life. A lot of them said, "You need to get started on this, because you need to apply to these colleges," or whatever. A lot of the information– yeah, they gave me a lot of good information since nobody else in my family could help me. It's just like, "Okay, any school, any university." I know I didn't want to go to a community college. Like, I want to go to a four-year university. I want to get the four-year experience.

My friends and the influential people that were there when I was at El Valor influenced me. I worked closely with a guy that was doing reception work there at the time. He had just graduated out of college, so he would talk to me about "Oh yeah, I just graduated from college at Southern Illinois, and I was in a fraternity, and these are things that you can do," and all this other stuff. And I was like, "Wow, I want to be a part of that stuff too." And another summer, I worked at another El Valor and worked closely with the receptionist there too. Her daughter had just gotten admitted to the university and told me, "You can get scholarships. You can do this and that." It turned out that that receptionist–she was a founder of an organization here, Youth Struggling for Survival. And that organization was founded by her as well as her husband, who happens to be a writer and has written a couple of books based on his story, his gang experience back in East LA.

So I was around a lot of educators at the time, a lot of people who wanted to help out our community, kids that were struggling that lived in these neighborhoods that sought out gang life to do whatever they wanted to do or whatever. They were there to kind of guide us and tell us that it's not the correct route to take. Their intentions were good, and I think that's what helped me. Also, besides my parents and having people like that in my life, the organizations I was into in high school, the student council–our adviser there would always talk about, "What college are you going to go to?" Even though the school was, "We want to get you out of here so you don't start working at Mickey D's and you have an office job at least," she was someone that saw it differently. And even once we were in junior year, she would ask, "What schools are you applying for?" So she was very helpful.

I try to do the same thing with as many people as I can. I do it with all my sisters, my brother more than anything, because that's home, and I want my sisters and my brother to go in the right direction, so I share my experiences with them: "I struggled here; maybe you need to do this." My sister–she's the third one of us. She's four years younger than me. She was in high school when I was in college. I tell her, "You know what? I notice that I slacked off in this class. Maybe you need to start paying attention in math, and maybe you need to start doing this," or whatever. She was a little bit more rebellious: "What do you know? You're just trying to be like my mom." And so she wouldn't listen to me. When she got out of college, secretly on the side, she'd tell my mom, "I wish I would have listened to Dolly. She was right." My mom would come back and tell me, and I'd go, "Yeah!"

College–it was a challenge. I felt bad. I felt bad because I felt like I was doing so much in high school. I kind of felt cheated. I did so much: Why didn't they push a little harder to have me prepared for this? It was very hard. My first two years at the university were very hard, to the point where I felt like I couldn't do it, even though I went through the LATIS program. They had a Latino program to help kids of Latino origin get into college, and they will provide guidance counseling and a lot of school-related stuff.

I remember when they asked us, "What do you want to major in?" Because I dealt so much with computers in high school, I said I wanted to major in computer science. And somebody told me, "Based on your scores, I don't think you can do that." And then I'm like, "Well, is there any other route that I'm able to take to eventually get to computer science?" "Well, you could go through the business route, but even that might be a little bit difficult for you." And so I just thought, *Okay, they're saying that I'm not going to be able to do this.* That was discouraging, and I went home, and I told my mom that they're pretty much saying that I'm not going to be able to do what I want to do, because "It's going to take too long, and based on your scores, if you didn't pass at the level you are supposed to in math, what makes you think you're going to do it later?"

That upset me, and then I started off with the liberal arts and sciences college, but then I was like, "No." And then I took English classes, and my first English teacher told me–she's like, "Wow, you're pretty good when it comes to English. Are you sure you don't want to become an English major? I could see it in you. I could see that you like to write." I love to write. Whether I write it the right way, I don't know. And she's like, "I see it in you. Are you sure? There are these routes that you can take. You can even write for the student newspaper and everything." It all sounds interesting, but right now, I don't know, though. And I joined a fraternity. I did—a coed Latino fraternity on campus. I thought, *Wow, all these people are in the same boat. We all suck at math, and we all suck at English. We all have to take those same classes; there's something going on here.* And one of my friends, most of my friends—they wanted to do the business side. And that's what I also had kind of considered. And I'm like, "I've heard it's hard," this and that.

And then I was talking to one of my friends who told me to just apply: "I'm applying to get into the College of Business. My GPA's like one point short of what it needs to be. You'll be fine." So I applied, and I got into the College of Business. And I'm like, "They said I couldn't get in. And I'm in." It felt really good. But I stopped going to them for help. They obviously don't know that I'm willing to take it. I'm willing to take a hit, but that's not going to stop me. I'm going to do what I want to do, and I have my goals in mind, and I'm going to achieve them. And that comes from my dad, because my dad would always—I would come home, and he would see how I'd worry. "You can do it," and he'd just turn around and continue watching TV. I'd be, "How do you know I can?" "You can do it"—and turn around and continue watching TV. And I'd look at my mom, and she'd talk to me more. And she'd be like, "I pray to God every day, and I know that as long as you put in, he's going to be there every day, and you do whatever you can." I struggled with accounting; I struggled with finance. I cried, and I cried again and again. My mom would see how much I would struggle, but I would tell her, "I'm not going to stop. Like, I'm going to get through."

Like I mentioned, a lot of my friends were business majors, so we all—a lot of us—knew where our weaknesses were and everything, and we would ask each other for help. And that's how most of us ended up graduating, because some of us were weaker in some areas and some of us in others. I have friends that graduated as finance majors, economics majors, management, marketing, and entrepreneurship. We all leaned in for help, and a lot of us would take classes together for that same reason: "Hey, we're taking this class together; we're going to study together so that we finish this class." A couple of times, we dropped. I dropped Accounting 1, and I dropped Finance 1 because I knew going into it it wasn't going to end up right. I know myself, and this is not the right time. I would drop those classes, and then I would retake again. The second time I took accounting, I got an A. The second time I took finance, I got a B. See? I did it right. I made the right decision. Most people that I know that are at UIC or in college–they are English majors or whatever. I remember calling my friend because we kind of lost touch, and she didn't manage to graduate from college. I told her, "Guess what? I just graduated with a double major." And she's like, "Really? What did you do–English?" "No, I actually did marketing and management." She's like, "Really? Nobody that I know has been able to pull that one off." Well, I'm not willing to settle. I guess not. I'm trying to move forward.

Community and Family Support

Community means a lot to me, and you know what? I can also trace it back to El Valor. I would work on and off during the summers there, and I loved the people there. And I had a few mentors there, but once I was in college, I also had a huge mentor; he was actually the director of the Youth Enrichment programs. I would do tutoring while I was in college to get a few bucks to buy myself food. And I remember he would tell us, "You guys are going to be big shots," because he would only hire college kids to tutor high-school kids or even grade-school kids. "Just remember, once you become a big shot, once you climb over that wall, remember to pull that rope back to help somebody else, because we need to help each other out." A lot of our community– and he was actually from New York, but he came and he started working here, and he'd tell us it's the same everywhere for Hispanics. "Look at the neighborhood that we live in. People look at us a certain way, and they think we are not going to end up becoming anything. What you see out there is what you're going to get, but obviously, we have people here who are willing to go to school, who are willing to make a better life, who are willing to be role models for these kids. Just always remember that somebody helped you. And the way they helped you, you need to help somebody else."

I do it with my siblings, and I'll do it with my cousins; I'll do it even with my husband's family. And that's something that I always talk about. It's education. I forget who told me this, because I've had a lot of influential people in my life. Somebody told me they can take anything away from you. You can become broke. They can take everything away from you, but the one thing they're not going to be able to take away from you is your schooling. To me, that's something that I hold close, and with my cousins, I'll always tell them,

> "Just remember, once you become a big shot, once you climb over that wall, remember to pull that rope back to help somebody else, because we need to help each other out."

"What are you doing?" My cousin was kind of heading in the wrong direction, and he was only twelve. "What are you doing? This isn't what you want to do." I felt like it was kind of my responsibility to keep on top of what everybody was doing. It was hard for me to know what was going on, but then it got back to me. Hey, this kid came out with the wrong crowd in school. It got to a point where he got kicked out of school because he started selling drugs in, like, seventh grade. You don't do that. It got to a point where I had my uncle dropping off my cousin at my house twice a week. And I would just say, "Hey, let's do homework, or let's pick up a book and read it."

And I remember what my parents would tell me. And that's exactly what I would tell them: "What do you want to become? What do you want to do? Do you want to do that? I'm sure you don't. I'm sure you want—" I would see what they would be into. They would look at these cars. "Do you want that car? I'm sure you can't afford it." From what I hear now, one of my cousins is doing really good in high school. And so I'm proud of that. But you can't always get that, though, because his brother's not doing so good. You can only do so much. Another one of my cousins, same thing; I helped her with her essay and everything for UIC, to get into UIC. Unfortunately, she didn't get in, and she ran away from home before she even got a letter from them on what the status of her application was.

I don't know if she ever got accepted or not, but I try. I definitely do try. And all those kids that I would tutor when I was at El Valor? A lot of them are from the community. A lot of them go to my church, which is also in the community. I still go there. I see a lot of them, and I'll talk to them. I'll be like, "What are you doing now?" I know they're about to graduate; I can pretty much keep track of how old they are. "Do you need help with your application? Do you need help with what schools [you are] considering?" And then I know it's just one person; it's just me. But sometimes you also see them with their parents. Some of the parents know that the way they grew up was okay: you are meant to start working as soon as possible. That way, the family's better off immediately. I can't change that.

My parents' goal for us was just finish your bachelor's degree. I don't think they knew there was anything beyond that. But it was also my mentor at El Valor that started talking to me about this MBA. And obviously El Valor was joining with National Louis in bringing this out. So I always knew. When I was in high school, I was going to get my bachelor's degree. But even then, I knew I'm going to get my master's degree, and I'm going to get my doctorate. It's just going to happen. That's what I want. Not right now, but those are plans for the future. Right now, it is to finish that MBA.

We can do it. We can do it as long as we have the support, and we've always had it from our families. And we've been very fortunate in that. Those are my plans: to get my PhD once I'm done with my MBA. I'm actually considering getting a concentration in either finance or accounting. I'm leaning more toward finance. I love human resources right now. I just got a new boss, and I'm learning so much from her. She's young, and she's an HR director, and she's done so much. It's motivation also. I'm thinking, *Hey, I might stick it out with HR.* If HR doesn't work out, just do something else with my MBA.

Goals and Persistence

But for sure, eventually, I would want to go back and teach, though. I would love to teach grade school; I love the kids, because I work so much tutoring kids. I would love that or go to a university and teach there. Ideally, that's what I would love, and I told my mom I would love to. Everything that I've learned from my work experience–I would love to share that. I would love to share that with somebody and have them learn my experience. So in the long run, that's what I would love to do. Obviously, kids and everything, but after kids, I'll go back and get my PhD. That's what I want to do.

You just have to want to do it. It's not about who's the smartest, because something that I also told my mom is even when I was in the eighth grade, I hung around with probably the smartest kids in the school, and I felt very fortunate to hang out with them, because, wow, they're just, like, so smart. I always felt they were smarter than me. I knew they were smarter than me, and I would try hard to be as smart. Once we got to high school, I would keep in touch with a lot of my friends, and I want to say that 90 percent of them didn't graduate. Some of them had kids, and some of them got into drugs and things that probably weren't good for them in the long run. I told my mom, "It's not who's the smartest. It's who really wants it." Because you can learn things–if you put your mind to it, you can learn it. Like I was, and the proof is there. I'd see some of the smartest kids. They were so smart; people made fun of them. They felt they needed to fit in, and they ended up getting into gangs and doing things that weren't good for them.

I even recall when I was a freshman in high school, one of my friends–we had the same lunch break. It was open campus; we were able to go out to restaurants and eat. She would do it for fun. She would cut school and go to house parties during the daytime. And she graduated, but she's not doing anything, really, with her life now. And those were like my closest friends and girls and guys that I knew were very smart–very smart. We would take Iowa tests, competency tests, when we were in grade school. They would always score so much higher than I would. They actually got the opportunity to apply to a magnet high school, and I didn't. I would try really hard, and I really wanted it–probably wanted it more than them. I didn't get those opportunities, but they got them, and they didn't take advantage of them. And they were good even in sports and everything. They were involved in school, clubs, and everything. I told my mom, like, I don't know–it has a lot to do with our parenting, because my parents, luckily, they were always there.

Reflections

Dolly is the model of resilience and determination. Even when the schools had low expectations for her, she knew she was going to college and would earn her degree. She was ridiculed in school due to her lack of English, but she persevered and became proficient in both Spanish and English. Spanish became a coveted part of her heritage, and Dolly is determined to pass it on to her children someday.

Her parents provided much emotional support, but they couldn't come to school due to work and obligations related to raising their other children. They never learned to speak English, but they knew how important it was for their children. Her father always encouraged her even though he did not have a formal education.

Dolly tries to be a positive role model for her younger relatives and others in the community. When she went to college, Dolly was discouraged by her lack of preparation, but she was determined to succeed. She and her friends helped each other succeed, and she continues the cycle by reaching back to help others in her community attain their goals. This is how Dolly defines *community*.

18

Carmen and Angela

I met Carmen and Angela in Carmen's office at the community medical center. They were close friends and colleagues who had an enormous amount of respect for each other and wanted to tell their stories together. They had been leaders in the Pilsen community for several decades. Together, they were behind many significant initiatives, including the development of a high school and a medical center to serve the community. Throughout our time together, their passion and serious commitment were evident, as was their wonderful sense of humor. Carmen and Angela were dreaming forward for the well-being of their community and its residents.

Background

Carmen: My name is Carmen. I'm the executive director of the community medical center, and we are in charge of a federally qualified health center. There are three sites. We service seventeen thousand patients. Our population, as a majority, are undocumented, predominately Mexican community, bilingual, Spanish speaking. The community medical center is a topic all unto itself that you need to look at, because you can't do this community without including the medical center.

Angela: Okay, I'm Angela. I'm working as an educational consultant because after thirty-nine years in education, I'm avoiding having an employer. So I do a lot of consulting and a lot of volunteer work. If you want to know specifically, I'm on the second legislative committee of a state senator and have worked on a report on the status of Latinos in the public schools. I'm working now with three other volunteers to update that report from the original that was issued in 2004. It's been on his website since then. We had it translated, and it's in English and in Spanish. I just had one hundred hard copies printed because it was difficult getting money. It costs like $4,000 just to have it translated, so we saved our money for that. I'm also a member of the Community Colleges Board and a variety of education initiatives in the city and state.

Carmen: I was born in the heart of the community, where the university sits right now. There is a love/hate relationship with university. In the early '60s, when the university was built, people were then moved west, and you had what was a German, Croatian, and Irish community become the port of entry for the Mexican community. I went to elementary school here, not to a public school but a Catholic school, and right next door was a public school.

But we moved out of the neighborhood, and I was a fish without water, so really and truly, any work that I've done evolved on the community issues in this neighborhood. We moved. My father bought a piece of land where every Sunday after Mass, we would go to see where he was going to build a house. [laughs] So he finally did, at Seventy-Second and St. Louis. Yes, we were the first Mexicans, and that was in 1950.

Angela: Shall I go now? I'm just going to repeat a conversation with a student. Many students I've worked with have asked me if I grew up here, especially when I worked in this community. I would tell them, "Well, this neighborhood, as a Mexican community, did not exist when I was growing up." So I too was born in a hospital, which is now a condo just west of the university. As a child, before we moved out west to a Jewish community because my father was drafted into the army in World War II, my mother and I went to live near my godmother. So I lived on the west side for a very long time and went on to college. I was determined not to go into education. It was too traditional a career.

My father told me I must go to college before I figured out that that's what I had to do, but I was absolutely determined to stay away from education. And I did for a long time. I was married, and my son was born. There was this desperate need for teachers, and I read an article in the newspaper paper one day. It was maybe in '62 or '63, and I received a provisional certificate to teach in the city.

I was provisionally assigned to a fourth-grade classroom that included a child who couldn't speak English. Once I became certified, I was reassigned to a first-grade class. Within a couple of weeks, they had moved him with me to first grade because the teacher had no control; she couldn't communicate with him. It was then I realized I needed to work with children who spoke Spanish, who were bilingual, and whose culture was either Puerto Rican or Mexican. I requested a school that was predominately Latino, and I ended up in this community because the principal recruited me to come and be with her as an assistant principal.

That never happened, because I took off to Mexico for a year in a teacher exchange. But when I came back, I did begin working here. From there, I was recruited to be assistant principal at a public school nearby, which now also has another name. I was assistant principal there. I was there five years until I was recruited to open up the new public high school. By then, it was '79, and I was recruited by Carmen through the superintendent of schools.

I spent many, many years at the new public high school. One of the reasons is I'm Mexican and wanted to work with Mexican and Puerto Rican children. I wanted to work with Mexican children because I saw a tremendous great need, and being Mexican, you realize that without even thinking about it, that you become a big role model with the students when you work with them.

A New High School

Carmen: The dream for the new public high school was that at the existing high school at the time, there were a lot of problems, gangs, and not too many success stories.

Angela: There was high absenteeism and a high dropout rate.

Carmen: There were not too many role models. And there was always issues: no bilingual, bicultural, Spanish-speaking counselors. So it was not the place to have your son or daughter at. I was on the board of education between 1974 and 1980, and the community decided to challenge the system and wanted a new high school because it would give hope and success stories through education, and they organized and succeeded in getting it. There was a big fight. It didn't happen overnight. But it came to the board. The other issue that was part of that was the elimination of a major thoroughfare because it cut through. Remember? The businesspeople– they were opposed to it because it eliminated some businesses and cut down on the traffic they needed as businesspeople. It used to go straight through

> The community decided to challenge the system and wanted a new high school because it would give hope and success stories through education.

the property of the school. In order to build the school, they had cut off the thoroughfare at Eighteenth Street.

You had several organizations, and they were very grass roots, with the purpose of organizing and really sitting up and be counted. And so, of course, the Neighbors worked with the schools and the parents. They asked, "How are we going to convince the public schools to buy this land and give us a new school?" And it was a huge school, about a thousand students.

Now, the other aspect, as we sit back and talk about it–the other part of that issue was who are we building this school for? We have always been threatened by living too close to downtown, so if we build this school, are our kids going to be the ones who are going to be in this school? Is that going to help the dropout rate? Are we going to have our teachers? Are we going to have kids going to college? And again, there was no hope. I think the local high school didn't give hope to the community. And I believe in education–I mean, that is what spins everything off on life.

Angela: The existing high school was mostly Mexican and black students. One of the peculiar things about it was the big, old, ugly building was not in very good condition. It was a general education program. They did have a bilingual program, transitional bilingual-education program, but it was at another building two or three blocks away. It was in an old elementary school that had been built in the nineteenth century and was even in worse condition than the high school, and that's where all the bilingual students were going. They were sort of segregated–those that were predominately English-speaking at the high school, and all the transitional, bilingual-education students were at this other building.

It was very sad, you know, the condition of that building at the branch of the high school. All the Latino teachers were at the branch, and they had inadequate lamps or no lamps at all, because I observed the teachers teaching there when I was hiring for the new school. So you put those two things together–students being segregated, a building being decrepit–and you begin to get the message: the education for our children doesn't matter. That's obvious. There were cultural issues between the administration and the parents in our community, who expect to be welcomed when they walk into an institution–not necessarily fluffed with but at least smiled at. You have to be able to communicate with them, and that was not happening at the existing school.

Carmen: You had a composition of eleven board members: one was the head of all the unions in the city, and one was the African American professor from the university. Then you had the mucky muck Anglo-Saxon lady. You had a Jewish woman at the table. You had Pat, who was Irish, and Kay, who also lived on the north side, Presbyterian-wife lady, and you had

Mrs. Cary Preston, whose only interest was to desegregate the public schools no matter what cost.

I understood what the issue was in relationship to the African community. But when we went through that whole process of the desegregation, my position is I didn't support it, because I believe that if you had four children, you'd be involved in the children's education at four different schools, and to desegregate our kids was crazy.

The whole issue of bilingual education—it was like immigration today, the hottest issue in the country and in the city. So you know, we took some positions around the environment for our children. Look at nomenclature with the U.S. Census Bureau. Not until 1989 did you have white, nonwhite, Hispanic, and all the breakdown that went with it, and then Asian and then, quote, "Other." Then what happened? Right now, in 2006, they don't even want you to say "Hispanic." They want you to say "brown Mexican," "white Mexican," or "black Mexican." Bioethnicity! Whenever I see that, I go like this, and I put this: the word I wrote down is *Mexican*.

I'm ferocious about being clear about being Mexican, because we have clarity as a community. Do not try to confuse my identity. I think another piece is that the challenges we face as Mexicans make us very clear about who we are, and we are passionate about that. They're always trying to play mind games on us in that they want us to feel guilty because we say "Mexican," not "Latino," because you're including people. Bullshit! You know? No, it's *Mexican*. For me, I was born here, but I still have a double nationality.

> I'm ferocious about being clear about being Mexican, because we have clarity as a community. Do not try to confuse my identity. I think another piece is that the challenges we face as Mexicans make us very clear about who we are, and we are passionate about that.

Angela: Within the Mexican community itself, there are those who say "Mexican American." There are those who say "Mexican." To me and to Carmen, I think, "Mexican American" is redundant. All Mexicans are Americans. Then there are the Chicanos and Chicanas, who are much younger than us, and that was a term that arose in the '60s during the civil rights movement in California, in the Southwest. In our age group, we have generally not identified with that name. I know some women who are around forty who do identify with it. To them, it's more activist in nature. Really, activism is in your actions.

Carmen: All I've been saying to you is very important. The conversation about the new high school is meaningless without this conversation.

That's why it's very important for our youth, whether in the public or the Catholic high school, to be determined who they are. Because if you're clear of who you are, your self-esteem—no one can take that away. And then no one can say or imply directly that you can't do something or you can't be something. And the other piece of that is the whole issue of entitlement. I'm not talking about entitlement. There's a segment of our youth who think they are entitled. They're entitled, shit. But I think there is the segment of our children and youth who need to know that they can do it with the support of other adults and people close to them. If they have the inner strength because of their families and who they are, can just say, "I'm real clear where I need to go. Just get out of my way."

Angela: It's so important for your family to believe in you and what you can accomplish. As an educator, I've seen that over and over again. Sometimes even the fact that counselors in our schools discourage our Mexican youth to do and accomplish many things that they still go forward. I would meet them at the university, and they would tell me how a counselor said, "Why do you want to go to college? You're only going to get married and have babies." This is in the late '90s, and she said, "I'm so angry that I know I'm going to graduate from this school." Her anger certainly helped her in the end. I think her family helped her a lot, but she was just appalled. And we were all appalled that in the late '90s, this continued to happen.

At Juarez, there was a tremendous focus on the Mexican culture, and we had a terrific bilingual-education program. We had many Latino teachers. Ah, many more Puerto Rican teachers compared to Mexican. We've always had tremendous shortage of Latino teachers in our schools. We had a lot of bilingual, bicultural teachers, both Mexican and Puerto Rican. Everything we did as a general group generally revolved around the culture in the community. There was very deep involvement with community organizations and parents from the very beginning. They dictated certain things they wanted in terms of a dress code, which, at the time, didn't go over very well in many of the high schools. Because of the gang activity in the area, it was decided we would have closed campus. We opened with that in mind. We may have been the first closed-campus high school at the time, because it was not a popular thing to do. People wanted the kids to go out, but unfortunately, they didn't come back. So we decided that in order to keep the kids and not lose anyone, that we would have a closed campus. They would eat here and go directly back to class.

It happened mostly because of the parents and community support. They signed off on "Yes, we will have a dress code." And one of the reasons is because of gang colors. We did not want to have gang colors. We gathered students before the school opened at the church in the basement. We brought as many students that were going to be coming from the elementary schools to our school and from the existing high school. It was a really large group, and they voted on which color would represent the school, which was extremely difficult because of all the gang colors. We ended up with awful beige and awful brown, but at that time, it didn't represent any gang colors. That's the way decisions were made.

There were two neighborhood groups, and they were not seeing eye to eye on a lot of issues. It becomes an issue on who's going to decide whose territory it is. And that is one of the things I had to work with. I had to work with both groups so we could eventually agree on how the school was going to open up. One group took a more radical approach. They were younger. And younger people always seem more radical. They were more involved with curriculum issues than the other group was. They wanted ESL instruction this way. They had a whole idea how instruction should go, and many of them were at the university as students at the time. But that was the young group; the other group was a more parent-type community activist. So the two groups didn't see eye to eye at the beginning, but by the time the school opened, we had resolved all differences, whatever they were.

One of the reasons I even came on was that the school was not even going to open, because there were major, major problems going on—the principal that was selected.

Carmen: The process of selection! Everybody wanted a Mexican principal, and it was someone else who was finally selected. Not by our choice—it was politics that brought him to the table. Am I correct?

Angela: I'm assuming that. There weren't too many people qualified. At the time, you had to pass an exam to become a principal. I hadn't even taken the exam. I certainly didn't pass it; I don't think I had taken it. I had only been in the system twelve years. I had just finished earning my master's, so I know I hadn't taken it yet. And so there weren't very many qualified people that had a principal's certificate and who were Latino who could take over the school. I don't know how many Mexicans there may have been—two or three—so it became a problem for the community to accept the selected principal. He withdrew his name because, he told me, he received threats. He was supposed to be principal. He had been selected at some community meeting or something. I was busy with my own school. So I would just hear what was going on, mostly from Carmen. But he was selected, and he withdrew his name.

Carmen: I forgot that.

Angela: He withdrew his name, and the superintendent was really up against the wall, because the school was. He had already seen the protests from the community about the fact that the conditions at Harrison were terrible, and this school was going to be opened, and there was just no *but*s about it. So they had to do something. That's where I came in.

Carmen: Yeah, okay–yeah, yeah, yeah.

Angela: I received a call one afternoon that said, "You are to report to the superintendent's office Monday morning at eight."

Carmen: Oh God, how can I forget about that?

Angela: I had the temerity to say, "Which superintendent?" I had district superintendents. There are all sorts of superintendents above me, and I think it was Jones on the other end of the phone who said, "There is only one superintendent!" [laughs] I got the picture. So that's what I did. That was so strange. One day, you were at one school, and the next day, you were just gone. And that's exactly how it happened.

I became administrative head because I didn't have a principal's certificate, and they couldn't name me principal. It was my job to open up the school, and I didn't know if I was going to stay. I didn't know how the politics were going to go. Just the fact that I was opening up the school was a pretty big deal, because I was not a high-school person, which, in the system, is a big deal. It's like a university saying "community college."

You know, the high-school teachers see themselves as a great, big, fat notch above elementary school, but here I was, coming from an elementary school to take on this big job, which I had to learn very quickly. I knew there was going to be this arrogance and antagonism toward me because I was in elementary school. There were just so many obstacles you could not believe–being female in a predominately male administrative system, being a Mexican.

Carmen: Not having the appropriate criteria.

Angela: Not having a high-school certificate–I didn't qualify for one. I just didn't apply for one, because I was working in elementary. I didn't live in the community, but that had never bothered me or anyone else I knew. That issue certainly didn't come up. But there were all in the community groups that saw things in their own way. So it was a big challenge.

To open up the new high school, you just plod along with the politics of the community. We are also talking about politics of the central administration, which is not any less antagonistic, not any less challenging to the school, because at one point, they removed, I think it was, $700,000 from my budget that was specifically geared toward the library. I'm having to deal with budget. I'm going in with the hard hat into construction. I'm going out and interviewing teachers and counselors with the focus on bilingual people or the people who understand ESL instruction. There are so many, many issues.

My budget was several million, but to establish a library takes a lot of money, and by then, we're talking computers and furniture and books and media. They thought no one would notice, and they wanted to use it somewhere else–and not for Juarez.

Carmen: This speaks to expectation and respect, and again, what do we need the library for? And we dared buy the books in Spanish, too!

Angela: And then I called the community and said, "I have discovered that there's this money missing to open up the library. I've gone and verified it. I want you to know because you're going to need to get that money." I did that in one afternoon, and by eight o'clock the next morning, I got a call: "Someone at the district would like to meet with you in fifteen minutes." I had already hired the librarian at that point, and she was Mexican. I thought this is about the money, so when she happened to be there, I said, "We've got to go. They're going to ask me about this money, and you're going to have to explain why we need the money. I can't do as good a job as you." I walked into the room, and it's a room I'd never seen before in that place. It's not one of those obvious conference rooms.

And they were all there. They were around the table, seven of them.

Carmen: I can picture them.

Angela: And I went, *Uh-oh.* So anyway, we presented our case for getting money out. And they sounded like they might be putting it back. I didn't ask, "Why'd you take it out? Where'd it go?" I don't care. It's the money for the school. And that afternoon, I get called to another meeting in the community. It happened so fast. And for whatever reason, I didn't get there. I might have been one or two minutes late. All I remember, they were all seated around his desk, and he was sitting there, and he had saved one seat for me. That was the only time I was willing to sit next to him. We discussed the money, and he said, "You'll get it back. Tell the community it'll be back in your hands." One of the community organizations had demanded to meet with him because of the money, so he quickly put together this meeting.

I was in charge of curriculum, and I wanted the departments to examine if they were really meeting the goals and standards that were required by a high-school curriculum, whether it was the city's or our own, because we had done some of our own curriculum development since the city had not really updated its curriculum guides in high school for over twenty years. It had been a long time. We started this exercise. Some departments really did well and seriously sat down and said, "Are we reaching our goals? If we're not, why aren't we, and how do we know we've accomplished it?" Typical goal-setting and administration type of thing.

The administration met, and so we sat down and started to talk about what we saw as problems: attendance, and because attendance was so low, we suspected the dropout rate. The dropout concern was supported by the fact that when we admitted our freshman class, it was at least six hundred students. When we graduated, it was—

Carmen: How many students, Angela?

Angela: Six hundred usually came in. This is like in '83, and I realized that we have six hundred incoming students. In our graduating class four years later was usually two hundred or less. Clearly, something was going on, and it couldn't be all transfer outs or anything like that. We decided to really seriously look at our dropout rates and came to the conclusion that we had a serious dropout problem. And we proceeded to do something about it. And this was in spite of the fact that we were considered the terrific school. The ambiance *was* terrific, but the ambiance can fool you and help you to avoid looking at the reality of some of the problems.

Clearly, if you start with six hundred and you end up with two hundred or less, there's something going on. So we began to look at absences and some kids. We knew a lot of anecdotal stuff about kids who had to work the third shift and come to school after the third shift, because they were supporting their family–kids for who we tried to adjust their program so that they could work, and it still was too much for them. But there were a lot of problems. In some cases, families are just so poor.

English language was the cause of the dropout problem. In terms of the transitional bilingual-education program, we would find that, at least when I left, 45 percent of our graduates had been in a bilingual-education program at a certain point in their education. And I remember talking to someone about this, and he told me it was over 50 percent. But if you were in the bilingual-education program, it appeared–no one did a study on it–that you had a better chance of graduating than if you were not.

I don't know what the statistics are today, but one of the things about a bilingual-ed program is that it is a smaller community, and the teachers tend to collaborate because they've got such a narrow curriculum–they have to deal with that; they have to communicate in order to support the students and support their own program. And of course, you have to have a good coordinator that makes sure there's some continuity going through the program. The departments at a high-school level are just like a university level. They're all competing with each other, and you can't tell me what to do. Language becomes such an issue in those programs.

All those curriculum issues come up, including "Are we going to teach Spanish to Spanish speakers and not just Spanish to non-Spanish speakers?" We were part of–not the academic decathlon, but there was a time that all the west-side schools were involved in the academic competition. I forget, but it was an academic competition, and there's all these subject matters. And most of the schools were African American. Our African American teachers had to fight to include the Latin American studies part, because there was no African American studies program. So they actually had to rationalize it. You had these whole big committee meetings. The other issue was they wouldn't allow us to compete in the Spanish competition, because they said that it was too easy. Everybody agreed that we would have non-Spanish speakers compete. Those who were English dominant and had studied Spanish at the school would compete. They wouldn't allow it. The committee of the schools wouldn't allow it. What the language department did was say, "We're going to show them. We're going to compete in French, and we're going to win." And they did. They got first place in French! You can imagine how all of this helps kids to really firm up their identity, who they are, especially when you see teachers going, "This is wrong." They would not let Juarez compete in the Spanish portion, so they went on and won in the French.

Today, the administration does respond to community demands. That's why we have community high schools. The mothers and grandmothers went on a hunger strike. They will respond to that. But the issue is, why do we have to do that? Doesn't it make sense that morally, you feel responsible to do something? The Mexican community has been overcrowded since the late '60s in the schools. That's how long? And I keep saying–I say to the CEO, "Haven't you figured it out yet?" No one's figured it out. A new administration comes in and forgets about all the old problems: "They're not mine." That's how long. I've been teaching in overcrowded schools for 90 percent of my career in the schools.

> Today, the administration does respond to community demands. That's why we have community high schools. The mothers and grandmothers went on a hunger strike. They will respond to that. But the issue is, why do we have to do that? Doesn't it make sense that morally, you feel responsible to do something?

It's not true everywhere in the city. If you find a TIF district that is gentrifying, you will find underutilized schools. The first school that I was assigned to had a large Puerto Rican and Mexican population, is being considered for closure because it's underutilized. There aren't any kids there. Lot of condos! I was principal of a school where there is big gentrification. As those new property assessments came in, those For Sale signs went up. It was an underutilized school, and many of the kids came from the northwest side. People that were middle class don't send their kids to the schools. Lane was a very poor school, and it could only be because it was predominately Latino; it wasn't based on scores. I took my scores with me, to my parents, and showed them. Where is this a bad school? So you know, I don't see that we have the power at the administrative level. I don't know who's taking the leadership to serve our students.

Partners with Community

Carmen: There is also education going on in the community, like here at the community medical center. Early on, for example, we would have a summer program and ask the Boy Scouts, Girl Scouts, and Health Explorers for names and how we would identify who would come. The youth who said they wanted summer jobs would apply. They would give me a batch of names of kids who were interested in health careers. We would help them prepare a résumé and all that. We did a couple things. We developed a curriculum over the years, because we had that program around seven or eight years. In fact, the curriculum was utilized by new high school teachers.

For example, when the students came in, we did a pretest and a posttest. We wanted to have a survey, and they developed it. It asked what they thought about the health issues, and they kind of ranked what the issues were, and then we kind of talked about that. Initially, we started out with dual sexuality, which showed the miracles of life and what their responsibilities were to each other. We would have some of the students give little workshops. They would demonstrate how to use a condom and things like that. And we did it, I think, for around seven years. We had binders, and teachers from Juarez would come and get ideas from them.

Now we have partnerships within the schools. There's a component that says if you have comprehensive activities going on at a school that involve not only learning activities but other kinds of playful things happening to the kids, their parents learn English. Offer a lot of aerobic classes, and you're partners per item, depending on what item. Be a health partner, and we then have a lot of health education and prevention, cancer awareness—things like that. We also have a school-based health clinic. Well, that gives us another kind of opportunity. Yes, in many ways, community-based organizations absolutely give probably what you call the educational aspects of on-the-job training.

I still believe that I look at the new high school as "What does the community think?" I personally believe we have lost. I was trying to figure it out. We were on the board between '74 and '80. Are we playing games in the sense of "Okay, we once had two hundred kids. Then the second year, it was one hundred seventy-five; the third year was less; and the fourth year was even less"? And this was in the 1970s. We are now how many years later?

Angela: Thirty-five.

Carmen: To me, we have lost, if you're just taking it by tens, three generations. I think we've lost more than that, and by "lost," I mean that it's the manpower, the brain power, the society power to make a difference. Not the ABCs that they learned, because I'm a product of a Catholic school. I had the same shit in the public schools that I had in the Catholic schools. They expected nothing of me; I gave them nothing. To me, it's an individual making a difference, giving people hope, individuals hope. How would you like to be undocumented and female, depending on a male for "Do I go out? Do I know how to drive? Do I know how to speak the language? I have to wait until he gives me money to go out and buy bread."

Angela: So there are also some cultural issues that don't help the situation.

Carmen: And girls not being allowed to go to where you show them different colleges.

Angela: One of the STEP programs we developed at the new high school was at the university, and originally, two high schools were asked to join the discussion. Unfortunately, when they invited one of them, they didn't invite anyone from the school; it was just community people. It becomes a challenge if they don't have a good relationship to carry it through. The program started exclusively at one school, and we would identify students in the eighth grade that were graduating that appeared to want to go to college, were doing pretty well in school–didn't matter if they were English proficient. They could be in bilingual education, or maybe their grades weren't too great but their teacher felt they could do well. They were recruited for this program.

Carmen: It was run by a couple, a man and wife–very committed individuals.

Angela: They touched hundreds and hundreds of students.

Carmen: The parents knew the couple. They were a married couple. There was respect for them. The kids respected them. They had an opportunity not to be threatened by their peers, and it worked. They had to work.

Angela: The students would go on Saturdays. The parents became part of the program immediately. That was the only way we could convince the parents that their kids didn't have to stay home on Saturday and do chores. The better option for them was to go to the university. And initially, they were going to start off with math, because it was the quantitative areas we were trying to get students into. It ended up with a little literacy and basic math to start, because there were bilingual students as part of it. The other thing was buses were rented to pick them up in the Juarez parking lot and then take them to the university and bring them back. There was no messing around with this program. There were a few students who thought, *Well, we'll go out to lunch, and we're not going to come back.* If you did that, you're gone from the program. It was very strictly run and the kind of thing parents would want.

Carmen: High expectations.

Angela: And there was a very good completion rate for those kids. One of the top researchers at the public schools right now went through the program. She went to Princeton or Yale, and a couple of years ago, she earned her PhD from University of Chicago. She went far beyond expectations in terms of the students in general. There were many other students who also went to places like MIT, who went to just a lot of different universities. It's a real challenge if you're undocumented, because you don't get scholarship money.

Carmen and Angela: Many were.

Carmen: What are our challenges today? It's racist. We're good enough to take care of the babies. We're good enough to feed you, to work in the factories. There is no respect. There's no value that is given to us. That is our problem. All the others: health education, low-income housing, environment—those all fall in. Our numbers are speaking to power. It's not going to be our challenge anymore. It's down to society's challenge.

Angela: You know, in the educational system, we just need many more bilingual, bicultural teachers. I know from my own experience walking down the hall, I would have two of our female students stop me in the hall: "Okay, are you Mexican or Puerto Rican?" And I would say I'm Mexican. And the Mexican girl would turn to her Puerto Rican friend and say, "See? I told you!" [laughs] It matters; it matters because they see someone in a position that they consider not bad. That's pretty good. We don't see enough of that. We can even have non-Mexican people who are empathetic for the culture and language.

Carmen: For example, whether it's education or health, of all the nurses in this country, 2 percent are bilingual, bicultural—2 percent! When we opened this facility, one of the rules were anyone who is going to have direct patient care had to be fluent Spanish speaking. That was f'ing hard. I'll bet you I wouldn't hire you. I wouldn't hire my own niece. I wouldn't hire my mother.

Angela: And when I was at the new high school, I had bilingual special-education programs. I had my contacts with the universities. I hear about someone graduating from the university, and I recruited a lot of teachers from there. I understood that people liked to have teachers for a long time. It's hard to recruit all the time, but I understood that if I hired a qualified bilingual special-education teacher, I had, at most, a year and would have to go looking again, because they would just be recruited away.

Meeting the Needs

Carmen: We have the public schools, we have the Catholic schools, and now we have the Jesuit school. For sure, it has success stories—absolutely. I believe, and I don't have this knowledge intimately, but I can document it.

It would be very interesting to see, if there are two elementary schools—one Catholic and one public—where they go to school, who succeeds not only academically but socially. Because I think the academic part is very important, and especially depending on your career, but the social aspect is key to making a difference in your community.

Angela: Do they have bilingual education? Do they have special education? Do they have bilingual special education? In the Catholic schools, I don't know if they have any bilingual teachers that teach bilingually. I don't know if they have English-as-a-second-language instruction. And we know they keep closing schools. So it's not that they're holding onto students.

Carmen: The Jesuits came around asking kind of the same question, asking, "What are parents looking for? What do kids want?" They want to be in a safe environment. They want to be cared about. We're not talking about the ABCs. We're talking about the human aspect.

Angela: *Personalismo.*

That's one of the reasons the university is so successful with Latino students graduating. Personalismo is part of their mission. It doesn't mean they're great with all their kids, but there's an *alismo*. It's certainly a key factor, and that's what the new high school has: personalismo. That's what the medical center has. I know that when I was there, the new high school certainly had that. If a person from central administration walked in the building, our students would ask, "May I help you?" That sort of shocked the hell out of the school superintendent. She had to tell me, "I walked into the building, and a student came up and asked me if he could help me." This is someone who went into high schools all the time, and that didn't happen.

So personalismo is really important. And when that is established, some people think that that's where it ends—that once you get through with that role, you don't have to worry about anything else. Well, not true. There's certainly the educational development of kids. When I was hiring, someone in the community came to me and said, "Oh, you have to hire Senora So-and-So; she's just wonderful with kids—bilingual, bicultural." I looked at her straight in the eye and said, "But can she teach?" They didn't know. She had this wonderful personality, but it's not enough. We need good teachers—personalities, personal, bicultural. We need teachers who are committed. A teacher who says to me, "This is just a job"—you're gone. This is not just a job. This is kids' lives, so you need that kind of commitment. In spite of all the shit that goes on in the school, you have to remain focused on the kids.

It's very tough to do.

Reflections

Angela and Carmen both worked diligently to strengthen their community. They recognized the existing inequalities and collaborated with city officials and local residents to advocate for and implement a new high school to serve their community. They both describe how politically charged that initiative was and how they developed the skills necessary to collaborate and bring it to fruition. They ensured that services previously denied, such as special education and bilingual education, were delivered with high standards. Driving their commitment was the concept of personalismo: treating everyone with respect and listening to their needs. Underneath it all was a strong sense of who they were and helping to preserve the community's cultural and ethnic heritage while dreaming forward.

They were also instrumental in developing a medical center located in the heart of the community to provide services not available earlier. They talked about the importance of reaching out to the community for input and serving entire families. They both emphasized the importance of developing partnerships with colleges and community groups to get everyone involved.

19

Joel

Joel was a student in the College Bridge dual-enrollment program, and he offered to tell me his story after hearing about my request for interviews. Joel came to my office and opened up as if he had never before had the opportunity to talk about his life. He told what it means to be undocumented while wanting to continue with his education. His story is one of hope laced with an anxiety about his future.

Family Background

My name's Joel, and I'm eighteen years old. I'm currently working at a factory, and I'm going to a two-year college. I have one younger brother, fifteen. His name's Pedro, and I have a younger sister who's eight now, and her name's Andrea. My mom's living with us, and my dad right now's in Mexico because of some family issues he had over there. So right now, we're the only family we got. There's nobody else in the U.S. for us—just us.

I'm not sure why we came to the U.S. I'm still a little confused because over there, we had a house that was paid for, and over here, we don't have nothing. We only have each other. Over there, my mom had a job; my dad had a job too. From what my mom tells me, she wanted a better life for me and my brother; she just wanted us to be raised and know everything we could possibly know about anything. She said that from what she knew, the U.S. was the place to get all that. So basically, at a young age, we came here. My aunt came this summer and told me I was eight when we came here, but I don't remember. We still have a home there. I don't remember it, but I know we have a home.

I have not been back. I'm shown pictures of my family, but I could care less. I guess because I don't really know them or remember them. I talk to them, and they're like, "We miss you." It's cool. I miss them too, but I just don't know who they are. Both my grandparents on my mom's and dad's side just passed away. It kind of sucks, because I see my mom, and she's all hurt. I don't know what to tell her, because I don't really remember my grandpa that much. I know it's her dad, and I feel for her because she's my mom; I honestly don't know how to attack the situation. My heart goes out to her, but I really don't know how to feel. I totally wish I knew him. Maybe I could understand where they're coming from, and they could understand me, but I didn't really talk to them.

When I got to the U.S., things got so annoying, because my dad was here before my mom. He sent for us. My dad had a house, and we were living in Arizona at the time; he had some money, because he sent us to private school. The school was nice; I'm not complaining, but the teachers weren't as nice as the school. The teachers were horrible. Like I said, I had trouble spelling things in Spanish. I didn't even know English, and these people didn't go out of their way to say, "Oh, we're going to get you somebody who understands you, somebody who speaks your language." The only person who spoke Spanish there was the principal, and how often did I get to see him?

Early Education and Language

My dad understands English, and he is able to ask for directions, but that's it. He doesn't know a lot. My mom understands it now, but back then, she didn't know anything. I didn't know what I was supposed to do. I'd ask my mom, "Can you help me?" She would say, "I don't know English." My dad would say, "You'll figure it out." My dad never translated anything. He didn't know how to read English, and the few words that he did understand would be things that he would have trouble even explaining to me, because he himself didn't fully understand them. So I would just have to show up to school with a half-assed assignment, and my teacher would take it just for the sake of me not whining. The only people helping me translate were the students, and they didn't really want to help me.

I hated school. I didn't understand math, and people wouldn't help me. I was horrible at writing; I was even bad at saying the alphabet. That's how bad

I was. I misspelled words; the whole little comma on top of the letters would throw me off all the time. It was just bad; it was a wreck. My mom would try to help me out whenever she could when she got home from work. But that was late, and I had to do all the learning by myself.

I remember after school, I would be picked up by my aunt because my mom's work was not near my school. I would do my homework with my cousin. We would help each other. I really didn't get this; nobody wants to help me out. My mom's not here. My brother's out there crying and going crazy because we basically raised ourselves. I raised my brother, and I know my brother is raising my sister. We kind of, like, teach each other. My parents were always working. Whenever we would hang out as a family, it would be so weird. Me and my brother would tease each other because we were hanging out with my mom.

> I remember after school I would be picked up by my aunt because my mom's work was not near my school. I would do my homework with my cousin. We would help each other. I really didn't get this; nobody wants to help me out.

My teachers–they never really asked who helped you with your homework or how it was that you did this so fine and yesterday you couldn't even spell this word. Oftentimes, I would lie: "Oh, my mom helped me," just so they would get off my back. And then this kind of like crashed, and we're having the whole student-teacher and parent-teacher meetings. My ma was there, and she's like, "What do you mean this is not your work?" She blew my cover. "This is your cousin's! This is way too out of your league; how are you going to use a word this long?" So that's basically how she blew my cover, but my teachers didn't care: I'm showing up with something.

I felt alone, like kids didn't want to hang out with me. They didn't want to talk to me, and they would be making fun of me behind my back. They would talk to me in Spanish and say something about me in English. I would hear my name, and they would look at me. The teachers–I don't know if they knew what was going on. I wouldn't say anything, though. My parents told me not to say anything, because when report card pickup in Arizona came, I was making As and Bs. My parents were like, "If you're making it now with As and Bs, keep your mouth shut; you've got a good thing going. Don't say anything." I think they were giving

> I felt alone, like kids didn't want to hang out with me. They didn't want to talk to me, and they would be making fun of me behind my back. They would talk to me in Spanish and say something about me in English. I would hear my name, and they would look at me.

me fake grades. The only homework I would do would be stuff that required me to draw something or draw some type of emotion with a drawing; that's what I would do. That's the only assignment I would do.

I guess it was a pretty well-known school, because I remember my principal coming into classes with other people in suits, going around and checking over kids' shoulders to see what they were doing. Sometimes they would sit in class. Some guys were important. During those times, they would tell us to go somewhere else. They're like, "We got something set up for you at this class. Go and do whatever you're told." Okay, and half the time, I was sitting in an empty classroom with dudes just staring at me. My brother and I didn't say anything; we were scared.

I honestly was hoping immigration would come and get me so I could leave. I honestly didn't understand why my family came to the U.S. This was making me and my brother fall behind in school. I didn't get anything at all school-wise. I didn't understand nothing. In Mexico, I usually got some sense; they were speaking my language. If anything, I understood what I was supposed to be doing. I would think, *If you work with me, I will do it. I will put that extra energy to get my assignment done.* But over here, they just wanted me off their back, and I guess I got the grades I wanted.

It was not as bad when we moved to Los Angeles, because there, my teacher would sometimes talk to me in Spanish. He would tell me about the assignments. There, I was at least turning in something. Whatever it was, at least I tried, and he will know I tried. But I would get to school, and kids would ask me, "Hey, did you do this assignment?" I only thought we had one. "No. We had five homework assignments." Five? I had no idea there were all these other assignments due. Either I forgot, or I guess it skipped the teacher's mind to tell me. There the grades—all my As turned into Fs. Like, all my grades were real now. They were like F, F, F, C, F.

This was still elementary school. When I got here, I was in fifth grade. They opened up a school around my neighborhood called the Explorers Academy. My mom tried so bad to get me and my brother in there because she thought they would help us out. My mom would wake up early and make sure that my name and my brother's were the first ones on the list; she made sure that my name was there. My mom would go to school and would ask so many people, "What's going on? Are they name picking this week? Next week? I want to know." She dragged us with her. Me and my brother were there even though we were already in school somewhere else. In the meantime, I was learning to speak English a little because I was forced to. I ended up doing bills at the age of ten because my mom didn't know how to read them. She would have me read them to her; that was my practice of English.

By some miracle, me and my brother were both picked out; we both started school. I was a grade behind, and I was placed in fourth grade because my math was horrible; my English was not good at all. I didn't really know how to speak it, and I didn't know how to write it that well. So instead of putting me in a class with just an English-speaking teacher, they put me in an ESL class, full-time ESL. The whole day, I was there in ESL. You would still do history and English, math, and all that, but it would be in Spanish. Everything else was in English; everything that we wrote was English, English, English. They really forced it down my throat.

I would get into my class with my teacher, and we would do English in the morning–basic, really easy English. He would help us on the Spanish a lot, way more. He would do the most help ever. After English, he would do history, and he wouldn't do American history; he would teach us a lot of Mexican history. He would be going back from Spanish to English. That was really the rule of the day: "I get this. He's teaching me in Spanish, and I kind of understand it in English when I'm reading it." So it really helped me out a lot.

This time, I had friends; I felt like I was part of something. I would get in trouble, and he would make us write a thousand times, "I will not do this" in English. I really got my *will*s and *I*s, and I understood all that. I would be at home, and I would do it for fun. I knew I would get in trouble, so just for the hell of it, some days, I would write them for the next time. I would have a piece of paper with five hundred "I wills." Just in case I get in trouble tomorrow, I already had them done.

But we were stuck: it wasn't like a regular class. It was a classroom/ storage space, so he had, on one side of the classroom, a big old closet where they kept books. The cool thing about this class was that it was very chill, very laid back. We'd do the work, get in groups, help each other out, and basically, the classroom was ours. We'd go study somewhere. Me and my little posse decided to hang out in the closet. All the books were there, and we would climb the stair to the roof and throw books at each other from the top. I don't know why we would do that; I guess it was fun back then.

We always got caught because this teacher was a strict man. He was raised in Mexico with Mexican parents. I honestly don't know why he was being so tough, and he's got to be the toughest teacher I've ever had. But it worked; with me, it worked. I guess I needed that extra push because I already had the nobody-cares attitude. So what if I don't do my work, and what if I talk in class? I'm not going to get in trouble. But this guy–you really couldn't do that. If you misbehaved, there were consequences with this guy.

Even though we hated doing the "I wills" and the "I won't do this in class" and "I will not talk," it was nice to just have somebody, a teacher, actually care enough to get us in trouble or tell you that you did a good job. Feedback on anything was, at that time, better than nothing. And this teacher wouldn't be like my other teachers, who wouldn't call my parents. If I did something wrong, my parents would find out before I did. He would let me know at the end of the class, and by then, my parents already knew that I did something wrong. So my mom got a report on my schoolwork, and she was always down there. Half the time, it wasn't because it was bad; it was because he saw improvement, or he thought she should be helping me out with my English.

Even though we hated doing the "I wills" and the "I won't do this in class" and "I will not talk," it was nice to just have somebody, a teacher, actually care enough to get us in trouble or tell you that you did a good job. Feedback on anything was, at that time, better than nothing. And this teacher wouldn't be like my other teachers, who wouldn't call my parents.

Fifth and sixth grade, my classes were never mixed; ESL class was full-time, all the time. Seventh grade, after lunch, they would take me out for a good hour to my ESL class. When school was over, since I had bad grades before, they put me in after-school classes all the time. I would stay for an hour of ESL classes. My friends saw, and they didn't have to stay. They'd just go home. I'd have to stay with other students who I had never even met. I was getting extra help after school, but it really sucked when summer came along, because everyone got their summer off, but not me. By seventh grade, the school told my parents it was optional, but they made me go. Anything I could fit into that brain, I had to take it. No questions asked. It built up my GPA.

Actually, after seventh grade, after I started asking my principal for me to be put in English classes, my mom would make me speak to her in English: "Speak to me in English. I want to learn." She learned it well enough to understand it but not to speak it; there is always the pronunciation. I guess she is scared of saying it wrong, and it will mean something else, so she doesn't speak it.

Language in the Workplace

She doesn't need it at work. I know because I was working with my mom this summer, and I lost a job for knowing English; I was working at a plastics factory. This was June, and I had just graduated. My mom had worked there for a year, and she got me the job. Basically, you're like a zombie in there; you don't talk. You just do what you are told. They give you a big old machine to take care of and spitting out big old baskets of plastic; you have to cut the extra plastic that's coming out the end. You cut it and stack it, and you're done. You repeat for twelve hours.

This is my first job, right? It was a twelve-hour shift: we started at 6:00 at night and worked until 6:00 in the morning. I'm not sure how the working laws are. I'm not real well informed about that, but they were only giving us one break at midnight. At midnight, lunch, forty minutes, and after that, they would ask us, like around two in the morning, if you wanted to go to the bathroom. You better believe that I wanted to go to the bathroom, because if you didn't get that five minutes to sit down, you stood the whole time. If you didn't get that five minutes to sit down, it was a long night.

I got the job through a staffing agency. They send out workers to factories that need workers. My mom talked to her supervisor, and they looked for my name, and I got the job. Nobody told anybody that I spoke English; nobody said anything. The only people that spoke English there was the supervisors that spoke broken English. They kind of knew well enough to talk, to say basic things in the working areas. The mechanics were all black. So I'm working; nobody's talking to me. I don't have any friends, and this mechanic comes and tells me by hand gestures that my machine was going to be shut off. I said, "That's cool, man. I got it." He said,

> "Don't speak English in front of the supervisors. They've got some major, like–they're breaking the law here, man." I said, "I don't understand. Why are they breaking the law, dude?" "Dude, you only get one break in twelve hours, and that's your lunch break. Honestly, do you think that's fair?" "It's my first job. I wouldn't know."

"Wait. You speak English? I didn't know anybody spoke English here. Don't speak English in front of the supervisors. They've got some major, like–they're breaking the law here, man." I said, "I don't understand. Why are they breaking the law, dude?" "Dude, you only get one break in twelve hours, and that's your lunch break. Honestly, do you think that's fair?" "It's my first job. I wouldn't know." "How much are you getting paid?" "I think seven fifty." "Seven fifty? You know, the minimum wage now is eight dollars." "Really? I didn't know none of this." And my mom–I guess she didn't know, or if she knew, she wasn't saying anything. I told my mom that we were supposed to be getting eight dollars, and she didn't know that.

During lunch, they have these posters up on the walls, and they're talking about the laws and all this. So I'm reading them during lunch, and I found out that guy's right: June 1, 2009, eight-dollar minimum wage goes up. I'm afraid of losing my job, so I didn't say anything to the supervisors. I only talked to the mechanics all the time, because they loved me. They always would come talk to me, because the mechanics didn't like the Mexicans; the Mexicans blamed everything on the mechanics because they didn't know. So the mechanics didn't really get along with anybody else, only me and the supervisors, because I spoke English. The mechanics are like, "Don't let them find out that you know English." "Why not?" "Because you can lose your job, or you can be out of here; they're afraid of people like you that know English, because you could say something about it. If they catch you speaking to me, you could be in trouble." Actually, that's around the time a supervisor passed. He came up to me and the mechanics, and he just laughed. The supervisor says in Spanish, "If you don't understand them, it's fine. You don't have to talk to them; just look for one of the supervisors. They have these blue coats. Look for one of us, and we'll translate."

That's when it got me. They're speaking to me in Spanish, and I responded in English. Like, I know English; I'm more comfortable speaking to them in English than I am to any worker in here in Spanish. Then she looked at me weird, like, "You know English?" "Yeah, I know English." That's when I started noticing a lot of the supervisors hanging out in my area, making sure I was there, making sure I wasn't talking to them. A week afterward, it was a Friday. Friday was my last day. On Monday, when I showed up back at the agency, they called everyone's name but mine. And they pulled me aside and made me go back behind the little counter thing. "We have been informed that you were caught stealing." I was like, "Stealing what? I don't understand. Stealing? I'm standing in one area twelve hours. If I wanted to steal one of those big old buckets, there's no way I could get it out without anybody seeing me. What did I steal?" They're like, "You stole some tools." They weren't even specific on what I stole. Apparently, I stole something that was of value, so they took it from my check. I wasn't paid that week. I was paid fifty bucks because whatever equipment I had stolen was one hundred and some dollars. I lost my job. I wasn't allowed to go back to that agency anymore; that agency wouldn't employ me anymore.

Moving into High School

At my high school, the teachers cared. If I were like five minutes late, there was a text from my teacher, asking, "Where are you at?" I'm like, "Man, chill, there was traffic." My school became like my second home. I would rather be at school than be at home, because school fed me; school taught me. I was there most of my time. My teacher became like my mom, and my principal, my dad. My principal's always there. He would have lunch with us, and we would talk to him. He was cool. He was down to earth. It was like I was talking to a dad I never had. He was always there. And everything with him was education–everything. And he would always have these cool little lectures to get us to do things education-wise. And my teacher, my adviser, always cared. If we were doing an assignment for a different class, she was like, "Whoa, what's going on? How come you didn't do your assignment for the history?" And we're like, "We had something at home." "Well, what happened at home?" Meetings after school with the teacher, just you and them talking–just talking, nothing grade related. Everything was loose, just you and a person talking, which was awesome because that's what I wouldn't get at home.

Throughout my high school and even now, my mom's still working at this factory, and luckily, they raised their check up to eight dollars now. I guess because they were afraid or something. My mom's been working from 6:00 to 6:00 forever, ever since she's been working there, which has been like two years already. If it wasn't at that factory, it was a different factory. It was kind of by luck she would get a job, because she basically had to beat everybody else to the agency to make sure she was there first so she could be signed up first to a factory. So throughout high school, my mom worked from 6:00 in the morning; she was gone before I woke up, and she was gone before I got home. Then I started taking university classes, and I really didn't see her then. I would see my mom maybe a good three hours a week.

Even though I didn't see her, I knew she knew what I was doing. Like, me taking classes at a university was good, so that got through her head. And it was hard convincing her to let me take classes, because she's like, "You need a social [social security number] to take classes." I told her that my teachers have reassured me that you don't need one. So the whole social thing has been a wall between her and wanting to move forward in her life. It's the same thing with us. If we ever want to do anything at all, like go anywhere job-wise, school-wise, we have to ask, "Do you need one?" And if you do, then you can't do it, because it's just a risk my mom is not willing for us to take, because we're her kids, and she doesn't want to be split up.

My teachers convinced me to take College Bridge classes. I was on my mom's side on this one. I saw that my mom knows best. And my principal would take me and my friend out to lunch. After school, he would take us out to eat, and we would talk about home, school, and he basically convinced me, "You got to do it, man, especially because you don't have a social. And school after high school's going to be tough for you. You got to do it now. You can do it for free." So that really got to me. Now that I'm out of high school and taking college classes already and paying for them, I got to tell you, it really sucks when you save up a good $2,000 and then they're gone like that before you even spend them, because you need to pay for your classes.

The Path to College

I decided to go to this college because we took a school college field trip to visit this school. At the time–it was during junior year–I wasn't really taking college too seriously. I don't think I can go to college, because my mom needs help. My dad's not there already. She needs an extra provider, someone to help put food on the table. And then I started–I met more people, and my friends were coming here too, and a lot of them were in the same situation I was in. They had a different mind-set. They're like, "No! Going to school is what's going to keep me out of working at a factory." I'm like, "You know what? That's right."

If I already have an associate's, that's thumbs-up for me. That's an open door right there. And even if it's not, if I go back to Mexico, I still have that degree. I know English, so that's another plus. But yeah, my friends helped me through that, and I see my mom struggle. I don't want to work at a factory the rest of my life, no. I want to be far from them. It really sucked when I graduated from high school that I had to crawl with my tail between my legs to my mom that I can't get a job. And it sucks it had to be in a factory, but I needed the money.

Now she supports me. She says, "You're going, and you're doing this for yourself and for us. You're setting an example for your brother and your sister." She's really sentimental about that. Because I'm her oldest son, and I'm doing something. I'm taking up after her; that's what she says instead of after my dad. I'm studying and working a job at the same time. She knows the schedule I'm working with, and it's kind of crazy. I don't see her any more than she sees me. So I basically go to sleep, wake up; she goes to sleep, and I'm out. So if that's what I have to do to pay for a class. Right now, I can only afford to go part-time, so I'm only taking two.

I am way prepared for this. Classes here in college are an hour. I feel, if anything, they're stealing my money, because my classes at the university College Bridge program were four hours long. I would go there and really feel like, "Okay, I understand this, and I got four hours ahead of me. If I don't get it right now, I'm going to get it before I'm out of this door." And now you come in, and your teacher's late, like fifteen minutes; there goes a good chunk of your class time. It really sucks because my teachers do come in late. And what the hell am I learning? That's money going down the drain, time that I pay for that I'm not getting. It's up to me now to do the extra learning on the side. So if I'm not sleeping in the library because I'm too tired from work, I have to read that bio book, because I know I'm not doing good in bio, and I got to learn it.

It's funny, because I'm taking 102-level classes; these are sophomores, juniors. These are people who are twenty-eight years old. Here I took classes with like older people, in their thirties. They weren't as young. These are really tall people, and I'm just like the shortest one in class. I'm the only Latino in there. I'm just like, "Whoa!" It's really funny to see, like, all these people—they're like towers above me. Okay, man. Because I was studying with older people here, it was like I'm studying with a relative; this could be my mom, as long as she's helping me out. It made me feel like I'm not too far from home. They were older people, understanding people. At Morton College, they're younger.

Gangs in the Community

My brother is now in high school. He's going to a charter school, the high school that just opened up on Forty-Seventh. He doesn't take any ESL classes now. He went through that with me, and now Uno is very, very strict, so he's up at 6:40; he's there at 7:00, starts school at 8:00, and gets home at 5:00 in the afternoon. He hates going there, because it's the time; it's so crazy. My mom made sure he went to a charter school, and even if he didn't want to, he was going to go over her dead body. My brother wanted to go to the local school with his friends. My mom's like, "No, you're not going to go to there, because we're growing up in a bad neighborhood, and there's a lot of gangs."

My brother and I—not to say we're affiliated with gangs, but we know a lot of gang members who are our friends. We don't treat them as gang members; it's just like, "Hey, you're my friend. I met you before you were in the gang; we're still cool with each other." My mom knows that a lot of our friends are in that situation. And a lot of our friends go to places that have gangs. I'm guessing she has friends who have kids in those schools that tell her that they get into a lot of fights. And she finds out. I don't know; I guess it's that motherly instinct. She just finds out that it's a bad school, and she's afraid that because of friends that already joined the gang, we might join the gang, I guess. Not to say she doesn't trust us; she's just fierce for us that we might fall into that mind-set that since my dad didn't care for me, they're going to care for me. They're my brother and sister.

That's what my mom believes. That's why she steers us from that, because she knows that a lot of our friends don't have fathers there for them or somebody to encourage them to go to school. They don't have moms or dads who went that extra step to take care of them, do the stuff she did to get us into fairly tough education. So she's like, "Hell, I'm going to get you there if it kills me. Even if I have to pay your principal extra money, as long as I know I'm going to keep you safe. If you can't be safe around this neighborhood, I at least know you can be safe at school." She doesn't have to go to work worrying like crap: *My kid could get into a fight tonight because there's this gang at that school.*

When I was going to a community-based high school, I worried a little because during winter, it was dark, and I actually got into some trouble with that. I was jumped once, and that really scared my mom; it really, really, really scared her. *This is my oldest son, and he could have been taken away from me*—so that really scared her. I guess this was around, like, my junior year. I'm like, "These things happen." But my mom must not want to think like that. She said, "No. They happen for a reason, and that's because you weren't being cautious or because you were doing this the wrong way." But just the fact that I got jumped and I got beat up and my stuff was stolen away from me, that would boost her up on why we should be more careful in school, because if you can't be safe in the streets, at least be safe in school. And she sometimes— because I know, okay, so I don't have a social.

Persistence and Goals

So I'm going to school, and it kind of gets depressing when you talk to the people at work. They're like, "Why do you go to school?" One lady asked me, "Why do you go to school?" I said, "Because I don't want to work here forever." She said, "Do you have a social?" "No, I don't." She thinks, "You're going to get that degree, that piece of paper that tells you you went, took classes, and you're going to end up here. You don't have a social. No one in a professional field is going to hire you if you don't have a social." That kind of gets to you, because in Mexico, I don't have anything. Like I said, I'm more comfortable speaking English than I am Spanish. When I'm speaking to my mom in Spanish, I'm fighting to get the right word. It's easier for me to speak to her in English. If I go back to Mexico, it's going to be like, "What the hell am I going to do over there?" People speak Spanish. My Spanish is not as good as it used to be back then. I can definitely understand it; speaking it could take me some time to come up with the right words.

But in a sense, they're right. You got to keep up that optimism. You got to be like, "Things are going to change," because if they don't, you know you got to deal with it or make the change. You got to do something. If I have this degree already, I'm not going to have it up on the wall. I'm going to do something. I already have this knowledge—why not use it? Use it for the better and help other people out, and maybe start a movement. Make sure things get changed, because if they don't, what the hell's the point—getting up, go to work, going back home, sleep, pay bills? That's not a life. That really sucks.

I think for change to happen, I would start with the family. This is something I assumed because I grew up with a broken family, and from what teachers told me, it starts in the family. If you already have a dad who really doesn't care about education, a mom who was never really there for you, and you're basically raising your brother, like I was, then that's really messed up. I was changing diapers at the age of ten because my mom was at work. Luckily, she was at work. I don't know what would have happened to me if I didn't have a mom who cared so much. I could only imagine all the other kids who don't have parents. I'd die. I think you would start with the family, and then from there, you would go to the community to start something.

In three years, hopefully I'll be out of college for sure. Whatever degree I may have, I'm not quite sure. I'm not quite there. But I know I'm going to be working a good job. Hopefully, everything with the whole social gets fixed. That would be great. If not, I got to go around it. I can't give up, because if I do, what are my brother and sister going to do? It's up to me, basically.

It's a tough question about leaving the community, because me and my friends grew up with each other, and we're all in the same situation. If I leave, I guess I'd feel like, damn, I made it, and they didn't. Why the hell am I leaving now? I can't leave them behind. I can say, I guess, I would like to, but I don't think I would. I feel responsible. I don't know about my mom. My mom is a totally different thing. My mom grew up with the mind-set of grow up, get a job that pays well; if you don't enjoy it, well, you got to stay because it pays well. I've never been that type of person. If I don't enjoy my work, then what the hell? There's no point. Money's just paper that buys things. It means nothing if you're not doing anything with it.

I work at factories; I feel like a zombie. I don't do anything. It's basically the same thing, repetition over and over again for twelve hours. That's horrible. I cannot imagine myself doing that for the rest of my life. And for my mom to think in that mind-set, I don't know how she does it. It's really hard for me even to think about seeing myself in twenty years from now working in a factory with my back all messed up because of menial manual labor—no. I've had so many, so many internships with youth. So hopefully, I will work with them. I really dig that whole working-with-kids thing. It's real cool knowing that you're helping somebody else. It's definitely something to feel good about. So working with that, I think I would like to do.

Two Roads

A lot of students after high school who were like me really got two roads if you're undocumented. You could get education and keep a job to pay for the education, or you could say, "Screw education. I need to help my family," because that's what happens to a lot of students in my situation. And right now, there's got to be three of me to be doing the amount of work I'm doing. Because I'm doing work, and I'm working to help my mom pay my school. And the same time, at school to get something out, you have to become something–something better than just a damned factory worker. Not to say they're bad people, but I just don't see myself doing that job. They could decide to get their papers fixed and go back to Mexico for a long time, ten years, but like I'm saying, like, a lot of us don't have anything back there to go, because most of us were raised here. I don't know my family. If I go back there, I'm just going to be living with strangers that call me family. And then now, the whole language barrier starts when you're over there; when I was in Mexico, they teach me how to read and write in Spanish. And when I get here, you forget about Mexico because this is not the same thing. So they taught me how to read and write in English. In high school–it wasn't until high school I started to write in Spanish, because I had to take Spanish and read in Spanish. This is tough; this is really hard.

If anything, I'd rather be with my family and not have papers in hand than to not have them with me.

Reflections

Joel grew up in a broken family, as he describes it. His mom was always at work to put food on the table, and he was responsible for his younger brother. As much as it would have helped for him to stop school and work full-time, he and his mom believed in the power of education. They both knew that he needed to continue no matter what it took. His mother speaks little English, but she is always aware of his activities and was there when he had trouble at school.

Joel was not a citizen at the time of this interview, and he worried about how that status could impact his future. He always felt the tension of continuing his education with no guarantees of a future with legitimate employment. He no longer speaks Spanish and is concerned that if he is sent back to Mexico, there would be nothing there for him. He doesn't know his family living there and cannot speak the language. He is studying hard to ensure that he doesn't end up working in a factory. He would love to stay in his community and work with children but worries about his future.

Despite his concerns, Joel values being with his family and persisting toward his dream of becoming a citizen and staying in the community in order to support other young people. He persists in the face of continuing challenges.

Epilogue

The Voices in Unison

These stories are filled with hope. But they go beyond simply being hopeful. The individuals we have gotten to know here are committed to finding solutions to the problems they have experienced. They do not try to hide the barriers and challenges they have faced; rather, they want to face them and make things better for their children, their families, their coworkers, and, most importantly, their communities. Despite their frustrations with the schools and the crime, they do not leave. They do not give up. They dream forward to communities that have rigorous schools, less crime, and resources equal to those in other communities. These individuals are not expecting change to come on the backs of others; they want to be the change agents themselves.

These storytellers are deeply reflective. They talk about their parents and their reasons for making the difficult trip to the United States, often leaving other family members behind. They know how they came to live in their communities and understand the hard work and dreams that got them there. They readily discuss how they have made the decision to stay and find ways to make it work for their own children and the generations to come. None of these individuals thinks of himself or herself as a victim of circumstance; rather, they are proactive community members who understand what it takes to get to the opportunities that their parents sought for them.

Completing the Mosaic

In the preface, we introduced elements that were common across all the stories, including history, family and community, safety, the English language and education, and encouragement. As we stand back to connect the stories and their common elements, we can see how they give shape to the overall mosaic.

Is the mosaic complete? Do the pieces fit together to complete an overall image? What will it take to complete the image? As we said in the preface, mosaic images are rarely completed by one artist and are often under construction. Our storytellers, like the mosaic artists, have provided significant pieces, but the overall image is not yet complete. What pieces might come next to bring an end to this phase of the construction?

Three major elements would help to move the dream forward and complete the mosaic: meaningful school reform, immigration reform, and the development of sustainable partnerships.

Meaningful School Reform

As we can see through this collection of stories, in order for school reform to be meaningful, it will need to embrace entire communities and set high expectations for all students. The schools must become hubs that are open to all community members beyond the traditional operating hours of 8:00 a.m. to 3:00 p.m. Collaboration with the community to house services, such as health clinics, English language classes for parents, after-school activities, and employment centers will encourage parents and children to think of the school as a welcoming and safe place that is integral to a healthy community.

Students are clearly looking for a more rigorous curriculum and academic support system. Their lack of English-language skills cannot be equated with a lack of overall ability, and there must be a meaningful transition from bilingual to English-language classes. When they need academic support outside the classroom, the schools need to provide the appropriate resources. Those resources could include quiet places to study, trained tutors, cohorts of students who are trained to work together, and programs to teach families how to help their children at home.

It is also important to address the social and emotional issues that can prevent students from being successful. The students repeatedly raised the issue of safety. Simply going to and from school is often a stressful time for the students and their parents. The schools must take a holistic approach with students to ensure they have time during the day to talk about these nonacademic issues that impact their ability to focus on course work. Professional counselors should be an integral component of the staff, with reasonable counselor-to-student ratios.

Creating opportunities to talk to families about the social and emotional issues impacting their children can provide an excellent resource. Together, the schools and families can help create safe passages to and from school. School counselors can help parents identify early signs of trauma or distress in their children, and they can collaborate to find ways to help them.

Students are discouraged by the low expectations often held by teachers and counselors. Teacher training programs must emphasize the importance of setting high expectations and building the scaffolding to ensure that students can meet those expectations. Students need to feel that their schools believe in them and are there to help them set and reach their goals. This approach starts from the day they enter school and concludes by preparing them for life after high school. Students need to develop a personal and meaningful academic plan from the start to guide them through the curriculum and the requirements for graduation. They also need support to think through a menu of options related to meaningful employment, job training, or further education following completion of high school.

Immigration Reform

We also heard in these stories how discouraged students can be as a result of their undocumented status. That status frequently impacts the educational and employment goals they set for themselves. No matter how high they set their educational goals, they will hear from others that without documentation, they cannot afford to attend college. They will also continue to hear that it doesn't matter how well they do–there will be no meaningful employment for them if they do graduate. In addition, teachers and administrators continuously treat them with less respect than their documented peers. This often leads to low self-esteem and fewer expectations for themselves. When this happens, the community loses young people with the potential to contribute meaningfully and make a difference.

Immigration status also impacts the family unit when there is constant concern about being separated. Parents can be deported, leaving young children with friends or relatives and an insecure future. In a culture where family means so much, it is unconscionable that individuals are not able to cross borders to provide support for aging family members. Young people without documentation are also not able to visit extended family outside the country, depriving them of a piece of their heritage.

There must be reasonable pathways for individuals to attain citizenship. Without such pathways, we discourage individuals from pursuing education, fulfilling their dreams, and contributing meaningfully to society. We discourage individuals from setting goals and reaching their potential. Creating pathways leads not only to personal fulfillment but also to the development of healthier, more-sustainable communities and is a more representative model of democracy.

Development of Sustainable Partnerships

The storytellers here are committed to driving change and working with others to make a difference. They have collaborated over the years with the churches, schools, police forces, politicians, businesses, and others to help fulfill their dreams. These collaborative efforts must continue and be developed through sustainable partnerships, relationships that will endure for the long term.

Businesses need to locate in the community, hire locally, and provide training for those who need it to succeed. They can work with schools to offer their employees the opportunity to mentor students, facilitate motivational discussion sessions, lead after-school activities, tutor, and serve on local school councils. They can also create internships and opportunities for students to visit their organization, shadow their employees, and talk about leadership and career paths. Educational scholarships can be created that are independent of documentation status.

Schools must continue to work across the community with families, local colleges and universities, and other organizations. Students need to see that their families and schools are working together to ensure their success. Family members must feel welcome and respected when they visit the schools. In partnership with the school, they can develop opportunities for more formal involvement, such as forming focus groups around special issues. The school board must give local school councils a measure of authority and an opportunity to present their ideas, knowing they will be heard and that resources are available to them for focused initiatives.

College Bridge programs are effective partnerships between high schools and colleges and universities. High-school students are enrolled in college courses at no cost to them after their normal school day. They participate in classes alongside college students and receive grades and college credits. This gives them the opportunity to see what college is like and raise their expectations to include attending college in the future. By giving them college credit, the program decreases the number of requirements they will eventually need, which also reduces their tuition.

The police force must continue its work with churches, schools, and local businesses to ensure cooperation and a sense of security. It needs to work with and train local residents to form safety coalitions and develop strategies for effective communication. Together with families, the police force can develop strategies for collaborating on how to create barriers to gang recruitment and also safe passage to and from school. Officers must also work with school administrators to ensure an appropriate presence in the schools so that students feel safe and comfortable enough to approach them with as little drama as possible.

The Overall Image

We've read the stories. We've highlighted the common elements running through them, and we've added three more that have the potential to complete the mosaic and move the dream forward. As we stand back to view the overall image, we can see how all the pieces fit together to tell the story of a community that is proud of its heritage, committed to its future, and determined to continue dreaming forward.

Many of our storytellers have already experienced the outcomes of dreaming forward. Eliamar was dreaming forward to understand better what it meant to be Mexican and ensure the preservation of the Mexican culture in her community. She now owns a successful store that specializes in Mexican artifacts. Francisco dreamed forward to a community where the school would be the hub of activity. He took his teachers into the homes of his students and invited families to come to school for community meetings. He now has 99 percent of parents coming to report-card-pickup day. Carmen and Angela worked together to dream forward for the well-being of their community and its residents. As a result, their neighborhood has a high school and a community medical center, both serving thousands of residents every year.

Dreams can move us forward, or they can hold us back. For these storytellers and their communities, dreaming forward is the dynamic process leading to the completion of a mosaic that tells the story of a healthy community.